Principles
of
Discipleship

Principles
of
Discipleship

Charles G. Finney

BETHANY HOUSE PUBLISHERS
MINNEAPOLIS, MINNESOTA 55438
A Division of Bethany Fellowship, Inc.

Published by Bethany House Publishers
A Division of Bethany Fellowship, Inc.
6820 Auto Club Road, Minneapolis, Minnesota 55438

Printed in the United States of America

Library of Congress Cataloging-in-Publication Data

Finney, Charles Grandison, 1792-1875.
　Principles of discipleship

　　1. Christian life—Congregational authors.
I. Parkhurst, Louis Gifford, 1946-　　. II. Title.
BV4501.F448　　　1988　　　248.4'858　　　87-34108
ISBN 0-87123-860-8 (pbk.)

CHARLES G. FINNEY was one of America's foremost evangelists. Over half a million people were converted under his ministry in an age that offered neither amplifiers nor mass communications as tools. Harvard Professor Perry Miller affirmed that "Finney led America out of the eighteenth century." As a theologian, he is best known for his *Revival Lectures* and his *Systematic Theology*.

LOUIS GIFFORD PARKHURST, JR., is pastor of Christ Community Church in Oklahoma City, Oklahoma. He garnered a B.A. and an M.A. from the University of Oklahoma and an M.Div. degree from Princeton Theological Seminary. He is married and the father of two children. This is his eleventh volume of the works of Charles G. Finney for Bethany House Publishers.

OTHER BOOKS IN THIS SERIES

OTHER BOOKS BY FINNEY

CONTENTS

INTRODUCTION

In this day of necessary contending for the truth of the Christian faith, in both word and deed, the great evangelist Charles G. Finney becomes an example of learned humility, compassion and gentleness. His sympathetic heart shines through the words of the letters in this book, while at the same time his courage and mental acumen is manifest as he argues for the Christian truths he had discovered from God's Word. Finney's personality, as a loving champion of Christlike living, nowhere shines with more evidence than in these warm and personal letters sent to those who had heard him preach his famous revival sermons throughout America.

In many ways this book is a bridge to some of Finney's other writings, and a companion volume to several in the Finney "Principles Series." First, these letters from *The Oberlin Evangelist* complete the collection of Finney's letters from that source. Donald W. Dayton compiled and edited Finney's "Letters on Revival" from *The Oberlin Evangelist* in his book *Reflections on Revival*, also published by Bethany House Publishers. With *Principles of Discipleship* and *Reflections on Revival*, the student of Finney's works has available for the first time in book form Finney's letters to the readers of *The Oberlin Evangelist*. Finney intentionally wrote these letters as though he were addressing the individual *personally*, and asked that people read them on their knees in prayer and apply his ideas to their own particular situation and needs. He used some of his letters to answer questions people sent to him after they heard him preach or read his books and lectures.

Second, *Principles of Holiness* (Finney's sermons on Christian holiness mostly from 1843), *Principles of Sanctification* (Finney's lectures on Christian holiness from 1840), *Principles of Union with Christ (Finney's meditations on Christian holiness from 1847) and Principles of Discipleship* (Finney's letters on Christian holiness from *The Oberlin Evangelist* mostly during 1841) are all companion volumes which examine this topic from different perspectives. All four volumes challenge us to live wholly consecrated to Jesus Christ in a faithful and loving relationship with God and our fellowman, but each one explores the meaning of sanctification a little differently. Sanctification discussed more thoroughly with reference to the baptism of the Holy Spirit can be found in *The Believer's Secret of Spiritual Power* by Andrew Murray and Charles Finney, also published by Bethany House Publishers.

Principles of Discipleship is both *practical*, with advice to parents and pastors, and *theoretical*, dealing with the critics of the doctrine of sanctification and making helpful applications and clarifications using categorical syllogisms. From this collection of letters, we see how unfair many of Finney's critics were in their refusal to really try to understand what he was saying before they criticized him, and we also see with what patience and forbearance Finney replied to them, when necessary. He is an example to all of us! Finney never wrote to vindicate himself, but replied to the criticisms of the doctrine of sanctification because of the importance of its truth and because people needed a clearer understanding regarding Christian Holiness. (I would especially suggest that Finney's letter in chapter 42, be read prior to the censure of Finney's views by the Troy Presbytery reprinted in that chapter. The Troy Presbytery so misrepresented his views that to analyze their comments before reading Finney's reply will lead to needless confusion.)

A few of Finney's ideas on diet will seem novel to us, and out of date, with regard to sanctification. However, when we remember that diet books and exercise books still make the bestseller lists in the secular book market today, Finney's comments do not seem totally out of place. Finney argued for simple frontier living, and he worked with students in a frontier college they had literally carved out of the forest wilderness; therefore, what he had to say was certainly appropriate. He tried to be current in his understanding of whatever concerned the human condition, and when we recognize that his references to the ideas of Sylvester Graham on diet are from a two-volume work published in 1839, and his letters were written in 1840, we see just how current he was in a day when books were not easily obtained.

Some of Finney's ideas regarding home schooling in comparison with public schooling are accepted by many families today, and his very protective ideas regarding the raising of children should cause people to reflect, especially when confronted with the rampant child abuse of today. All in all, through these letters we see a side of Finney not seen through his sermons and not captured in his *Autobiography*. No matter how active Finney was as a revivalist, theological teacher, pastor, and writer, he took seriously his duties as a father, and gave good suggestions regarding the importance of keeping our priorities in place.

Bethany House Publishers should be commended for their efforts to make Finney's works more widely accessible to the modern reader. A fine blend of Finney's works; collections of sermons, lectures, daily meditations, and letters, combine to introduce, educate, and inform new and old Christians alike. Finney tried to keep a very careful biblical balance, neither antinomian nor legalist, neither Arminian nor hyper-Calvinist: he understood the dangers of extremes. Finney cannot be easily pigeon-holed in a day when we prefer to label people and their ideas; therefore, with the many books by Finney now available, people can acquire their own understanding of truth and use Finney as a catalyst to help them think through biblical concepts and their contemporary application. Because some people who read Finney are legalistic, we cannot assume that Finney was legalistic, and because some people who read Finney are perfectionistic, we cannot assume that Finney was perfectionistic. Legalists, perfectionists, and critics of Finney, would all profit from an unbiased reading of these new books and new editions published by Bethany House Publishers.

I would like to personally thank Kathy Lytle for her typing of much of this manuscript, and for her fine editorial assistance in the midst of many pressing concerns.

For the sake of His Kingdom:
L. G. Parkhurst, Jr.

PART 1

Letters to New Christians

CHAPTER 1

To the young Christians who have been converted in the great revivals of the past few years, scattered up and down in the land, wherever the providence of God may have cast your lot

January 1, 1839

Beloved in the Lord:

My body is so far worn and especially my organs of speech so far exhausted that I cannot visit and preach to you the word of life. I therefore address you through the press, as the most direct and effectual medium through which I can communicate my thoughts.

I propose, the Lord willing, to address to you through the columns of the *Oberlin Evangelist* from time to time a series of short sermons on practical subjects that I deem most important to you and to the kingdom of our Lord Jesus Christ.[1] When I shall have said what I desire on those more immediately and highly practical topics, if the Lord permit, I design to give you a series of sermons on some doctrinal topics, especially the moral government of God, including the atonement and the influences of the Holy Spirit in the administration of that government.

A great many of you I know personally, but many more of you know me than I have the honor of a personal acquaintance.

---

[1]Many of these sermons from the *Oberlin Evangelist* are being reprinted for the first time in book form in the Finney "Principles Series," edited by L.G. Parkhurst, Jr. The sermons accompanying the first four letters in this book can be found in Charles G. Finney, *The Promise of the Spirit*, compiled and edited by Timothy L. Smith (Minneapolis: Bethany House Publishers, 1980).

You do me the honor to call me your spiritual father, and I have the unspeakable happiness of believing that God has made me instrumental in doing you good. Those of you who know me personally *know* that it is my manner to deal with the souls and consciences of men with great plainness of speech and directness of address. You remember that this was my manner when I was with you. I have the greatest confidence that this is still the only way to do you good.

Now the thing that I desire to do, so far as I am able, is to lay open before you the very secrets of your hearts, and also to lead you to an entire renunciation of everything that grieves the Spirit of God, to a relinquishment of selfishness under every form and in every degree, and to hold out before you those "exceedingly great and precious promises" whereby you may be made "partakers of the divine nature." The editors of this paper are willing that I should make it the medium of spreading before you my thoughts, as the providence and Spirit of God shall enable me. I shall give you a sermon as often as my health and other duties will permit; and whenever you receive this paper containing one of my lectures, I wish you to consider yourself as personally addressed by me. I wish you to read for *yourself* and feel that I mean *you*, as though it were a private communication made to you from my own pen, or as if I had a personal interview and addressed you "face to face." If I probe your conscience, I beg of you not to be offended and throw the paper aside and refuse to hear me. "I beseech you by the mercies of God," no, I adjure you by our Lord Jesus Christ to hear me patiently and with candor. Beloved, I expect candor from *you*; and many of you will not only hear me with *candor* but with *joy*. I will try to write as if I had you all before me in one great congregation, as if I beheld your countenances and were addressing you "face to face." In fact, I will consider you, and I desire you to consider yourselves, as in such a sense members of my congregation as to steadfastly fix your attention on my preaching. I shall take it for granted that you read every lecture, and of course address you from time to time as if you had candidly read and attentively considered what I had already said.

Unless I can engage you to grant me one request, I have little hope of doing you good. And that is, as soon as you receive this communication you will make me, yourselves and the subject of the proposed lectures subjects of earnest and constant prayer; and that whenever you receive a paper containing one of the proposed lectures, you go upon your knees before you read it and lay open your heart in solemn prayer before God and to the influence of truth, and implore the aid of the Holy Spirit to make the word to you alive and powerful. We shall all soon meet at the bar of God. I earnestly desire to do you all the good I can while I am in the flesh; and as I do not intend to write for your amusement but solely for your spiritual edification, will you pledge yourselves on your knees before God to examine the truth candidly—make a personal, faithful and full application of it to your own hearts and lives—and to use it profitably since you will answer to God in the solemn judgment? If these are your resolutions and purposes, I am confident the Lord will bless you. I shall not cease to pray for you and intend to make those of you whom I remember special and particular subjects of prayer; and I entreat you to do the same for me.

Charles G. Finney,
A servant of the Lord Jesus Christ

CHAPTER 2

To the Christian readers of
The Oberlin Evangelist

January 30, 1839

Beloved:

You can see that I have already commenced one of the promised courses of lectures. Before I proceed any further, permit me to bring distinctly before your minds the main objective I have in view and the reasons for the course I intend to pursue.

My objective is the sanctification of "your whole spirit and soul and body."

My reasons are the following:

When I was first converted and entered the ministry, my mind was powerfully drawn, as I then thought and now think, to labor for the conversion of sinners. Upon that one grand objective my heart was set, and to the accomplishment of it many of you can bear witness that all my powers were devoted. My study, preaching, prayers, visiting and conversation were devoted to that end. My mind was, of course, occupied almost exclusively with that class of truths that were calculated to work the conviction and conversion of the unrepentant.

I generally spent but a few months in a place, and during that time my preaching and influence were directed, as I have said, almost exclusively to the conversion of the ungodly. I only spent so much time in preaching to the church as was indispensable to arouse them and get them out of their sinful life.

About the same time, and subsequently to my laboring as an evangelist, a number of other evangelists were and have been called forward by the Spirit of God, who have labored mainly for the same objective. The attention and labor of pastors have also been directed mainly to the same end during the extensive revivals of the past few years.

To my own mind it appears that this unity of design and effort were, to say the least, to a great extent indispensable to the accomplishment of the great work that has been undeniably achieved. That hundreds of thousands of sinners have been converted to God by these instruments I have no doubt. And I think I can see very clearly the wisdom of God in calling up the attention of so many evangelists, pastors and churches to the immediate conversion of the ungodly.

It has been reported that I wholly disapprove of my own course as an evangelist and that I wholly disapprove of the course of other evangelists and pastors in this great work. Now this is by no means true. I do not by any means pretend to justify all that I have done, nor suppose that my course was faultless. Nor do I pretend to justify all that other evangelists and pastors have done to promote this work. Nor do I pretend that in everything our views of what was best to be done have been exactly alike. But with respect to myself, I feel bound to say that the more I have looked over the course in which I was led, the class of truths I preached, and the means that I adopted, the more deeply have I been impressed with the conviction that, considering the objective I had in view, namely, the conversion of sinners, the course in which God led me was upon the whole wise, and such a one in almost all respects as I should pursue again, with my present experience, had I the same objective in view.

I am also convinced that God has been wise in leading other evangelists and pastors in their preaching and measures. And although much of human infirmity may have and doubtless has appeared in what we have done, yet upon the whole I do not see what better could have been expected or done, under the circumstances of the case, for the accomplishment of so great and good a work.

In the midst of my efforts, however, for the conversion of sinners (and as far as my knowledge extends, it has been so with other evangelists and pastors) we have overlooked in a great measure the fact that converts would not make one step of progress unless they were constantly urged with means as well adapted to their sanctification and growth in grace, as were the means for their conversion. Believing and feeling as I did then and do now that if persons were once converted, God in faithfulness would save them, I overlooked the necessity of the constant, vigorous and pointed use of means to effect this end.

By this I do not mean that I did not at all feel this necessity. But it was not so fully before my mind as the necessity of the use of vigorous means for the conversion of the ungodly.

It is true that not being impressed with this necessity, my stay in every place was too short to accomplish much in the work of leading converts to manhood in religion. The same has been true of my brethren who have been and are evangelists. And I have reason to believe that the great desire of pastors for the conversion of sinners in those congregations where revivals have prevailed, and the great success that under God has attended the use of means for their conversion, has led them in a great measure to neglect the church—to leave out of view the more spiritual truths of the gospel that constitute the food of Christians and are essential to their sanctification.

In revisiting some of the churches in which I had formerly labored, my mind was some years ago from time to time deeply impressed with the necessity of doing something for the sanctification of Christians. And after I had been settled two or three years in the city of New York and had labored almost exclusively for the conversion of sinners, I was fully convinced that converts would die, that the standard of piety would never be elevated, that revivals would become more and more superficial and finally cease, unless something effectual was done to elevate the standard of holiness in the church. And in attempting to present to the church the high and pure doctrines of grace and all that class of truths which are the food and life of the Christian soul, I found to my sorrow that I had been so long in pursuit of sinners with the law, to convict them, and only enough of the gospel just to convert them, that my mind had, as it were, run down. And those high and spiritual truths had not that place in my own heart which is indispensable to the effectual exhibition of them to others. I found that I knew comparatively little about Christ, and that a multitude of things were said about Him in the gospel of which I had no spiritual view and of which I knew little or nothing.

What I did know of Christ was almost exclusively as an atoning and justifying Savior. But as a JESUS to save men from sin, or as a sanctifying Savior, I knew very little about Him. This was made very clear to my mind by the Spirit of God. And it deeply convinced me that I must know more of the gospel in my own experience and have more of Christ in my own heart, or I could never expect to benefit the church. In that state of mind, I often used to tell the Lord Jesus Christ that I realized I knew very little about Him; and I besought Him to reveal himself to me that I might be instrumental in revealing Him to others. I used to pray especially over particular passages and classes of passages in the gospel that speak of Christ, that I might apprehend their *meaning* and feel their *power* in my own heart. And I was often strongly convinced that I desired this for the great purpose of making Christ known to others.[1]

I will not enter into detail with regard to the way in which Christ led me. Suffice it to say, and alone to the honor of His grace do I say it, that He has taught me some things that I asked Him to show me. Since my own mind became impressed in the manner in which I have spoken, I have felt as strongly and unequivocally pressed by the Spirit of God to labor for the sanctification of the church as I once did for the conversion of sinners. By multitudes of letters and from various other sources of information I have learned, to my great joy, that God has been and is awakening a spirit of inquiry on the subject of holiness throughout the church, both in this country and in Europe.

You who read my lectures in the *New York Evangelist* while I was in the city of New York may remember the manner in which God was leading my own mind—through what a process of conviction and to what results He brought me previously to my leaving there. Since then God has been continually dealing with me in mercy. And how I have longed often to unburden myself and pour out my whole heart to the dear souls that were converted in those powerful revivals.

And now, dearly beloved, I have commenced this course of lectures in the hope that, should God spare my life, He will make them the instrument of doing you good. You need searching and trying and purifying and comforting. You need to be humbled, edified, sanctified. I think I know, very nearly, where great multitudes of you are in religion; and will endeavor, God helping me from time to time, to adapt truth to what I suppose to be your circumstances and state of mind. As I said in my former letter, I cannot visit you and preach to you on account of the state of my health. And besides, I think the Spirit of God calls me for the present to remain here. But through the press, I can hold communion with you and preach to you the gospel of Christ.

In addition to the sermons which I design to preach to you,

---

[1]See Charles G. Finney, *Principles of Union with Christ*, compiled and edited by Louis Gifford Parkhurst, Jr. (Minneapolis: Bethany House Publishers, 1985) for 31 meditations on the names of Christ, and how to know Him more fully and deeply as a personal Savior.

I shall probably from time to time address letters to you, when I have anything particular to say that cannot well be said in a sermon. If any spiritual advice is asked by letter, as is often the case, upon any subject that can be answered in a sermon, you may generally expect to find my answer in some of my lectures-concealing, of course, the fact that I have a particular case under my eye. If, in any case, the answer cannot well be given in a sermon, should providence permit, you may expect an answer either privately to the individual who makes the request or in a letter in the *Evangelist*, which may not only assist the inquirer but that class of persons who are in a similar state of mind. In this case also, of course, I shall not disclose the names of the particular inquirers.

And now, dearly beloved, do not suppose that I do this because I suppose that I am the only man who can give you spiritual advice, but because I am willing to do what I can. And as I have freely received, I wish to freely impart whatever of the gospel the blessed God has taught me.

One more word: I have noticed in several papers a garbled extract from a remark that I made in one of my lectures published in the *New York Evangelist*, which I here mention simply because it is dishonorable to God and injurious to you. In that lecture I said, "that those converted in the great revival in the land, although real Christians, as I believed, and the best Christians in the church at the present day, were nevertheless a disgrace to religion on account of the low standard of their piety; and if I had health again to be an evangelist, I would labor for a revival in the churches and for the elevation of the standard of piety among Christians."

Now you perceive that I have here asserted my full conviction that those revivals were genuine works of God, "that the converts were real Christians," that "they are the best Christians in the church," and yet that on many accounts they are a disgrace to religion. Now this I fully believe and reassert. And it is to win you away, if possible, from the last remains of sin that I have undertaken this work. The papers to which I allude have injuriously reported me as admitting that those revivals were spurious and the converts not Christians. I do not complain of this on my own account nor speak of it, if I know my own heart, because I have any regard to its bearing upon myself, but because it is a slander upon those precious revivals, and injurious to you, as in substance denying that the grace of God ever converted you.

And now, dearly beloved, I must close this letter, beseeching you to make me a subject of earnest prayer that God will enlighten and sanctify me, fill me with the spirit of the gospel of His Son, and help me to impart to you the true bread and water of life, rightly dividing truth and giving to everyone a portion in due season.

May the grace of our Lord Jesus Christ be with you forever.

Charles G. Finney,
A servant of the Lord Jesus Christ

CHAPTER 3

To the converts of the great revivals that have prevailed in the United States within the last few years

February 13, 1839

Beloved:

I closed my last letter by referring to the fact that several professedly religious periodicals have so referred to what I had said in regard to your being "a disgrace to religion" as virtually to represent me as denying the reality, genuineness and power of those glorious revivals in which you were converted. I denied having said anything in that connection to that effect. But I did assert in my lecture and reassert in my last letter that I believed many of you were by your lives a disgrace to the religion of Christ. Now, beloved, I did not say this then, nor do I say it now to bring a bitter accusation against you, but for the purpose of preparing the way to put some questions to your conscience, with the design to turn your eyes fully upon your own life and spirit as exhibited before the world.

And here let me say that when you receive this issue I desire each of you to consider this letter as directed to you individually, as a *private letter to you*, although communicated through this public channel.

I will write upon my knees, and I beg you to read it upon your knees. And when you have read it as written to *yourself* and received it, as I adjure you to do, as a private communication to *you from me*, in the name of the Lord Jesus Christ, I entreat you to hand it to all your Christian friends in your neighborhood and within your reach, beseeching them to re-

ceive it and consider it as a private letter to *them*, in the name
of the Lord Jesus Christ.

Hereafter, should the providence of God permit, I may more
particularly address different classes of individuals than I can
in this letter. I intend to address fathers, mothers, husbands,
wives, children, ministers, church officers, editors of religious
papers, young men and young women—all distinct classes of
individuals to whom particular truths may be applicable.[1] In
this, I address you without reference to your age or sex, calling,
or position but simply as a professor of the religion of Jesus
Christ.

I have said that I fear and believe that many of you, at least,
are a disgrace to the religion you profess. By this I mean that
instead of fairly and truly representing the religion of Christ
in your life and spirit, you in many respects grossly misrepresent it. Do not at this point let your temper rise and turn upon
me and say: "Physician, heal thyself." I might, to be sure, confess my own sins; but my business now as "an ambassador of
Jesus Christ" is with your own conscience.

And now, dearly beloved, bear with me while I put the questions home to you, as by name.

Are not your life and spirit and habits a miserable *misrepresentation* of the religion you profess?

You are a professor of the religion of Jesus Christ. Your
profession of religion has placed you on high, as "a city that
cannot by hid." You are not hid. The eyes of God, of Christians,
of the world, of hell are upon you.

And now, precious soul, do you sincerely believe that you
feel and *act* and *live* and *do* as the Lord Jesus Christ would
under similar circumstances?

Are those around you forced by your *life* and *spirit* to recognize the divine features of the character of Christ in you?

Would those that know nothing of Christ be able to catch
and *understand* the true *spirit* and *meaning* of the religion of
Jesus by an acquaintance with you?

Would they obtain from your *life* and *example* such an idea
of the *nature*, *design* and *tendency* of the gospel as would lead
them to value it, to understand its necessity and importance?

Are your spirit and temper and conversation so *unearthly*,
so *heavenly*, so *divine*, so much like *Christ*, as to accurately
represent Him? Or do you misrepresent Him?

---

[1]The letters in this book bring together for the first time in book form Finney's
letters to all these distinct classes of Christians.

Is not the *temper* that you manifest, the *life* that you lead, your *behavior*, your *pursuits*—are not all these in many respects the very opposite and contrast of the spirit of the religion of Christ?

My beloved brother, sister, father, mother, whoever you are, *remember* that while you read these questions God's eye is pouring its *searching blaze* into your *inmost soul.*

What is your temper in your *family*, among your *friends*, in your *private* life, in your *domestic* relations and in your *public* walks?

Is your behavior in heaven or is it "earthly, sensual, devilish"?

What is the testimony of your *closet*? Can it bear witness to your sighs and groans and tears over the wickedness and desolations of the world?

Are those who observe your good works constrained to "glorify your Father who is in heaven"? Or is the name of God blasphemed on account of your earthly and unchristian life and spirit?

Can those that remain unconverted in the place where you live bear witness that a great and divine change was wrought in you by the Spirit of God?

In the name of Christ I inquire, are your unrepentant acquaintances *constrained* to confess that there *must* have been a work of God to have wrought so great a change in you, as they daily witness?

Do you think that the interests of religion are *really advanced* by your life and that you are continually making an impression in favor of holiness on those around you?

Do they witness in you the "*peace* of God that passeth understanding"?

Do they see in you that *sweet* and *divine satisfaction* in the will and ways of God that spreads a heavenly *serenity* and *calm* and *sweetness* over your mind, in the midst of the *trials* and *circumstances* to which you are subjected?

Or do they behold you annoyed, anxious, worried, easily disturbed and exhibiting the spirit of the world? My dear soul, if this is so, you are a horrible disgrace to religion; you are unlike Jesus. Was this the spirit that Jesus manifested?

Let me inquire again: what are you *doing* for the *conversion of sinners* around you, and what for the conversion of the world?

Would one hundred million such Christians as you are, and living just as you live, be instrumental in converting the world?

Suppose there are a thousand million of men upon the earth

and suppose that one hundred million of these were just such Christians as you are, in your present state and at your present rate of usefulness; when would the world be converted?

Are the church and the world *better* and *holier* on account of your profession? And are they really *benefited* by your life?

If not, your profession is a libel upon the Christian religion. You are, like Peter, *denying* your Savior; and like Judas, you have kissed but to *betray* Him.

Now, beloved, I will not take it upon myself to decide these questions that I have put to you on my knees and in the spirit of love. Will you be honest and, on your knees, spread out this letter to God our Maker and Christ your Savior? Will you not upon your knees read over these questions, one by one, and ask God to show you the real state of your life as it relates to each of them?

And here, beloved, I leave you for the present; and may the Savior aid you and make you honest in meeting cordially and answering honestly these questions. You must be searched and humbled and broken down in heart before you can be built up and made strong in Christ.

Do be *honest* and in *haste*, and address yourself to the work of self-examination without delay. I beg of you to prepare yourself to receive the consolations of the gospel of Christ, for my soul is panting to spread them out before you.

Providence permitting, you may expect to hear from me again soon.

Charles G. Finney,
A servant of the Lord Jesus Christ

CHAPTER 4

To the Christian readers of
The Oberlin Evangelist

April 10, 1839

Beloved:

The object of this letter is to state a little more definitely than I have before some of the reasons why young converts have not grown more in grace, and why I have feared, as I said in a former letter, that revivals would become more and more superficial until they would finally cease.

I have from my earliest conversion been led to notice more and more particularly the fact that there are four classes of professors in the church.

The first class seems to have had very little conviction of sin, and consequently there is not light enough in their experience; that is, they have not experience enough to understand the Bible so as to be able, under God, to convict others of sin. They pass along, and nearly their whole lives seem to be worse than useless so far as the interests of religion are concerned.

A second class seems to have had frequent and deep conviction of sin but appear never to have been truly regenerated. They understand the Bible measurably on the subject of depravity, so as to be able under God to bring others under conviction and distress of mind; and here they stop. They rarely if ever are instrumental in the regeneration of a sinner. Having no experience on the subject of conversion themselves, they are all in the dark. And when the inquiry is made by an anxious sinner, "What shall I do to be saved?"—although they may give him directions in the language of Scripture, yet as a matter of fact they cannot answer his inquiries and shape their direction and remove his difficulties so as to bring him into the kingdom of God. This class is very numerous. And I have been astonished to find how seldom it is that professors of religion know what to say to anxious sinners. From long and close observation, I am led to believe that the difficulty lies in their total lack of *experience* on the subject of regeneration.

The third class have been really converted and understand the way through the gate of regeneration well enough to direct others. Knowing themselves what it is to be converted, thus far they can go with sinners. They know measurably how to use the law to produce conviction, and enough of the atonement and of Christ as a justifying Savior instrumentally to bring sinners fairly into the kingdom; for this they have personal experience.

But they have gone no further than this. Their time and thoughts and lives have been employed with these two classes of truths: the law, and so much of the gospel as to produce conversion. They have, though, advanced no further than "the first principles of the oracles of God." They continue to lay again and again "the foundation of repentance from dead works and of faith toward God, of the doctrine of baptism and the laying on of hands, the resurrection of the dead and eternal judgment." They go round and round in the circle of these first principles of the doctrine of Christ and never "go on to perfection," either in doctrine or in practice.

Hence, having never given their attention to those higher and more spiritual truths of the gospel which are the more appropriate food of the Christian soul and indispensable to his growth in grace, they make little or no progress in holiness and often in a few years become mechanical in their efforts to convert sinners. Their spirit, not being sweetened by deep and constant and increasing communion with Christ, becomes bitter and hypercritical. They know very little what to say to an anxious Christian struggling against remaining sin. Let them be consulted by a Christian who has made any considerable attainments in piety and who well understands the plague of his own heart and is panting after the utter annihilation of sin in all its forms and to be raised up "to the measure of the stature of the fullness of Christ," and they are in the dark. They will generally insist upon such persons going to work for the conversion of sinners and reproach them with not being at work for God and for thinking so much about themselves and their own sins. The fact is, they are in the dark in regard to the real state and necessities of such persons. This state of mind is entirely beyond their experience. They seem to be totally destitute of that which Paul refers to in 2 Corinthians 1:3–6: "Blessed be God, even the Father of our Lord Jesus Christ, the Father of mercies, and the God of all comfort; who comforteth us in all our tribulation, that we may be able to comfort them which are in trouble, by the comfort wherewith we ourselves are comforted of God. For as the sufferings of Christ abound in us, so our consolation also aboundeth by Christ. And whether we be afflicted, it is for your consolation and salvation, which is effectual in the enduring of the same sufferings which we also suffer: or whether we be comforted, it is for your consolation and salvation."

Here the Apostle found that God gave him deep Christian experience and comfort that he might be able to understand the distresses and administer comfort to those in like circumstances.

Now as a general thing I do not believe it is possible for a Christian to go much beyond his own experience in administering the consolations of the gospel or in removing the difficulties that obstruct the paths of others. Even Christ himself was, in this respect, made perfect through sufferings: "for in that he hath suffered, being tempted, he is able to succor those that are tempted." The New Testament, and especially the Epistle to the Hebrews, seems plainly to recognize this truth that Christ having been in the flesh "and tempted in all points like as we are" is thereby qualified to sympathize with us, because He "can be touched with the feelings of our infirmities." It seems plain from the very nature of mind that in order to lead others, we ourselves must be acquainted with the way; and it is alarming and affecting to see how few Christians there are in the church who have experience enough to direct those who are struggling after high attainments in piety. Whenever a teacher attempts to go beyond his own experience he becomes a blind leader of the blind.

This class of converted Christians who are able, at least for a time, to labor successfully for the conversion of others, without ever having grown much in grace themselves and in the knowledge of our Lord Jesus Christ, has been much increased during the great revivals.

The fourth class, and I am constrained to say that they are comparatively few, have learned so much of Christ as a *sanctifying* as well as a *justifying* Savior, have drunk so deeply at the fountainhead of love and of the waters of the sanctuary, as to be able not merely to direct an inquiring *sinner* but an anxious *Christian*. I have always observed that this class of Christians feel peculiarly solicitous for the weak lambs of the church. The weak and stumbling and God-dishonoring state of the church is what most peculiarly afflicts them. Their compassions are greatly moved when they behold the haltings, complainings, anxieties and follies of the church.

Now, it seems to me that there is something in the history of Paul that ought to be instructive to the church on this subject. He seems to have spent a number of years almost exclusively in the conversion of sinners and in the establishment of churches. But during his confinement at Rome and in the latter part of his ministry, he appears to have had his attention turned particularly to the subject of strengthening the church. And it is very edifying to see in all his epistles this prominent feature of his character: a great eagerness to promote growth in grace among Christians. It is not to be supposed that he omitted to labor for the conversion of sinners. But it is, I think, obvious beyond all dispute that his mind was mainly engrossed with the sanctification of the church. And it is evident from his epistles that he did not believe that the church would ever be sanctified merely by pressing them to labor exclusively for the conversion of sinners or by dwelling upon that particular class of subjects that were referred to by him as "the beginning of the doctrine of Christ." His letters were, I think, undeniably designed to lead Christians into a fuller knowledge of Christ—in all His relations—to the necessity, means and practicability of entire sanctification.[1] The same seems to have been true of all the apostles whose epistles have come down to us.

I have made so many preliminary remarks that I must omit until my next letter my main design which is to notice some of the reasons why converts have not grown more in grace.[2]

Charles G. Finney,
A servant of the Lord Jesus Christ

---

[1] In 1840, Charles Finney preached a series of lectures in the *Oberlin Evangelist* on sanctification. These lectures were published that year in a book *Views on Sanctification*. This book has been republished as *Principles of Sanctification* (Minneapolis: Bethany House Publishers, 1986). *Principles of Holiness* (Minneapolis: Bethany House Publishers, 1984) is a book of his sermons published in the *Oberlin Evangelist* in 1843.

[2] See chapter six in this book for the letter to follow this one.

PART 2

Letters to Ministers

CHAPTER 5

To editors of periodicals who are professing Christians

January 15, 1840

Dear Brethren:

It is appropriate for me to speak with genuine modesty and humility in addressing you on a subject of the highest importance to this nation and to the world. It is no part of my design to enter into any controversy with you, nor to take it upon myself to decide in regard to the manner in which you shall discharge your duties. But I beg to be allowed to speak to you in love as a Christian brother, and to suggest several things, or rather to make several inquiries in regard to the influence which your periodicals are exerting upon your numerous readers.

Is it not a well settled truth that "evil communications corrupt good manners"?

Is it not also a well-settled truth, that the spirit of a disciple is almost certainly, in a great measure, modified and molded by the spirit of his teacher?

Is it not a fact, to which the experience of almost every man can testify, that "like priest, like people," is a maxim of unerring truth—that the spirit of a church partakes in a great measure, of the spirit of its pastor and that those who love and have confidence in him will almost certainly drink in his spirit and strongly sympathize with him in whatever engages his heart and draws forth his soul? If he is secular, his church will be so. If he is sticklish about orthodoxy, or has no settled views at all, such in general will be the character of his church. In short, whatever he is, so far as he has influence, his people will be. Those who are not at all influenced by him, who have little or no confidence in him, may, and very likely will be almost the reverse of his spirit. But it is plain, that in proportion to their confidence will be the degree in which their characters will be molded by his influence.

Does not the same truth hold good with regard to the authors with whom an individual and a people commune?

And does not the same truth hold good in regard to periodicals? Will a man take and pay for a periodical unless he is pleased with it? And can he be pleased with it unless he drinks in the spirit which it breathes? And do not the periodicals and literature of the day modify and mold the character of a people or nation, as a pastor does that of a particular congregation?

Is not the present a day of general rebuke, criticism, strife, bitterness and mob rule, both in and out of the Church? Do not the openly ungodly display the turbulence of their spirit by breaking forth into the most outrageous anarchy, setting aside all law, and trampling under foot everything that is lovely and of good report? And do not somber clergymen and professed Christians trample on the constitutions and laws of their respective denominations, setting aside the ordinary and constitutional modes of procedure, and in the true spirit of ministerial mob-rule proceed, without law or order, to a spiritual lynching of those who are subject to their jurisdiction?

Now, beloved brethren, I would humbly inquire, is not the press, to a very great extent, chargeable with all this unruliness? Is it not certain that the periodicals of the day to a very great extent breathe this spirit, and have been the principal instruments of enkindling and diffusing it through every department of society? Was not the press, in the city of New York, justly chargeable with the mobs that prevailed there some years ago; and has not this been the case throughout the length and breadth of the land? Was not the press chargeable with the horrors of the French Revolution? Are not the commotions of the Church, its arguments and misrule, chargeable in a great measure upon the professedly religious presses? Are not the pastors and religious teachers throughout the land greatly excited and their whole character and influence greatly modified by this same press? Is not every minister's preaching upon the Sabbath, in a great measure, suggested and modified by his reading through the week; and where his periodicals are filled with highly inflammatory, sectarian, slanderous, and hypercritical articles, does he not drink in their spirit and by degree come to feel that these are things that ought to be preached and insisted upon, and does he not thus to a great extent become the echo of the religious press? If he reads much he almost certainly does preach accordingly, whether he is aware of it or not. What pastor has not felt the constant and I might say, uncontrollable, influence of periodicals in his own congregation?

Now, beloved brethren, if these things are so, what awfully responsible positions do you fill. Is it not of the utmost importance that you should be eminently holy men? And if you are not highly spiritual men, is it not true that the greater your talents, the more is the Church and the world cursed by your influence? Ought not a man to have as particular regard to the periodicals which he reads and the editor whose thoughts and selections are pouring their constant influence over his mind and the minds of his family, as he would in the selection of a pastor under whose instructions he and his family were to have their characters molded for eternity? For myself, I must say that I could no more suffer a newspaper edited by a man who has a bad spirit to come into my family, and breathe its silent influence over our souls, than I would willingly have the plague or any other evil influence come in among us. I regard editors as sustaining the most important relations to the world, of any men in the world, for they give to themselves, through their publications, a kind of ubiquity. They live and move and breathe their influence over the whole heart of the nation. Their influence is felt over hundreds of pulpits, thousands of domestic circles, and millions of hearts; and in fact the whole land is molded by them as it were by a king of omnipresent influence.

Dearly beloved brethren, is it not then of infinite importance that you should fully appreciate the solemnity and responsibility of your positions and have a special regard to several things which you will now permit me to mention?

In regard to the spirit of the writers whose productions you allow to find a place in your columns: Were you promoting a revival of religion, as a pastor of a church, would you allow a man with a fiery, sectarian, bitter, sarcastic, hypercritical and denunciatory spirit to preach to your people? You would neither encourage nor allow such a man to take the lead in any meeting and exhort, pray, and diffuse his spirit through your congregation. Or, if it were not a time of revival you would not, if you could prevent it, allow such a spirit to be diffused among your people. Who has not, in seasons of revival, seen a single prayer or exhortation in a bad spirit do immense mischief in a congregation? And who has not witnessed the disastrous influence of the spirit of such writers in periodicals, changing the sweetness of Christian love into the bitterness of gall, and pouring in a current of death upon the gardens of spiritual life?

Should it not then be the universal practice of editors to exclude from their columns everything that is inconsistent with the spirit of holiness and perfect Christian love?

It is of the utmost importance that articles bearing injuriously on the character of any man, or set of men, be published with great care, and only under such restrictions and upon such conditions as cannot reasonably be expected to injure the cause of truth, by a prodigal-like disposing of the periodical's Christian influence. Is it not a great error for editors to suppose that they have a right to publish anything, however slanderous, if the writer will only give his name; and to give anything to the public which the malice, or prejudice, or mistaken zeal of any man shall suggest? Are editors exceptions to the common rules of Christ's kingdom in this respect?

In the days of Jeremiah, the prophet complained of the people in this language, "Report say they, and we will report it. All my familiars have watched for my halting." The doctrine seems to have been in those days, that if anyone would originate a report, they were at liberty to retail it whether true or false, and leave it to those against whom it was reported to contradict it or not as they chose or were able. Of this the prophet complained as a grievous wickedness. And I would humbly inquire whether there is not something extremely like this in the conduct of many editors? I have good reason to know from my own personal knowledge and observation for many years past that it has been customary with some editors to publish things which I knew to be absolutely false and slanderous. And most of this could have been, to be sure, easily disproved. But in this way the defamed individuals were required to spend most of their time repelling slander. When editors give themselves up to spreading such threatening influences over the land, either a great multitude of persons must spend their time in contradicting and correcting such statements, or the public mind must be allowed to become deeply and bitterly prejudiced, and the cause of Christ suffer immense injury from their influence. For myself, I have seen so many statements and things reported as facts, which I know to be false, that I am compelled to place but very little confidence in the religious publications of the day. I cannot but reason in this manner: that, if in respect to the dearest interests of religion, the most sacred things, and character, and proceedings, such utter misrepresentations are unblushingly published in so many instances within my own

knowledge, what *reason* have I to believe those things where I
have not personal knowledge—no, what *right* have I to believe
them? Now is it not a great evil when the spirit of the periodical
press is such that a most disastrous influence is avoided only
by giving very little credit to its statements? I design to speak
with the greatest kindness. But my heart is too often and too
much pained upon this subject to remain silent any longer. If I
hear any report of a brother, whether it be true or false, I have
no right to give it to the public without laying the subject before
him, admonishing him to repent and knowing what he has to
say to the charge. If the thing is untrue, I have no right to
publish it at all! And if it is true I have no right to give it to
the public without the most urgent necessity. Can it be right
for me or for any man on earth to give publicity to whatever I
suppose myself to have good authority for believing? Simply
because I believe a thing to be true, have I a right to send it
into circulation as upon the winds of heaven and leave it for
the individuals concerned to contradict it or not as they may
be able? Is not this as far as possible from the spirit and rule
of the gospel? Are editors any more at liberty to transgress this
plain principle of Christian law than other men? And is not a
most fearful amount of transgression in this respect causing
the religion of Jesus to bleed at every pore?

It is of the utmost importance that the tendency of every article should be well weighed by the editor before he gives it a place
in his columns. Is the editor to allow the writer to be the only
judge of the tendency of his article, and to suppose himself to have
no responsibility in this respect? He might as well fire a loaded
cannon upon masses of human beings, simply because another
man had loaded and leveled it and bade him apply the match.
Shall a man in such a case shut his eyes, apply the match, and
say I am free from the blood of all men? Or is he bound to open
his eyes, see what is before him, and determine whether the
contents of the gun are likely to do mischief if he applies the
match? Whether therefore an article prepared for your columns
be true or false is not the only question. Is not its tendency a
thing for which you are personally and in the highest sense
responsible? I have been astonished that editors should sometimes admit and sometimes deny this principle to suit their
own convenience and prejudice. Sometimes they will refuse to
publish articles on the ground of their evil tendency, alleging
that they are responsible for their tendency; and at other times
when called to account for publishing certain articles, will contend that they are not responsible for the tendency of articles

written by others. And thus we often find it impossible to depend upon the stability and consistency of their policy.

Again, it is of the greatest importance that editors should keep their own minds free from the influence of prejudice, and not suffer themselves or their correspondents to publish what will beget or perpetuate prejudice. Suppose a minister were to allow himself to become prejudiced in regard to members of his own congregation, and spread and perpetuate the prejudice; would not his words eat like a canker? And how amazingly injurious must be the influence of an editor who allows his own mind to become prejudiced on an important subject, and to increase and perpetuate such a prejudice on so large a scale!

In regard to editorial articles, permit me, dear brethren, to make two suggestions. First, is not great evil often done by editors replying to the personal reflections of other editors upon themselves; and would it not be altogether better for the cause of truth and for the spirit of this nation and of the Church to take no public notice of any personal reflections whatever? I have supposed it to be the duty of ministers and editors to attend to God's business and let Him attend to theirs—to defend God's character, and let Him defend theirs. Upon this principle I have endeavored to act, and I have never had reason to complain of a lack of faithfulness in my Divine Master in regard to these things. Always when I have been the most eager to attend to His business and His interests, He has been the most careful of mine. And when I have taken the most pains to defend His reputation and the least to defend my own, I have found by experience, that He has been caretaker of my reputation in proportion as I have been alive to His. And I have always remarked that in proportion as any man or set of men betake themselves to the defense of their own character, and the keeping of their own reputation, just in that proportion God leaves them to take care of themselves.

Secondly, it has been too much the case that editors have supposed themselves obliged to maintain the character of infallibility, and have thought that their influence would greatly suffer if they were frank and full in confessing any mistake or error into which they had fallen. Indeed I once heard an editor say that editors must be infallible, and that for him to confess would greatly injure his influence. I have known some ministers to adopt the same principle, and take the same attitude beyond which to my own mind nothing is more unreasonable and injurious. There are indeed some praiseworthy exceptions to this rule. For an editor, as well as other men, to confess his

errors, is Christian. It is truly blessed and heavenly in its influence. Few things come over the mind with such heavenly
sweetness as a frank, candid, humble, confession of a fault.

Again, let me inquire as to whether or not it is true that an
editor may, and often does, get into a bad spirit by immersing
his mind in other periodicals, many of which breathe a bad
spirit and gain an influence over him before he is aware of it.
He allows his reading to gradually poison his own spirit and
bring him forward into the arena of controversy, sectarianism,
and slander before he is fully awake to his danger.

A periodical published with a bad spirit may for awhile succeed in maintaining a large subscription list. But God is against
such a paper, and He will sooner or later put it down. Besides
there is a tendency in the periodical itself to work its own ruin.
It will in all probability, in the process of time, develop so bad
a spirit in its readers and lead them so far from God that they
will neglect paying for their paper, and finally feel so little
interest in religion as to refuse to take it at all. If I am not
mistaken I have known some periodicals to fail in this manner.
I know it is true that the editor may go so gradually into a
wrong spirit as to carry his readers so imperceptibly into backsliding that they will not perceive where they are, or what the
spirit of their favorite editor is. A similar course is observed
when a member of a church, under such preaching, sinks down
into a state of sin, without being aware that either his pastor
or himself is in a bad state of mind. But let this same man go
elsewhere and come under other influences, and get his mind
imbued with a sweet revival spirit, and how it will distress him
to return and mingle with the church, and sit under the preaching of his own pastor. How plainly will he perceive that they
are all entirely away from God, and know not what manner of
spirit they are of.

In the same manner a Christian may subscribe to a bitter
periodical without observing how contrary it is in spirit to that
of Christ, because he has the same spirit with its editor. But if
by any means he can be kept from reading his paper long
enough to get into a revival spirit—long enough to get his eyes
open and his heart broken—how terribly will his religious
newspaper grate upon his soul. He will soon find himself unable
to read it and preserve the spirit of Christ; and he will either
discontinue it or fall again under its influence, and be carried
by it away from God and holiness. For my own part I must say,
there are few things against which I have been obliged to be
more watchful than the promiscuous reading of religious pe-

riodicals. And I can heartily say that I do not know a minister of my whole acquaintance who is in the habit of acquainting himself with the periodical publications of the day, who seems to possess a high degree of spirituality. Their influence upon the ministry is just what it appears to be on editors themselves. And is it not often true that the correspondents of papers excite a bad spirit in the editor, and the editor in his turn excites a bad spirit in the writers, and thus a reciprocal influence is given and received, which often waxes worse and worse till the piety of the Church is well nigh extinct. I ask with pain and with the deepest humility whether this is not the case at the present time? Beloved brethren, how would you expect a pastor to keep his people free from a hypercritical spirit? Would it not be by abstaining altogether from such a spirit himself, and by pouring the sweet spirit of the gospel upon their souls from Sabbath to Sabbath and from day to day? And when disturbing causes come in upon his people, to do all in his power to divert their attention from them, and fix their minds upon those highly spiritual considerations which alone can promote their growth in grace?

Do not understand me, dear brethren, as insinuating that there is not much that is good and profitable in your papers. There really are many judicious and excellent things written both by yourselves and your correspondents, which are cheering to the heart of piety, and I trust cause many thanksgivings to God. But I inquire what is the influence of your periodicals as a whole? Does not the present state of the Church tell the whole story? Is it not obvious that while there are many good things in your papers, as there are many good sermons preached by the ministers of the present day, yet the influence of the good things in your papers is worse than neutralized by the many bitter and slanderous things contained in them?

The state of the human heart is such that a few caustic, sarcastic, bitter, sectarian sentences or articles will take a deeper hold, and make a more permanent impression than ten times the amount of spiritual matter that is calculated to counteract the influence of sin. A few pernicious paragraphs, catching the eye of a reader, will often poison his spirit more than a whole page of matter that has a good tendency will do him good. Who does not know that even if you let a minister preach the most powerful and spiritual sermon, under which the deepest and most salutary impression is produced, if he is followed by an exhortation or prayer just five minutes in length by an individual in a bad spirit, it will destroy the whole good effect of his sermon. And worse than counteract it, it will divert the whole flow of excited feeling into this pernicious channel. Consequently the audience will actually retire in a worse and more perturbed state than if they had heard nothing else than the bitter exhortation or prayer by itself when in a calm and unexcited state. So let your readers become interested by reading what is ever so good and powerful and moving, and then before they lay aside their paper, let them read but a short article breathing a bitter and slanderous spirit, and their whole excitement of mind will be turned into a wrong channel, and ten to one will rise from their reading and be guilty of slander and bitterness the first time their mouths are opened.

And now, dear brethren, how shall we promote a great revival of religion in the land? How shall a sweet and heavenly spirit be diffused through all our churches, unless the periodical press can be sweetened, and spiritualized, and made to exert a holy influence?

Beloved brethren, you are breathing your own spirit into the very bosom of the Church of God from week to week. You are constantly molding and forming the public heart, and continually influencing the characters and the destinies of the Church and the world! O how you need the prayers of Christians! How much you need to be eminently praying men yourselves! Much of your time must be spent upon your knees in direct and sacred communion with God, or you will poison the Church and the world to death. O brethren, do receive what I have to say to you in kindness. I say it in love, and with a full heart. I will try to pray for you. And may the God of grace guide you, and help you to exert wholly a right influence upon His Church.

Do not understand me as taking the attitude of a censor or a dictator. I would gladly get down at your feet and beseech you, and pour out all my heart before you in strong importunities that you will not be instrumental in diffusing a wrong spirit through the Church of the blessed God.

Were I sure that it would be kindly received, I would propose a day of fasting, humiliation, and prayer to be observed by the editors, ministers, writers, and especially for the editors and writers of religious periodicals. My soul is sick with the present state of things. May the Lord pour out His Spirit and direct us how to conduct ourselves so as to bless the Church.

I have many more things which I may suggest at a future time, if I have reason to believe that these are well received.

Charles G. Finney

CHAPTER 6

*To the professors of religion who were members of
the Church previous to the late great revivals*[1]

January 29, 1840

Beloved Brethren and Sisters:

In the last volume of the *Evangelist*, I addressed several
letters to the converts of the recent great revivals. Among other
things I pointed out to them some of the reasons why they had
not grown more in grace. I then designed, long before this time,
to address you upon the subject of your influence over those
converts, but have been prevented until now by the pressure of
multiplied duties.

And now, beloved brethren, permit me in the tender affections of Jesus Christ to approach your consciences and your
hearts upon this subject. In some places it has been somewhat
common for the old professors to complain of the spiritual state
of many who were hopefully converted in those revivals. And I
have no doubt there has been much reason for complaint. But,
beloved, let me inquire: How much of the guilt of their present
state lies at your own door? What, as a matter of fact, has been
your real influence over them? It must have been great in every
case, either to make them better or worse—to encourage and
press them forward, or to depress, discourage, and hinder them
in their Christian course.

When they were converted in the midst of you, they were

---

[1]By "professors of religion" Finney means those who profess to be religious,
"professing Christians," not teachers of religion in an educational setting.

like newborn infants thrown into your arms as nursing fathers and nursing mothers, to watch over, nurture, and guide in the paths of life. Now have you not these responsibilities, and what account can you give of the manner in which you have treated these young children of God? It is probable you will not deny that you were bound to exercise as much watchfulness over them as if God had really committed to your care a company of children in a state of infancy to train up in the nurture and admonition of the Lord. Now, suppose there *had* been committed to you the training up of a great number of children and you had paid very little attention to them—permitting them to go where they pleased by day and by night—to choose their own involvements, books, companions, and activities, and to spend their whole time according to their own inclinations, with very little counsel or reproof administered by you. And suppose that they had, as would almost certainly be the case, fallen into temptation, and the snare of the devil, and become anything but what was desirable. Now suppose also that you had been under solemn oath and covenant commitments, entered into in the house of God over the broken emblems of the dying body and shed blood of the Lord Jesus Christ, to watch over them with all fidelity and tenderness, to seek their purity, peace, and edification. And in spite of your promises, you had conducted yourself toward them as in the case I have supposed above. Now who can describe or even conceive the guilt of such persons under such circumstances? And if these children should become vagabonds, and outlaws, and pirates, and everything that is injurious to themselves and to their country, who would not hold you in a great measure chargeable with these results? And now suppose that under such circumstances, instead of blaming yourselves, you should complain of them behind their backs, and talk among yourselves of the state into which they have fallen—would not such conduct in you be regarded as an instance of almost unparalleled depravity?

Now, beloved brethren, I suppose that a great many of the converts of these revivals have, defying the pernicious influence of some of you, stood as high in point of spirituality as any members of your churches. They have been led by the grace of Christ, against all the unfavorable influences that many of you have exerted over them, to maintain a life of comparative devotion and zeal in the cause of Christ. Others of them have been discouraged, and stumbled, and finally have been turned back by the tide of influence poured down upon them by the example and instruction of old professors of religion.

And now let me inquire, have you not taught them, either by precept or example or perhaps both that they must expect to backslide and become cold in religion?

Have not your worldly spirit and temper, your carnal and sensual lives, been the most impressive lessons that you could urge upon them to lead them to backsliding and spiritual death? Indeed, have you not explicitly taught them that they must expect to backslide? A brother is with me now who says the first thing told him after his conversion was that he must expect to backslide and lose the peace of God which then filled his soul. And this was by an aged man who had been for years a Christian. For weeks this was the great lesson impressed upon him, and it finally contributed in a great measure to draw him away from God into a state of backsliding and sin.

Let me ask again, have you sought out young converts and conversed with them often upon spiritual subjects? Have you encouraged and strengthened them in the service of God and warned them against temptation?

Have you earnestly and affectionately inquired into the detail of their lives, into their business operations, and after their books and associates?

In short have you looked discriminatingly into those influences with which they are surrounded, and faithfully pointed out and warned them against whatever might naturally lead them astray?

Have you daily made them the subject of prayer?

Have you carefully attended all the prayer meetings yourself, and taken pains to ascertain who among them attended such meetings and who stayed away? Have you gone anxiously but kindly and often to those who stayed away and inquired into the reason?

Have you taken the alarm at any indication of backsliding among them, and done your utmost to reclaim and save them from injuring the cause of Christ?

Have you been careful that all your influence and example should be such as would naturally have a salutary and heavenly influence over them?

Have you carefully copied the example of Christ who says "For their sakes I sanctify myself, that they also might be sanctified through the truth?"

Have you avoided all parties of pleasure which you think Christ or an apostle would have avoided? Have you abstained from all those things and ways which had a natural tendency to divert them from walking with God?

Or have you, on the other hand, done the very things which have seduced them from the paths of holiness, and been the means of bringing them into the very state of which you complain? I hear that some of you have attended wine and card parties, that you have been deeply engaged in party politics, and have entered deeply into the speculations of the day, and in many respects have done all that was calculated to stumble and destroy the infant piety of young converts.

Now, my beloved brethren, I would get down at your feet and humbly beseech you to look at your responsibilities and guilt in these things. When young converts read this letter will not their minds revert to many of you as the instruments of their deplorable downfall? They may be too much hardened at present to deplore deeply their state, or very sincerely or deeply to blame you. But do let me inquire what you think will be their views of your influence if God in mercy should ever reclaim them from their backsliding? Will they not look with as much abhorrence and indignation upon your influence over them as they would upon the influence of Satan himself?

And now, my brother, my sister, have you not much to do to counteract the bad influence you have exerted over them? Have you not a mountain weight of sin to repent of, and confess to God and to them in this matter? Is it not your bounden duty at once to take up the stumbling blocks out of the way, to confess your dreadful breaches of covenant, to humble yourself and cover yourself as with sackcloth and ashes in the sight of God and in their sight, to deeply mourn over your own sin, and over them as having been led astray by you? Do you not know, do not they know, does not the world around you know and does not God know the vast amount of evil influence you have exerted over them? And do you ever expect to be forgiven without confessing and forsaking this iniquity? They have naturally regarded you as fathers and mothers in Israel. Your example has had that influence that parents have over children.

And now, beloved, are you acquainted with the real spiritual state of these converts in your midst? Will you not go to them and honestly inquire what influence your example has had over them? Will you not beg of them to be candid, and frank, and tell you the real truth in the case? Will you take up the subject seriously, and inquire on your knees before God what has been the moral tendency of your deportment, and spirit, and manner of life in its bearing upon their piety?

And let me ask again, have not the efforts of your pastors and religious teachers been in a great measure counteracted and nullified by a spirit and temper in you that has been the direct opposite of that urged by them?

At present I will say no more upon this subject, but leave these questions and suggestions to be deeply pondered by you, and will go down upon my own knees, and beg of God to search out the deep foundations of your heart upon these subjects.

Will you also take this letter and retire to your closet, and read it upon your knees, praying and asking God to make an application of every sentence to your own heart?

Will you, my brother, my sister, do this honestly, earnestly, and repeatedly, until you get a knowledge of your own standing in the sight of God upon this most solemn subject? May the grace of our Lord Jesus Christ incline you to do it, and to His name shall be the praise.

Your brother,
C. G. Finney

P.S. Will you, dear brethren, and sisters, consider this letter as addressed to each of you by name; and will you hand it to as many of that class of persons to whom it is addressed as you conveniently can, and request them also to consider it as a private communication from me to them?

CHAPTER 7

To ministers of the Gospel of all denominations

February 12, 1840

Beloved Brethren:

In addressing you according to the plan which I suggested in the last volume of the *Evangelist*, I would by all means commence by saying, and I beg you to understand and all along to remember, that I would by no means take the position of a censor or dictator in regard to those things that pertain to your responsible duties. But on the contrary, I would get down at your feet, and beg permission humbly to suggest some things for your consideration which have long pressed upon my mind. I have had almost nothing to do with the ecclesiastical arguments of any denomination of Christians, and never intend to have. But I have watched with great interest, and with much concern, the movements of the Church, and the results of the various influences that are acting upon the cause of Christ. Since by the Spirit and providence of God you are made the leaders of the hosts of God's elect, it appears to me proper that I should make my suggestions directly to you, and spread at least some of the thoughts that have been so long weighing upon my mind before you for your consideration. Permit me to begin by suggesting several things in relation to the present state of the Church.

Is it not evident that the Church as a body is sunk in gross sensuality, and that its members have lost sight in a great measure of the fact that "the flesh lusteth against the Spirit," and is one of the most potent enemies of the soul? Is it not true that very little is said or seems to be thought of the influence of the appetites and passions of the body upon the spirituality of the soul, that instead of eating and drinking for the glory of God, the Church, as members of a body, are as much enslaved by their appetites, and are as decidedly making a god of their belly, as any part of the world, that in regard to these things, they are almost entirely conformed to the world?

Is it not true that the Church is exceedingly blind and ignorant in regard to the philosophical and certain effects of sensuality upon the mind, that its members overlook in a great measure the fact that in this life the mind is dependent upon the state of the physical system for all its developments, and that every species and degree of intemperance, whether in eating, drinking, exercise, or dress, necessarily impairs the physical organization, through which and by which the mind acts, and therefore certainly and absolutely curtails the capabilities of the mind in all its healthy manifestation? In respect to the subject of alcohol, the Church is to some extent informed with regard to its action on the mind through the physical system. But are there not innumerable forms of intemperance, an immense amount of gluttony, and gross violations of the laws of life and health which are working disease and death, both to the body and soul, of which the Church is entirely ignorant?

Are not Christian churches almost universally given up to minding earthly things, extending their business operations and their worldly possessions as far as possible, and literally immersing their minds in the subject of money-making, politics, and other things that are earthly, sensual, and devilish? Are they not so far away from God as to not understand at all the philosophical and certain bearing of these pursuits upon their piety? These and other earthly things fill up their thoughts, time and conversation, insomuch that communion with God is almost entirely excluded.

Is not the Church in a state of great unbelief, so much so as to have lost in a great measure a right understanding of what faith is? They do not seem to understand that faith is a *felt, conscious assurance of mind that what God has said will assuredly come to pass.* And even the lowest exercise of real faith has come to be looked upon by the Church as a very rare attainment, and that to which very few persons ever do actually attain in this life. They suppose that unrealizing assent to the truth which almost all persons have, to be real faith, and that *realizing assurance* which in reality is faith, they suppose to be fanaticism; or, as I have said above, some very rare attainment which is not to be expected in this life, except by a very few.

The Church is in a sad state of division and sectarianism.

How few Christians of any denomination can relish the preaching, the prayer meetings, the revivals, the biographies, of other
denominations! And how lamentable is the fact that in little
villages throughout the whole land, where one minister might
instruct the whole population, some half a dozen or more sects,
and perhaps as many sectarian ministers, are occupying the
ground, scarcely able to sustain the ordinances of religion, simply because they are so divided! And thus thousands of ministers are retained in this country, who should be abroad teaching
the heathen, simply because of the sectarianism of the Church!
Is it not a great and crying and God-dishonoring sin in the
Church, to be so divided, to be so sticklish for their peculiar
sectarian notions, as to retain among them so many hundreds
and thousands of Christian ministers, *all holding the essentials
of the Christian faith*, who at once ought to be allowed, and
except for the sectarianism of the Church would be allowed to
preach the gospel to the perishing heathen?

Is not the sectarian spirit of the Church likely, in its results,
to destroy all the piety of the ministry? The sectarian interests
of every village and congregation lead them to feel that they
must have a talented minister, an educated, eloquent, impressive, and popular speaker, a man of genteel manners and
worldly refinement. Now is it not true that these qualities in
ministers are much more prized by the Church than humble,
devoted piety, and a deep experimental acquaintance with the
truths of the gospel? This is the natural and necessary result
of sectarianism in the churches. The denominational interests
of the different sects, of course, lead them to the selection of a
popular minister; i.e., a minister who will be popular, not with
the piously devoted few, but with the great mass of the people.

Is not the Church rapidly advancing toward the same state
of things that exists in Germany? Who does not know that the
cry for an educated rather than a holy ministry has, by degrees,
filled the church in Germany with little less than an educated,
infidel ministry? And I for one must say I tremble for the pros-
pects of the Church in this country, when I see that as a matter
of fact, so much more stress is laid upon learning than upon
piety; upon a thorough education of the head, rather than of
the heart. Is not the Church, in a great measure, in a state of
almost entire conformity to the world—in its spirit, temper,
business, politics, habits of life, dress, means of travel, tables,
furniture, and in almost everything—do not its members follow
closely in the footsteps of the world? I speak not now of conformity to the world in things that are necessary, and appro-

priate, and important to the comfort and usefulness of Christians. For I believe it is their bounden duty, so far as the providence of God puts it in their power, to provide things commendable, and suitable, and appropriate for them in their circumstances. But I speak of that conformity in those things that are useless, extravagant, and in multitudes of instances of a positively evil tendency.

Does not great selfishness prevail almost everywhere in the Church? And does not selfishness disclose itself in almost every form in which it shows itself among worldly men? Does not the Church to a great extent have the impression that selfishness is compatible with true religion; in other words, that selfishness and true religion can coexist in the same mind?

Is it not true that even those who are supposed to be the most pious in the Church have a legal and unhappy religion for they are warring against sin and their lusts in their own strength. They have very little practical knowledge of where their true strength lies, and are almost perpetually overcome and discouraged by the prevalence of their sins; while great multitudes in the Church have not had conviction enough even to make them unhappy, or thoroughly to feel the necessity of a salvation from sin?

Is not the Church amazingly inefficient, so much so, that in many places where there are hundreds of professors of religion, the whole of them will not, by their instrumentality, effect the conversion of ten sinners in a year?

Lastly, is not the Church in its present state a standing, public, perpetual denial of the gospel? Do its members not stand out before the world as a living, unanswerable contradiction of the gospel and do more to harden sinners and lead them into a spirit of hypercriticism and infidelity than all the efforts of professed infidels from the beginning of the world to the present day?

Now I have not made these inquiries in a spirit of bitterness or accusation, but in deep seriousness. They are not the language of revilement and hypercriticism, but of solemn truth. No, indeed, they are but a glimpse of the real facts as they exist almost everywhere. In my next letter, the Lord willing, I intend to hint at some of the reasons for this state of things, as they present themselves to my own mind.

Your brother in the bonds of the gospel,
Charles G. Finney

CHAPTER 8

To ministers of the Gospel of all denominations

February 26, 1840

Beloved Brethren:

In my last letter to you I glanced very briefly at the present state of the Church, and promised in this letter to notice some of the reasons for this state of things, as they present themselves to my own mind.

I would humbly inquire whether ministers themselves are not in a great measure under the influence of sensuality? Is it not true, my brethren, that we are given up very much to the influence of our appetites, that many of us indulge ourselves freely in the use of those things that give the flesh dominion over the soul? Are not ministers, as a general rule, so far sunk in sensuality as to be in a great measure blind to the influence of the body over the mind, both with respect to themselves and also with respect to the Church of God?

Are not many of us exceedingly ignorant in regard to the physiology of our own bodies, and of those dietetic habits which are most congenial to bodily health? Are we not exceedingly ignorant or utterly unmindful of the necessary connection between health of body and health of mind? Is it not true, my brethren, that the mind is, in this state of existence, dependent upon the physical organization for all its developments, and that every transgression of physical law tends strongly to a violation of moral law? This is known to be true as it respects the use of alcohol. But is it considered, even by ministers, that it is equally true in regard to every other abuse of the physical system? Are ministers aware of the immense number of causes of spiritual declension and backsliding which are at work in their congregations? Almost everyone knows, at the present time, that what used to be considered the moderate or temperate use of alcohol renders spirituality impossible. But is it understood and believed, even by ministers themselves, that the same is true to a greater or lesser extent of gluttony, of the use of narcotic substances, and of nonnutritious substances in general? The same general law prevails in reference to them all, that the use of any and every one of them is a violation of the laws of the physical system, an injury to the nervous tissues of the whole body, and always and necessarily abridges the capability of the mind in proportion to the extent of the abuse. These causes of backsliding are almost innumerable, producing their results with just as much certainty as alcohol, though the *connection* between the abuse and the result is not so *obvious* in the one case as in the other.

Is it not true that the ignorance and silence of the ministry in respect to the influence of the flesh, and the means of keeping the body under and bringing it into subjection, are leaving the Church quietly to slumber over the inevitable causes of backsliding without knowing what is the matter? For myself, I must say that my ignorance and silence on these subjects was a great hindrance to my own spirituality, the cause of frequent temporary declensions and spiritual bondage. I never made, as I can now see, any perceptible advance in real piety until my ill health and other circumstances turned my mind to look these causes of backsliding fully in the face and put them away.

I am frequently amazed that I so far overlooked all those passages in the Bible which speak of the influence of the flesh upon the mind. The three great enemies of the soul are represented in the Bible as the world, the flesh, and the devil. I used to preach against the world and against the devil, and warn Christians against their influence; but I must say with shame that I knew but very little of what was meant by those warnings in the Bible against the influence of the flesh. Such passages as these were not deeply pondered and well considered by me: "The fleshly mind is enmity against God." "To be carnally (or fleshly) minded is death." "If ye live after the flesh ye shall die." "Therefore mortify your members which are upon the earth." "He that is Christ's hath crucified the flesh, with its affections and lusts." "I keep under my body and bring it into subjection." "Be ye not deceived, God is not mocked, whatsoever a man soweth that shall he also reap." "He that soweth to his flesh shall of the flesh reap corruption." "They that are after the flesh do mind the things of the flesh." "For many walk, of whom I have told you often, and now tell you even weeping, that they are the enemies of the cross of Christ: whose end is destruction, whose God is their belly, and whose glory is their shame, who mind earthly things."

These and multitudes of other passages of scripture, I must confess with shame, have been till recently very much overlooked by me; i.e., I did not ponder and well understand their meaning. And I can now see that I confounded the influence of the world and the devil with that of the flesh. I am now fully convinced, however, that the flesh has more to do with the backsliding of the Church than either the world or the devil. Every man has a body and every man's body, in this age of the world, is more or less impaired by intemperance of one kind or another. Almost every person, whether he is aware of it or not, is in a greater or lesser degree a dyspeptic[1], and is suffering under some form of disease arising out of intemperance. And I would humbly ask, is it understood and proclaimed by ministers that a person can no more expect healthy manifestations of mind in a fit of dyspepsia than in a fit of intoxication? Is it understood and preached to the Church that every violation of the physical laws of the body as certainly and as necessarily prevents healthy and holy developments just in proportion to the extent of the infraction of physical law, as does the use of alcohol? In short, my brethren, do we understand, sufficiently consider, and proclaim the fact, that man is a compound being, that his soul is entirely dependent upon the physical system for all its manifestations, and that therefore, unless we eat and drink for the glory of God, or in such a manner as to promote our highest physical perfection, unless we render our "bodies a living sacrifice, holy and acceptable," it is naturally impossible that our souls should prosper? I am convinced, that the temperance reformation has but just begun, and that the total abstinence principle, in regard to a great many other subjects besides alcohol, must prevail before the Church can prosper to any considerable extent. I regard it as a settled and unalterable truth that until the physiological and dietetic habits of men are corrected, spiritual declensions and backslidings are inevitable. The laws of the physical system are the laws of God. They must be searched out and proclaimed by ministers, and obeyed by all men who expect to have their souls prosper.

I want to recommend to my dear brethren the careful, and prayerful, and repeated perusal of Graham's Lectures on "The

---

[1]One who suffers indigestion or some stomach condition.

Science of Human Life." I have been greatly edified by a careful perusal of those lectures. My health and the providence of God had, before their publication, led me to read whatever came within my reach upon these subjects. But still I felt the lack of much instruction which has been in a great measure supplied by this work. In recommending this book, I do not mean to say that I regard everything said in it as exactly correct. Yet as a whole, I consider it invaluable. I thank God for it. It should be read in every family, and persons of every age should as far as possible become acquainted with its contents.[2]

One thing more in relation to this point, my brethren. Let me recommend to you to adopt and practice principles just as fast as you are convinced of their truth, and that in your families, pulpits, and in all your ways, you hold up the light upon physical and dietetic reform. O, my brethren, I beseech you, turn not away from this subject as of little importance. I greatly sinned in this respect. I might have been instructed much earlier than I was, and saved much of strength and life for the service of God, had I been prepared to search out, embrace, and practice the truth, in every department of temperance.

It is manifest that Paul regarded dietetic reform as essential to thorough and permanent moral reform, and was in the habit of preaching and insisting much upon this subject. In writing to the Philippian Church he says, "For many walk, of whom I have told you often, and now tell you even weeping, that they are the enemies of the cross of Christ: whose end is destruction, whose God is their belly, and whose glory is in their shame, who mind earthly things." Now it is worthy of all observation here that he had often warned them before on the subject of making a god of their belly; and now, finding them so obstinately persevering in their sensuality, he told them again, even weeping, that they were the enemies of the cross of Christ, and that the evidence of this was that they made a god of their belly, and gloried in those habits of living that were a shame to them. Now if Paul, nearly eighteen hundred years ago, warned the Christian church often upon this subject, and wept over the sensuality of Christians, certainly it should be thought by ministers to be of some importance at the present time.

[2]Sylvester Graham (1794–1851) was the inventor of Graham flour and known today as the inventor of the Graham Cracker. He wrote *Lectures on the Science of Human Life*, 2 vols. (Boston: Marsh, Capen, Lyon, & Webb, 1839.) Due to Finney's numerous illnesses in his early ministry, probably due to exhaustion from overwork, we can understand his concern in this area. Good nutrition is still a vital concern of Christians today.

I beseech you, let no one say this is legal, and has nothing to do with Christian liberty. This is a sad and ruinous mistake. The fact is, there is a necessity founded in the very constitution and laws of our compound nature, for our knowing and doing the truth in regard to all our bodily as well as intellectual habits. And the gospel can no more save us from the necessity of correct physiological and dietetic habits, than it can save us from the necessity of abstaining from the use of alcohol. It is only through a proper knowledge of and obedience to the laws of our beings as we are constituted, body and soul, that the gospel has any power, and I may add, any tendency to save us.

Is not another cause of the state of the Church owing to a lamentable lack of spirituality in the ministry? I will not here enter into the discussion of the causes of this lack of spirituality. But, brethren, is it not true, do not our closets attest it, do not our own consciences attest it, that we live in a great measure in a state of spiritual bondage, and altogether too far from God? Do not the most spiritual members of our churches perceive and, in secret, grieve and weep over the obvious lack of spirituality in our prayers, preaching, and daily conversation? Do they not perceive that our conversation is not in heaven, that we do not daily walk with God, that we have not that deep spiritual experience and acquaintance with Christ that enables us to feed the lambs and sheep of the flock with that spiritual food and heavenly manna which they so much need? Beloved brethren, is it not true that the most spiritual members of our churches are sighing and crying over the great lack of spirituality in the ministry, and that while they treat us with respect, they look upon us with compassion, and in reality have very little confidence in our ability to guide them? They respect our station, they love us as men. Perhaps they regard us as Christians. But, beloved, I have good reason to know that great multitudes of the most spiritual members of the Church regard their ministers as exceedingly *in the way* of the advancement of the cause of true religion through a lamentable lack of spirituality. I am ashamed to say this; I mourn when I think of it; I am almost afraid to say it—lest blustering and hypocritical professors of religion should make it an occasion of criticism. And yet, beloved, somebody ought to say it. Our most spiritual members dislike to say it to us. They fear that it will not be well received, that it will be taking too much upon themselves to reprove their minister, that it will be regarded as an evidence and an instance of spiritual pride, and they fear, perhaps, that it will do more harm than good. They, therefore, pass along in silence, but with sorrowful hearts. As often as the Sabbath comes, they go to and from the house of God with mourning. They see us through the week. Our spirit, and temper, and deportment often shock and grieve them, and they fear that we have mistaken our calling. O brethren, be not offended at what I say; I say it in love and in grief. How long shall this be so?

Are there not classes of passages of the most spiritual and important character upon which we cannot preach, dare not preach, and should be regarded as hypocritical if we did preach, until we reform our lives and habits? Are not our own lusts, and lives, and habits virtually leading us to compromise on the subject of self-denial, bearing the cross, contempt of the world, and many of the most important subjects upon which the Church of God need to be instructed?

Is there not a great error among ministers, and in their families in respect to conformity to the world? Are not their wives, and sons and daughters, as well as ministers themselves in many instances, shockingly conformed to the world? Is not this the case so much that we cannot preach against conformity to the world, without being turned upon by our hearers and churches with the just retort, "Physician, heal thyself?"

Now I know that when there is in reality no fault in this respect, the wicked heart is apt thus to retort and to shield itself, under anything and everything, and nothing, rather than abandon sin. I have often observed that when ministers preach against conformity to the world in things that are useless and even pernicious, professors and worldlings are disposed to complain of them for allowing themselves to possess even the necessaries and little conveniences of life. They refuse to make any distinction between things really useful and necessary, and things useless, unnecessary, and even pernicious. In one instance a professor of religion who was reproved for squandering Christ's money and injuring his health in the use of tea, replied that if he gave up his tea, the minister, on the same principle, ought to give up his chair and use a stool.

But, brethren, there is a broad distinction and one, after all, that commends itself to the conscience and common sense of mankind and which we can compel them to see, between things useless or pernicious, and things really necessary or important to our happiness or usefulness. I would be as far as possible from suggesting that ministers have not a right to the necessities and comforts of life as well as other men. But in regard to extravagance in dress, tight-fitting clothes, injurious dietetic and physiological habits, conformity to the fashions of the world, and many other things, are not some of us and our families greatly at fault? Do not understand me, dear brethren, as excusing myself in these respects, for by the grace of God I intend to look well at home on these subjects.

Now brethren, is there not altogether too much silence among ministers in regard to conformity to the world, and is not this silence a great measure owing to conscious fault on our part, or on the part of our families, in these respects. Do not ministers pretend blindness at the extravagance of the Church, and in a great many instances allow them, unreproved, to squander Christ's money upon their lusts lest, as I have said, if they reprove them, they should meet the just retort, "Physician, heal thyself?" Beloved brethren, do we take pains enough to be "examples to the flock," in every respect? Do we see to it that, not only in our own, but in the spirit, deportment, habits and lives of our families, there is such a conformity to the principles of the gospel as "to commend ourselves to every man's conscience in the sight of God?" I must say that, for myself, I am grieved when I see the wife or the daughter of a minister follow on in the wake of fashion, and when the families of the ministers of Christ, instead of firmly resisting the tide of desolation that is inundating the world, fall in with, if not take the lead, in the extravagancies and worldly-mindedness of the Church. Beloved brethren, are we aware how much we and our families are watched and our spirit imbibed by the Church and the world? Do our wives and sons and daughters understand how much they abridge our influence and tie up our hands if they set an example of worldly-mindedness? How can we preach against abuses and things we practice ourselves and freely allow in our families? I have not said this because I do not suppose there are many godly ministers who are in a good measure alive to all these things. Nor do I say them because I have not been in many respects guilty myself; but on the contrary, because I have, and because I have witnessed them in such numerous instances, and because I regard them as a great hindrance and a great grievance to the Church of God.

I cannot pursue this subject further at present. I hope to be able to write you again in the next issue of the *Evangelist*.

Your brother in the bonds of the Gospel,
Charles G. Finney

CHAPTER 9

To ministers of the Gospel of all denominations

March 11, 1840

Beloved Brethren:

In pursuing this subject, permit me to inquire whether the sectarianism of the ministry is not the cause of the sectarianism of the Church? Is it not a fact that the spirit and bearing of ministers of different denominations toward each other, their preaching, and much of their influence, tend to promote sectarianism in the Church? Is it not a common thing, in revivals of religion, for ministers to feel and manifest a jealousy of the influence of other denominations? Do they not often take pains to indoctrinate the converts more with a design to guard them against the influence of other denominations than to promote holy living? Is it not common for ministers to take more pains to put the Church and the young converts on their guard in reference to denominational peculiarities, than to break them off from "all ungodliness and every worldly lust"? And is it not true of ministers of every denomination, that they are, to an alarming extent, more zealous in promoting denominational peculiarities and sustaining church order in reference to their own peculiar sect than they are to promote the sanctification of the body of Christ? Is it not a fact that doctrinal knowledge, especially on sectarian points, is more insisted upon by ministers than holiness of heart and life, and more than Christian love? Are not ministers more alarmed at the encroachments of other denominations than they are at the overflowing of sin, lukewarmness, pride, and worldly-mindedness in the Church? Will they not take the alarm sooner at the influence of other denominations; will they not display more zeal and promptness in exposing their supposed errors than they will to expose and denounce the ungodliness and worldly lusts that are disgracing Christ and ruining the souls of the people?

Again allow me to inquire, my brethren, whether the hypercritical disposition of ministers may not in a great measure account for the hypercritical disposition of the Church? Can it be denied that there is a fearful amount of transgression in this respect, among ministers of all denominations? Has not a spirit of distrust and evil speaking overspread the land and appeared very conspicuously of late among ministers of the gospel, until much of what passes in the business of ecclesiastical bodies and in newspaper articles savors strongly of slander and revilement?

Are not the legality and spiritual bondage of the Church owing in a great measure to the legal spirit of the ministers? Christ is exhibited as a Savior from hell, but not sufficiently and fully as a Savior from sin; as our justification, but not prominently as our sanctification. Justification by faith is abundantly, as it should be, insisted upon. But so far as my knowledge extends, sanctification by faith has not held a prominent place in the preaching of the present day. Hence, when Christians are brought under conviction of sin, they set themselves to war against it in their own strength. Like the case described in the seventh of Romans, they feel themselves condemned and struggling against temptation, but are swept away as with a flood.[1] Those that are accounted as the most spiritual in the Church seem to be in a state of almost perpetual bondage, complaining, grieving, and struggling because they do not apprehend Christ as an all-sufficient and present sanctification. They hope Christ will save them from hell, but they do not understand that He is a present Savior from all sin.

Beloved brethren, is there not even in the ministry a lamentable ignorance in respect to the practical truth, "The blood of Jesus Christ cleanseth us from all sin"? For one, I must say, that I mourn and am deeply ashamed before God that for so many years, I was so little acquainted with Him who was called Jesus, because He should save His people from their sins. [2] O

---

[1] See Charles G. Finney's sermons on Romans, some deal especially with Romans chapter seven, in *Principles of Victory*, (Minneapolis: Bethany House Publishers, 1981), and *Principles of Liberty*, (Minneapolis: Bethany House Publishers, 1983).

[2] See Charles G. Finney, *Principles of Union with Christ*, (Minneapolis: Bethany House Publishers, 1985). This little devotional book, compiled and edited from the 1851 edition of his *Systematic Theology*, discusses the titles of Christ and teaches how we can have a sanctifying relationship with Christ on the basis of these titles.

how little of what the gospel says about the Savior did I understand and receive. A great many of the most precious and sin-subduing truths of the Bible were entirely a dead letter to me. And I began to find, some years ago, that many spiritual Christians knew something about Christ that I did not know, but greatly needed to know. The fact was, I could not lead inquiring Christians to a sanctifying Christ. And now, beloved brethren, let me ask you, I pray without offense, is it not a matter of fact that there is among us comparatively little deep experimental acquaintance with the sanctifying power of Christ? Are not many of us in such a state of almost continual spiritual bondage and condemnation that we know but little of the great peace those have who love the law of God? Is it not also true that nearly all our sermons are upon texts that have a legal rather than a gospel bearing upon the heart?

Is it not a matter of fact, beloved brethren, that the declension of religion after revivals, and the backslidings of the Church that so deeply disgrace the gospel, are due to the fact that ministers do not sufficiently insist upon the renunciation and entire annihilation of the certain causes of decline and backsliding? A revival of religion implies reformation. There is no real revival of religion any further than there is actual outward reformation of life and habits. And certainly there is but one possible way in which permanency in religion can be secured; and that is by making reformation universal and entire, extending to all our habits of life, business transactions, and everything else that pertains to us. Total abstinence from all sin is naturally and even more indispensable to stability in religion than total abstinence from alcohol is to stability and permanence in the temperance reformation. Now, unless ministers set themselves in earnest to remove every form of sin from the Church, to hunt out and expose all the "fleshly indulgences that war against the soul"—all the erroneous principles and practices in business, and everything of every name or nature, that is inconsistent with walking with God, and with the self-denial of the gospel—except they expose the evils and hold up the remedy, carrying reformation thoroughly to the very bottom of every heart, and into the habits and whole life of every convert, then spiritual declension, backsliding, and virtual, if not open apostasy, will be the certain and inevitable result. If any form of sin is indulged, and not hunted out and reproved by the minister, no matter what or how trivial it may appear in the eyes of those who indulge it, it will grieve the Holy Spirit. It will bring certain darkness and leanness to the soul. It will be an inlet to a thousand lusts, and like the letting in of waters, it will cover the whole soul with darkness, and bring the mind into bondage to sin.

It often appears amazing to me that with the present experience of the Church in regard to adopting the principle of total abstinence as of indispensable necessity in the temperance reformation, that so little stress should be laid upon adopting and carrying out the same principle in religion.

Ministers say they do adopt this principle and preach entire consecration to God and total abstinence from sin. But, brethren, allow me to inquire in what way do you preach it? Do you, as a matter of fact, so insist upon it as to beget the ripe conviction in their minds that they are expected at once to abandon every form and degree of sin?

There are three classes of ministers. One class preaches that sinners ought to repent; but they so preach repentance as to leave the sinner under the impression that he cannot repent and must wait God's time. Consequently the sinner slumbers on under such preaching, till the knell of eternal death breaks up his slumbers and he finds himself in the depths of hell. A second class preaches repentance in such a way as to make the impression and beget the conviction that men can and must and are expected immediately to repent. This preaching arouses and alarms the sinner. He sees that the minister is in earnest and expects him to repent, and the anxious inquiry will soon be made, "What must I do to be saved?" The sinner is alarmed and makes the inquiry, because he sees the minister in earnest, and he really believes he can and ought to repent. This class of ministers really do expect sinners to repent. They are not surprised when sinners become alarmed and make the inquiry, "What shall we do?" And when sinners profess that they have repented, they are willing to believe that they have, and do not unbelievingly reject their pretensions as fanaticism and spiritual pride. This same class of ministers *claim* also to preach total abstinence from sin to the Church. They do not tell the Church that they may and must live in sin, and who does? They preach entire consecration; but after all, as a matter of fact, they fail to produce the conviction that they are really in earnest and *expect* them to live in a state of entire consecration to God. They no more bring Christians around them to inquire on the subject of entire consecration or sanctification than the first class brings sinners to inquire after repentance. This class of ministers will have inquiry meetings for sinners, and many sinners will ask "What shall we do to be saved?" But as a matter of fact, they do not preach entire consecration so as to arouse the inquiry after entire sanctification. Consequently, if any should inquire after this blessing, they would be as much at a loss to know what to say to them as the other class of ministers would be to know what to say to a sinner who should inquire after salvation. And if anyone should profess to have entered into a state of entire consecration or sanctification they would treat such professions with entire incredulity, and show that they never expected any such results from their preaching.

A third class not only so preaches that sinners must repent, as to awaken the inquiry after repentance and eternal life, and bring them around the preacher trembling in tears and agony for their souls; but they also preach the doctrine of total abstinence from sin, entire consecration to God, and so exhibit the blood of Christ as cleansing from all sin, as to bring around them throngs of anxious Christians earnestly and agonizingly inquiring after so great a salvation. The meetings appointed for the purpose of giving special instruction upon this subject are thronged with multitudes whose bosoms are heaving with emotion, and whose hearts are panting after universal holiness. This class of ministers makes the same impression and produces the same conviction upon the minds of Christians that they are expected to be entirely sanctified as they do upon the minds of sinners that they are expected to repent. And the results are the same in both cases. Sinners, by the grace of God, actually do repent; and Christians, by the same grace, take hold on full salvation and enter into the rest of faith.

Now, brother, to which of these classes do you belong? Do you preach repentance to sinners? If so, I humbly inquire, how do you preach it? Do you make the impression that you are in earnest, that you expect it, that God expects it, and that in all reason and conscience the sinner is bound at once to lay down his weapons and submit to God? Or do you preach in such a way as to leave sinners quietly slumbering in their sins; and would you feel disappointed should any number of sinners profess to have repented under your preaching?

Do you preach that Christians should entirely abandon all sin, enter upon a state of immediate, entire, and eternal consecration to God, and never, in any instance, again take up arms and make war upon God? Certainly you do not, you dare not preach the reverse of this. You do not, no, dare not tell the Church that they must of necessity and are expected to rebel against God, and serve the devil as long as they live. Should you tell them this, the common sense of all mankind would revolt at it. But, beloved brethren, do you say *nothing* which in reality implies this? Do you say nothing that after all leaves the impression that you really expect them to indulge in sin as long as they live? Do *you* lay aside in your own practice "every weight and the sin that doth so easily beset you," and set them such an example as to inspire the hope that they may even in this life get entirely above their sins? Bear with me, my beloved brethren, I speak in behalf of Christ. As on my knees, at your feet, would I address you. Indeed, I would implore you to inquire whether as a matter of fact you either preach or expect that Christians should give up all their sins? Do they so understand you? Do they inquire earnestly of you how they may get hold of this salvation? Do you know how to direct them? Do you so direct them that as a matter of fact they find deliverance from sin? Do you really succeed in causing them immediately to renounce "all ungodliness and every worldly lust"? Do you crowd this subject upon Christians as you do the doctrine of repentance upon sinners, and with the same earnestness and faith and expectation of success?

Let me inquire, I pray you, what would be the certain result of preaching repentance in such a manner as to leave the impression that sinners cannot repent? Why, under such preaching they would not repent of course. And do let me ask, my brethren, if you preach to Christians in such a manner as to create the impression that they cannot, or will not as a matter of fact, live without sin, will they not as certainly go on in sin? If you preach to sinners that they cannot repent, or say what plainly implies that they cannot, either with or without the grace of God, will they not virtually justify their unrepentance and show that they are not shocked and agonized at the fact that they are unrepentant? Just so, if you preach what implies that Christians cannot, or as a matter of fact never will, live without sin, they will not only live in sin, but will virtually justify their sins and show that they are not shocked and astonished at themselves for living in sin.

And now, brethren, do we not charge the unrepentance and lack of revivals in many congregations to a lack of practically preaching the doctrines of repentance and faith? We do, and no doubt justly.

And now, let me get down at your feet and inquire whether the state of religion in the church to which you minister is not due to the fact that you neither so *preach* nor *practice* entire consecration as to beget among Christians the conviction of its attainability? And let me ask again, were you to preach repentance to sinners as you preach entire consecration to Christians, do you believe there would ever be a revival among them under your preaching till the Day of Judgment? Should I ask the professors of religion who hear you preach, and who witness your life and spirit, whether they think you expect them to break off entirely from their rebellion and consecrate themselves wholly to God and indulge in sin no more, would they testify that they believe you do expect this of them?

Dear brethren, take it not amiss that I speak thus plainly; I speak in love. My heart is pained, my soul is sick that the Church is allowed to live in sin, and not so much as to be possessed with the idea that anything else is to be expected of its members till they die.

Let me inquire again, my brethren, do not every one of you require of the members of your church the solemn pledge contained in your church covenant, that he will deny all ungodliness and every worldly lust, and live soberly, righteously, and godly in this present world? Does not your church covenant bind your members as with a solemn oath to live in a state of entire consecration or sanctification to God? Now if this is so, and everyone knows it is, can ministers innocently let their churches live in the constant and open violation of this covenant, and still encourage them with the hope that they are in the way to heaven? Can you require such a promise, and consent that your members should make such a covenant, and then preach as if you did not expect them to keep it; and even treat the very profession of keeping it as an evidence of spiritual pride and fanaticism? Do you require such a covenant and then insist upon the dangerous tendency of preaching that this covenant should be fully kept? And do you, dare you, preach that to profess to live agreeably to this covenant is the result of gross delusion and fanaticism? My brethren, what consistency is there in this? What is it other than great impiety to require such covenant commitments as these, and then not only not insist upon their fulfillment, but maintain explicitly or impliedly that it is dangerous to insist upon or even expect to live in accordance with such a solemn vow? Is it not the solemn duty of every minister either to expunge that clause from the church covenant, or to admit and insist upon the practicability of keeping it?

How immensely injurious is it to the cause of Christ to bring Christians into a solemn covenant, entered into in the house of God, over the elements of the broken body and shed blood of the blessed Jesus, on the holy Sabbath, renewed and sworn over and over again as often as the communion season occurs, and then treat all insisting upon the keeping of this covenant, and even the profession of keeping it, as gross delusion, fanaticism, and spiritual pride?

Is it not most obvious that a lack of thoroughly taking up and pressing this subject of entire consecration upon Christians in revivals of religion is the very reason why they decline and react in such a way as to greatly dishonor the Savior? The very laws of the human constitution forbid that the great excitement that prevails at the commencement of revivals of religion should continue for a long time. This is neither possible nor desirable. But in proportion as the excitement dies away, the unconverted are apt to become careless and return to their former courses. Now what is lacking to keep the revival from declining among the real converts? It is obvious that something must be done that will set them in pursuit of the highest attainments in piety. Unless they are immediately cut off from their indulgences in sin, they will quench the Spirit and soon lose their ardor in working for the conversion of sinners. Unless every form of improper indulgence is pointed out and wholly abandoned by them, they will of course soon return to the world. Now beloved brethren is there any other way to secure them from this result than to set ourselves right at work to bring about their entire and perpetual consecration to God, laying down and insisting upon entire conformity to the great principles of God's government in every respect: in making restitution where they have done wrong, to the extent of their ability: in practicing all those degrees of self-denial; carrying the law of love through all the transactions of life, as fully, and thoroughly, and perpetually, as the gospel demands; holding up the cross as the foundation of all true reformation, and exhibiting Christ in all His relations and offices in such a manner as to make the saints partakers of His holiness and divine nature? This course of preaching would open to the convert a new world of immensely interesting light. It would fill him with pantings and longings after complete deliverance from sin, and would open to both minister and people the most enchanting fields of truth and usefulness conceivable. And Christians, instead of attempting to sit down upon the side of a slippery precipice from which they would surely slide to the bottom, would not think of resting or looking back until their reformation was so thorough and universal as to be able to say, "Blessed be God, we are free." Unless this course be taken, I am as well convinced as I am of my own existence that revivals will always, and certainly, and necessarily decline as they have done, to the great reproach of the cause of Christ.

Now I beseech my brethren to look at this subject and see if it is not a matter of fact, that revivals do decline in the Church, for lack of proper instruction and right example on the part of ministers?

One word in answer to an objection, and I will close. It is said that the Methodist brethren preach entire consecration or sanctification, and yet that their revivals soon decline. To this I wish to reply without offense to them: This doctrine is not insisted upon as universally among them, if my information is correct, as it was in the days of Wesley; that much of the instruction which awakened sinners currently receive is not sufficiently discriminating to insure sound conversions, and consequently many of their professed converts do not want to be holy. It also appears true, that in multitudes of instances the sanctification upon which they insist is rather a legal sanctification, and from the manner in which it is exhibited, is calculated to beget a self-righteous spirit and thus work decline in the Church. And finally, when they enjoy discriminating, thorough instruction, and have ministers that practically understand the subject, who live, and preach, and insist upon entire consecration, their revivals do not decline as is commonly supposed by other denominations. But under such instruction their prayer meetings, and the lives and influence of their members, prove the efficacy and excellence of the glorious and blessed doctrine of entire consecration to God in this life. As a body, I have long feared, and for some time believed that religion was on the decline among them. In the days of Wesley, and for a long time after, insisting upon this doctrine was the very life and power of that church; and precisely as this doctrine has fallen into disrepute among them, vital piety has declined. If these things are not true, I am wholly misinformed upon the subject.

Your brother in the bonds of the gospel,
Charles G. Finney

CHAPTER 10

To ministers of the Gospel of all denominations

March 25, 1840

Beloved Brethren:

Permit me to inquire whether another great difficulty with the Church is not that ministers have been endeavoring to promote spirituality in the Church without true piety? Has it not been too much overlooked that spirituality and communion with God are impossible any further than godliness is practiced in all our lives and ways? Have not attempts often been made, and are they not almost continually made, to keep religion alive and active in the *hearts* of Christians, while they are allowed, without reproof, to indulge selfishness in many forms, to transact business and practice self-indulgences that are entirely inconsistent with loving their neighbor as themselves? Has it been sufficiently considered by ministers that a *life* conformed to the law of love in all respects is indispensable to spirituality and heavenly-mindedness in religion?

Do not Christians in your own church live in a manner at home, while traveling, while transacting business, and doing many other things that must grieve the Spirit of God, when we consider the present state of the world, the calls for benevolent effort, and the deep feeling which Christians must experience in view of the fact that eighteen hundred years have already gone and but a small portion of the world has yet received the gospel? Are churches called by ministers to those degrees of self-denial demanded by the law of love in view of the state of the world and of the Church?

Again, are Christians called by the ministry to give up all attempts and all desire to surround themselves with creature comforts; and are they suitably instructed in regard to the fact that the more happiness they seek from the creature, the less they must necessarily find in the Creator; and the more they multiply earthly goods and sensual objects, and worldly attachments, the less of course they will enjoy of God; and that a life of self-denial, cutting off right hand and plucking out right eye sins, "laying aside every weight and the sin which doth so easily beset" them, are naturally and forever essential to the enjoyment of God?

Is there enough of the testimony of example on the part of ministers? Example is the highest moral influence that can be exerted. And is it not true my brethren, to a great extent, that while Christians hear our preaching, profess to believe it, and even praise it as excellent, their conduct is very little influenced by it because they do not believe that we expect them to live in accordance with it? And is it not true, to a great extent, that the reason why they do not believe us to expect this is that they do not see that we ourselves conform to the standard which we set up? Do they not see that in many instances we preach one thing and practice another? Now, when this is so, our example is the highest influence, and of course they will follow our example and not our precept. And is it not also true that to avoid this inconsistency some ministers do not preach self-denial nor insist much upon heavenly-mindedness? They do not preach entire consecration, so as to make it effective upon the hearts and consciences of Christians, for fear of the retort, "Physician, heal thyself." Now, is it not true that ministers and their families should take the lead, both by example and precept, in all those degrees of Christian curtailment, economy and self-denial that the state of the world and an enlightened benevolence would dictate? Of what use is it for ministers to preach against serving God and mammon, while they themselves are engaged in the speculations of the day? How shall they preach self-denial while they are living in idleness and feeble-mindedness themselves? How shall they preach against conformity to the world when they are attending parties, filling their tables with novels and light reading, and when in almost every respect they are as much conformed to the world as their circumstances will possibly admit?

But there is one subject to which I wish especially to call the attention of my brethren that I must not delay any longer. It is the fact that the *spirit of prayer* has greatly declined in the Church within the few last years, and the Holy Spirit has no doubt been greatly grieved by the course which the Church has pursued on this subject. The spirit of revivals is eminently a spirit of prayer; and so far as my information extends there was much more power and prevalence in the prayers of the Church ten years ago than there is at the present time. I would humbly inquire whether there has not been a fault in ministers in relation to this subject, whether they have not been afraid of the spirit of unutterable groaning and agonizing in prayer that pervades the hearts of those who are wrestling for a revival? I can say my own spirit has been more deeply wounded and shocked at the manner in which the spirit of prayer has been treated in the Church than at almost anything else since I became a Christian. So much has been said about order and against confusion that in many instances it is to be feared that even the ministry have gone to the opposite extreme, and not properly considering what in reality are order and disorder, they have grieved the Spirit of God and quenched the spirit of prayer by attempting to guard against what might, by some, be termed confusion. I have had occasion to know that in many instances ministers have feared and resisted what I have always supposed and now suppose to be the spirit of prayer. And if I am not mistaken, they have frequently crushed revivals in their very outset by causing Christians to restrain and resist the spirit of prayer. I have feared, that there were very few congregations in the land, and very few ministers, who would not resist the spirit of prayer, if it should be poured out upon them. If Christians should be seized with the pains of travail, their bodily strength taken away, and be exercised with such strong crying and tears as to wrestle with unutterable groanings, day and night, as they did in the days of President Edwards, as they once did in Scotland, and in various parts of Europe and America; if the Holy Spirit should come with such power that multitudes should be unable to stand or even to sit upon their seats, and be thrown upon their faces in the greatest agony of soul, and groaning out with such great pain as to arrest the ordinary proceedings of religious meetings, and fill whole assemblies with crying out, as have often been the case where He has not been resisted, and where revivals have been very deep and powerful—I say, I have feared that such things would now be so resisted as to be arrested in the very outset, and with the present views and feelings of ministers no such great revivals can bless the Church. The resistance which has been made to the spirit of prayer since about 1825 is, in my view, one of the most dreadful sins of the Church. One very prominent minister, about that time, published that the spirit of prayer had "run mad." There was so general an opposition to the spirit of prayer, as either to put revivals down altogether or render them exceedingly superficial in comparison with what they otherwise would have been. Indeed, from some things that have occurred is it not to be feared that ministers are so much afraid of the real *spirit* of prayer that, should it prevail in the Church to any considerable extent, they would consider it an objectionable thing, and instead of publishing it to the world as an illustration of the grace of God, would as far as possible conceal it from the world; and if any public notice were taken of it, they would feel called upon to apologize for it as a thing of very rare occurrence, and as something which they took great pains to counteract and control.

A few years ago there was so much of a spirit of prayer that in some instances Christians had been known to retire for secret prayer and to be so exercised with great agony in view of the state of the Church and of the world as to become oblivious to the length of time they were engaged in prayer, and continue their wrestlings for many hours together, covered with the most profuse perspiration, occasioned by the depth of their agony. And in some instances, when their strength was completely exhausted and their burden not removed, others would be obliged to lead them in prayer for the objects for which they were burdened for hours together, before they would get relieved; and in many instances their agony and travail of soul have been so deep that the men of strong nerves have fallen prostrate, and writhed and groaned as in the agonies of death. In those days there were such wonderful answers to prayer, such repeated and almost miraculous interpositions on the part of God to answer prayer, as to astound whole communities, and make it perfectly manifest, even to the ungodly, that the saints were prevailing with God. But things of this kind seemed to be considered as disorderly. Opposition was made to them in high and low places. Much was said and written against such things until the Spirit of God was grieved and there has been a great reduction of fear and restraining prayer before God. Since that time, revivals have been growing more and more superficial in their character, as I doubt not many of those ministers who have witnessed most of the spirit of prayer can testify. Churches have been less permanently benefited, and indeed the whole aspect of religious affairs has deteriorated in proportion as the spirit of prayer has been withdrawn.

And now, beloved brethren, I say not these things abusively. I could mention a great many facts which ought to cause the

Church to blush; but at present, suffice it to say that unless a different course is taken in regard to prayer, I do not believe that revivals of religion can extensively prevail. I have found for the last few years such a great fearfulness on the subject of admitting the spirit of prayer to pervade the churches as to forbid the hope of the Church being deeply and permanently revived, until their views upon this subject are corrected.[1]

Your brother in the bonds of the gospel,
Charles G. Finney

---

[1]See the "Trilogy on Prayer," Charles G. Finney, *Principles of Prayer*, (Minneapolis: Bethany House Publishers, 1980), *Answers to Prayer*, (Minneapolis: Bethany House Publishers, 1983), and *Principles of Devotion*, (Minneapolis: Bethany House Publishers, 1987).

CHAPTER 11

To ministers of the Gospel of all denominations

April 8, 1840

Beloved Brethren:

I am afraid in my letters to you that I shall appear dictatorial and as if I took too much upon me, and have often been on the point of resolving to say no more, lest I should appear assuming, and upon the whole do more harm than good. In continuing to write to you, if I am at all acquainted with my own heart, I would not assume any authority or occupy at all the place of a censor or a dictator. All I ask is to be allowed to speak to my beloved brethren as a little child, and to beseech my fathers and brethren in the ministry to hear the few things I have to suggest, although they are spoken in a great simplicity and weakness. I think I may say, that I speak upon these subjects only because I feel that they are of great importance, and because nobody else seems to open his mouth or use his pen to call the attention of ministers particularly to these subjects. I do not mean by this that the things I am saying and design to say are things upon which nothing has been said or written; but that it appears to me of special importance that these things should be more prominently before the minds of ministers at the present time than they are.

The particular object of this letter is to call the attention of my brethren and fathers in the ministry to the unreasonable prejudice that does, and long has existed in the Church, against what are called bodily prostrations and agitations in view of religious truth. By many this seems to be an insurmountable stumbling block. If the bodily strength is taken away, if swoonings and faintings occur, if persons fall prostrate in the public assembly, in the family circle, or in their closets, if they are seized with bodily agitations or trembling, multitudes take alarm at this and infer, as a thing of course, that it is either the workings of a disordered imagination or the result of devilish agency. Now there are few more unreasonable or ridiculous prejudices among mankind than this, or few things that set in a more painful light the ignorance and thoughtlessness of the Church and the world on some of the most important branches of human knowledge. A very moderate acquaintance with human anatomy and physiology, and a consideration of the compound nature of man, and that the mind always manifests itself through the nervous system, would forever put to silence "the ignorance of foolish men" upon this subject. And it does seem to me to be high time that ministers should take pains to inform the people in relation to the very natural connection there is between a highly excited state of mind upon any subject and bodily prostrations and agitations.[1]

It is very plain that bodily prostrations and agitations are no part of religion. But it is just as plain that these may be the natural effect of discoveries of religious truth. Several instances of bodily prostrations and agitations are recorded in the Bible as the result of such discoveries. Daniel fainted and was unable to stand, being overcome by the presence of the divine glory. Saul of Tarsus fell to the ground at a discovery of the glory of Christ. The Psalmist speaks of his flesh trembling. Now it certainly is not at all surprising, when we consider the compound nature of man, that his frail body should be overcome by clear manifestations of the glory of God. I never read or heard of any bodily effects that might not be most naturally and easily accounted for upon some of the plainest principles of physiology. Instances have frequently occurred when great and sudden excitement of mind has been produced by other than religious intelligence, in which persons have instantly fallen down dead. Now this is not at all strange when we consider the nervous system of man, its connection with the mind on the one hand and with the organs of organic life on the other.

Now such cases sometimes occur when sudden and great manifestations of the divine glory are made to the human mind. It is not at all amazing that this should be so. Some have objected to the bodily prostrations, agitations, and faintings of

---

[1] See Jonathan Edwards book *Religious Affections* for a thorough and competent examination of this point. Edwards based his book upon his experiences in the Great Awakening and includes many teachings from Scripture.

Mrs. President Edwards, of the Rev. William Tennant, and of multitudes of others both in ancient and modern times. The great Kentucky revival, as it was called, was notorious for the bodily prostrations and agitations that were common in that great work of the Lord. Now it certainly is a matter of extreme distress that so many minds, in many other respects enlightened, should stumble at such things, and feel as if no such results were to be expected as a natural effect, in proportion to the clearness and extent with which the Spirit of God makes known His truth to the minds of men. Why is it at all remarkable that the infinitely solemn, important, and awful things of eternity, when clearly brought home to the minds of men, should produce great tremblings and quakings and agitations and prostrations of body, with "groanings that cannot be uttered"? Truly, it is not at all strange. But the only wonder is that mankind are not a hundred or a thousand times more affected in this way than they actually are.

There can be no doubt that Satan can produce the same results by suggesting lies, and produce a great excitement of mind in view of things that are utterly false; for it matters not whether the things in themselves be true or false, while the mind regards them as truth, they will produce their effects and that in proportion to the vividness with which the mind perceives them, and the high import which the mind ascribes to them. It does appear to me therefore that bodily agitations, swoonings, faintings, or anything of this kind, are not to be regarded at all as objections to a work of grace.

As I have said, they are not part of religion, but they are very natural effects of a very high degree of religious affections and emotions. Nor is it true as some seem to suppose that none but what are called nervous people are affected in this way. It is true that all persons are more or less subject to bodily agitations on any exciting topic in proportion to the delicacy of their nervous system. But it is also true that there is enough in religious truth, if clearly revealed to the mind by the Holy Spirit, to wilt down the bodily frame of the strongest man on earth. It is not likely that Daniel was regarded as of so nervous a temperament as to be easily overcome by excitement. And Saul of Tarsus appears not to have been lacking in firmness of nerves. And in both ancient and modern times, great multitudes of the most sedate and orderly, men of the soundest minds and bodies, have been overcome by discoveries of the divine glory—by the infinitely great and overpowering considerations of religion. When, therefore, I hear it objected that bodily prostrations and agitations are something wrong in the proceedings of any religious meeting and to be denounced and opposed as fanatical and the works of the devil, I find it difficult to express the mingled emotions of shame, grief, and indignation which I feel: shame that professedly enlightened minds should know so little of human anatomy and physiology, so little of their own constitution and of the overpowering truth of God as to think of making this an objection to a revival of religion; grief that the Holy Spirit should be so resisted in making such discoveries as He is endeavoring to make of eternal truths to the minds of men; and indignation that so many of the Church of God should turn round and take sides with the ignorant and opposing multitudes, against that which of all things is to be expected, and might exist and often does exist, on any and every other subject that greatly and overwhelmingly interests the human mind. I have known a woman frightened to death because a building in the neighborhood was on fire, though no lives were endangered. I have known persons to go into almost instant derangement on account of events both greatly joyous and greatly grievous. I know of a woman who fell down dead on learning of the conversion of a near relative. Indeed, who has not known multitudes of such things? And why should it be thought strange that sometimes these bodily effects should be witnessed in revivals of religion? I must say, I am far from feeling alarmed at such things as these for the sake of the good they accompany, I could willingly see whole communities overcome and lying prostrate, if need be, for hours or for days, under the revelations of the divine glory.

I should abhor aiming to stir up an excitement *for the purpose of* producing such results as bodily agitations and prostrations. But if, while fulfilling my obligation to use all the means in my power to enlighten mankind in regard to the infinitely interesting things of eternity, some degree of bodily effects are produced, I ought not on that account stay my hand or take it for granted that anything is wrong.

I have not brought forward this subject now because anything of this kind exists at present in the Church to any considerable extent, either in this region or anywhere else, so far as my knowledge extends. But for precisely the opposite reason, because it does not exist. When such things do exist, have already excited alarm, awakened prejudice and the spirit of controversy in the Church, it is, as a general thing, too late to call public attention to an examination of the subject, because then the public mind is in no state to give it a candid and impartial investigation. It is of the highest importance, therefore, that the public mind should be prepared for a great and overpowering revival of religion, and for a copious outpouring of the Spirit and manifestation of the power of God and the gospel, since this can never take place without its resulting in great resistance and divisions in the Church unless the public mind is prepared to let the Spirit come in His overpowering influences without alarm. I have supposed, and do still suppose, that the great reason why revivals of religion have not been more deep, permanent and sin-subduing is that the Spirit has been unable to proceed beyond a certain limit in His work without meeting with a stern resistance on the part of multitudes of professors of religion and ministers. They seem, in their unbelief, to have prescribed certain limits within which revivals should be kept, have formed certain notions of order and endeavored to confine the Spirit down to a stereotyped mode of operation, and are ready to make common cause and unite their hand in opposing the Spirit whenever He should step over into what they suppose to be the regions of disorder. For myself, I am expecting, as soon as the Church will consent to it, and the ministry are prepared to lead the way, much deeper, more permanent and sin-subduing revivals of religion than the world has ever seen. The thing greatly to be desired is that the ministry especially should set themselves to prepare for this great work, take up the stumbling blocks out of the way of God's people, build a highway, and in the shortest time possible prepare the way of the Lord.

Your brother in the bonds of the gospel,
Charles G. Finney

CHAPTER 12

To ministers of the Gospel of all denominations

April 22, 1840

Dear Brethren:

Another topic upon which I wish particularly to address you is the fear of being thought to have changed your opinions upon religious subjects. There is something very astounding in the state of public sentiment to which the attention of ministers and all others needs to be called, and against which all good men should set their faces. It has, for a long time, appeared to me to be generally regarded as a crime for a man to make any advances in religious knowledge, and especially that he should suppose himself to have discovered anything that past generations did not know. The present state of the public sentiment seems to demand either that a man should assume at the outset that he is omniscient, or else make up his mind to remain forever in ignorance. It seems to be regarded as a sufficient objection to anything new which a man learns, that he did not always know it. And it seems to be regarded as something disgraceful and criminal for a man to advance in religious knowledge. As an illustration of this, to my present views of entire consecration to God in this life, it seems to have been regarded by some as a sufficient objection that I did not formerly believe and preach it as I now do.

Now several things are here assumed which are utterly untrue: that the former generations were the genuinely wise men, and that wisdom has died with them; that the Christian fathers knew all about theology, and that the divines (theologians) of President Edwards' day were so wise, that to differ from them in opinion is to be wrong.

It seems also to be generally assumed that for a man to hold any new opinions of which he was himself formerly ignorant, it is evidence of great instability of character and of a strong tendency to fanaticism. Now, certainly all these assumption are entirely unreasonable. The present generation ought to be ashamed if we have made not real addition to the religious knowledge of past generations. And every minister ought to be ashamed of himself, who is not, from Sabbath to Sabbath, bringing forth to his people new truths. A scribe that is well instructed will bring forth things *new* as well as old. And certainly it is a very absurd objection to any truth which a man may discover as taught in the Bible, that he did not know it before.

It is easy to see the bearing of this unreasonable prejudice in the public mind. Its tendency is to stereotype all our knowledge of a subject upon which of all other things it is most important that we should make rapid and constant advancement. Certainly the field of religious truth is infinitely extensive. The science of theology is as vast as the nature, attributes, providence, and government of God.

I have thought that ministers seem afraid to acknowledge anything new, simply because it is new. And, on account of public prejudices upon this subject, they fear to avow the fact that they have learned anything of which they were before ignorant.

Now if this principle or prejudice be applied to any other branch of knowledge, it is easy to see how disastrous its effects would be. Indeed it has been applied, in the dark ages of popery, to philosophy, astronomy, and to many other branches of sciences. Great and good men have been pronounced heretics for teaching anything new in philosophy, astronomy, etc. What was the result, but to cover the earth with a cloud of darkness, to exclude the light of science, and shut up the human mind in all the ignorance and hypocritical rituals of papacy? Now is there not still a powerful current setting in upon ministers and religious teachers calculated greatly to hinder advances in religious knowledge? Let any man, in these days, discover almost any new and important truth on the subject of religion, and make it known, and with the great mass of minds it seems to be a conclusive argument against it, that he did not always know it, and that such men as Edwards and Augustine did not know it. Now this is an unreasonable and ridiculous state of mind, and its downright absurdity and dangerous tendency would be seen if applied to any other than religious truth. God has revealed himself in many ways, principally in His works and providences and in His Word. The book of *nature* has always been open to the observation of mankind; but yet how little of its contents have ever been understood. Until the present century, comparatively little advance has been made in some of the most important branches of human knowledge. How little has been known, or is now known of vegetable, animal, and human physiology, and consequently of the true principles of temperance?

Now suppose that to the new truths that are continually coming before the public upon these and other important subjects of knowledge, it should be objected that they are new opinions; that their authors had never known them before; and that as they have always been discoverable to past generations, it is unreasonable to suppose that the great men of bygone days should not have discovered them, if they are true. The inconclusiveness of such reasoning would be seen at once. But the objection is just as good against advancement in any department of science as against advancement on religious subjects. It is no answer to say that past generations have had the Bible as well as we, and that it is unreasonable to suppose that it contains truths which they did not discover or which we ourselves have not discovered until now; for past generations have had the whole field of science, as well as the book of nature open before them as well as we, and whoever pretended to say that the revelation God has made in His works has more than begun to be understood? For myself, I am free to say, that the more I read the Bible, the more I am convinced that neither myself nor others of past or present generations, so far as my knowledge extends, have more than fairly begun to understand its glorious truths. And when I read it under the light of the Holy Spirit, I can scarcely get through a chapter or paragraph, without discovering new and thrilling truths. Indeed, wonders rise upon wonders, as often as I read and reread, search and research, pray over, and attempt to fathom the Word of God. I confess it has been far otherwise with me in much of my past religious history. I was, to an amazing extent, blind to my profound ignorance of the Word of God, till within about three years past. Since that time I have been enabled to read it with a degree of astonishment in respect to my former ignorance which I cannot express. I think the Lord has made me willing to acknowledge my ignorance and to profess a determination, by the grace of God, in the future to make some advancement in religious knowledge. And I pray the Lord to deliver me, and to deliver the ministry, from the absurd prejudice that chains them and the Church to a set of stereotyped opinions on all religious subjects.

In regard to doctrines, measures, modes and forms, public prejudice is and has been for many centuries so entirely unreasonable, as it seems to me, that ministers should thoroughly and unsparingly rebuke it. Attempts have been made to put down reforms on all subjects and in all ages by the cry of novelty and innovation, the likes of which are not two more unreasonable objections in the whole universe. Why, this objection assumes that everything is now right, and that any change will be wrong of course. It is as certain as that the world stands, that there *must* be great innovation, and an almost universal turning of the world upside down before it is consecrated to God. And if almost everything is wrong, as is certainly the fact, how infinitely unreasonable it is to put down reforms by the cry of innovation! Why, it is time the world should know that innovation is the thing needed, and that God has commenced a system of innovation by which He intends to change the whole moral condition of the world.

Christ and His apostles were often faced with the objection that their views were new, and their measures were innovations, and disorganizing in their tendency. Luther and Calvin had to confront the same impudent and unreasonable objection, for Judaism and popery were both sticklish for the stereotyped notions of the Church. In later days, Wesley and Whitefield in England, and Edwards and his associates in America, were considered and treated as disorganizers and dangerous innovators. They were all, in their day, more or less in advance of the age in which they lived and of mankind in general. And in looking back upon those periods, we can now discover the unreasonableness of those who brought the objections of novelty and innovation against them.

Should anyone object to these suggestions, that they are entirely uncalled for, and that there is no such thing in fact as a public sentiment demanding that no advances should be made in religious knowledge, or that anything is regarded as suspicious, if not false, because it is new, I would reply: such an objector would seem to me to not well understand the state of public sentiment. Not long ago a sermon was sent to me from a distance, preached by a prominent minister at the opening of a Synod, and published at their request, a leading design of which was to echo this public sentiment of which I have been speaking; and to rebuke, with no small degree of severity, the idea that the Church of the present day is to expect to make any advances upon the knowledge of past generations. I could mention many other facts, by adverting to the periodicals of the present or almost any bygone period, or by reference to the history of Polemic Theology, in every age of the Church, in confirmation of the assertion that such a public prejudice does exist, and long has existed, and that ministers are and ever have been very much under its influence. And I repeat it, if this prejudice is continued and allowed to cramp the energies of the ministry, to limit their inquiries, to rebuke their advances, and to restrict them from bringing changes upon the stereotyped technicalities of a Catechetical Theology, it appears to me plain that the Church must continue in a state of religious babyhood.

Now, beloved brethren, the object of this letter is not to recommend rash speculations and an incautious and reckless removing of ancient landmarks, nor a wild driving in every direction in search of novelty, nor the embracing of every or any opinion merely because it is novel. But the object is simply to call your attention to the evil of allowing yourselves to remain stationary in religious knowledge, and to look at the unreasonableness of refusing to embrace and proclaim any opinion simply because it is new.

Your brother in the bonds of the gospel,
Charles G. Finney

CHAPTER 13

To ministers of the Gospel of all denominations

May 6, 1840

Beloved Brethren:

The Lord is, in great mercy, visiting our churches again with precious revivals of religion. Will you permit me to make a few suggestions in respect to the course to be pursued to preserve the converts from backsliding? You are aware that in the providence of God I have had an opportunity of being in some measure acquainted with the course of things in these blessed seasons of refreshing from the presence of the Lord. I have watched with the deepest interest the rise and progress and decline of these seasons, and have inquired, with the deepest solicitude, after the best means of promoting them, and into the causes of their decline. After much reflection and observation upon the subject, there are a great many things that I would say to my beloved brethren, but for the present beg permission to drop a few suggestions in regard to the converts of these revivals. It has long appeared to me that errors in the management and training of young converts have been a principal cause of the decline of revivals of religion in the churches. I am very far from being of the opinion that revivals in this country have declined for many years as deeply and radically as many have seemed to suppose. It has been sometimes predicted that the revivals that have prevailed within the last twenty years had so declined so that a long night of death and darkness would ensue, like that which followed the revivals in the days of Whitefield and Edwards. I do not believe that any such thing has occurred or is likely to occur in this country, unless some revolutionary struggle, or great and absorbing political question should, for a long time, divert the public mind. We have great reason for gratitude that the decline of revivals has, for the last twenty years or more, been only temporary. And I think the fact that there have been only temporary seasons of declension can be accounted for on the plainest principles of philosophy and common sense. But I pass over this part of the subject for the present, for the purpose of saying a few things with respect to the converts.

The future character and influence of converts must depend under God upon the instructions they receive in the early stages of their Christian course. The notions that they first form—the shape and direction given to their religious character at first—will, in a great measure, determine what future instruction will suit their mental capacities, the infancy of their religion, and the circumstances with which they are surrounded. I repeat it, their instructions need to be individually suited to each convert. Infants should not be fed with strong meat, nor a child treated as a man. They ought to be made to see that they are children, that they are in a state of spiritual infancy and have everything to learn. Too many pains cannot be taken, therefore, to show them the perfection of their ignorance on spiritual subjects. They need, therefore, to begin with the ABC's of religious truth and duty, and be at the outset well grounded in the *first* principles of the doctrine of Christ.

Their instructions should be very thorough. It is no doubt a great error to suppose that young converts should not be instructed to make those discriminations that distinguish between true and false affections, between selfishness and religion. Unless these discriminations are made, and the convert rendered familiar with them, he will almost with certainty, for a time, imagine that he has much more religion than he really has, and afterward come to be very doubtful whether he has any religion at all. If selfish affections and emotions are allowed to be intermingled with holy ones, without discrimination, all will at first be taken as religion. But this process, long indulged, will soon root out and annihilate all holy affections, and leave the mind perpetually under the influence of selfishness. This selfish religion will soon so develop itself as to lead its possessor so utterly away from the Bible, as to force upon him the conviction that he is all wrong, and that he has probably never had any religion. But if he can be led to make the necessary discriminations, selfish affections, instead of being puffed up by them, will greatly humble him, put him on his guard to resist them and the occasion of them. He should therefore be made to flee from every form and degree of selfishness. He should have a clear idea of what selfishness is, and from week to week, the multitudinous forms in which it appears should be pointed out, and its deceitfulness exposed. When I have preached upon selfishness, the question has often been asked me by professors, "Why do not ministers preach more about selfishness? Why is not the fact that all selfishness is sin made more prominent in the instruction of religious teachers? And why is it not known that selfishness and benevolence are eternal opposites, and that their existence in the same mind at the same time is utterly impossible?" [1]

I confess that it has been, to myself, a matter of great wonder that the distinction between selfishness and religion is not made more prominent in the instructions of the pulpit, and that selfishness in so many forms, and in such disgusting degrees, is allowed to remain unrebuked in the Church of God. If converts are allowed to indulge selfishness; if they are allowed to overlook its malignant character; if they are allowed to *indulge* it in any form or in any degree, it will inevitably eat out all their piety. No, their piety is gone already, for the *indulgence* of any form of selfishness is a *state* of absolute rebellion against God.

Therefore, converts should be searched to the very core of their being. Their business *principles*, habits, and transactions should be thoroughly scrutinized and weighed in the balances of the law of supreme love to God and equal love to man. They should be made to see and feel that to pursue any employment or course of life for any selfish *end*, or in any selfish *manner* is downright apostasy from God. It should be insisted upon that they adopt in heart and practice the law of universal love as their rule of life.

Young converts must be made acquainted with the nature and degree of their spiritual needs and dependence. They should be guarded with the utmost caution against a spirit of self-dependence on the one hand; and on the other hand, guarded against regarding their dependence on God as a misfortune rather than the actual crime that compels such dependence. They should be made to see and feel that their *cannot* is their *will not*, in other words, that the lack of stability of disposition to do the will of God is the only difficulty in the way.

---

[1] See Charles G. Finney, *Principles of Love*, (Minneapolis: Bethany House Publishers, 1986) for a devotional guide to understanding how love in Christ casts out all selfishness. See also the "Unity of Moral Action" in *Finney's Systematic Theology*, (Minneapolis: Bethany House Publishers, 1976).

But that this instability of disposition is so great that they are as utterly dependent upon the influence of divine grace as if obedience to them were naturally impossible. I am aware, my brethren, that in churches where they have revivals these truths are taught, or there would not be revivals; yet, I have often thought that pains enough were not taken to make converts clearly apprehend the *depth* and the *nature* of their dependence.

I have found in my own experience that the greatest diligence and care is required to give young converts a just and sufficiently affecting view of their needs, and in the same connection to lead them to a just apprehension of the *fullness* and *nature* of the remedy. The law must forever serve as a schoolmaster to bring them to Christ. This, as long as the world stands, will be the use of the law in a world of sinners. But when they are brought to Christ, they should be brought to Him not only as a justifying, but also as a sanctifying Savior. No pains should be spared to make them understand not only that Christ has power on earth to *forgive* sins, but that His blood *cleanses* from the commission of all sin. The law, when properly exhibited, not only drives the sinner to Christ for pardon, but for sanctification. And the convert should be made to see that the main business of Jesus is to save him from the commission of sin, rather than simply to pardon his sins.

I am fully convinced that pains enough are not taken to lead the convert to seek earnestly the "baptism of the Holy Spirit, after that he hath believed." My own instruction to converts in this respect has formerly been very defective. The fact that the baptism of the Holy Spirit is something universally promised or proffered to Christians under this dispensation, and that this blessing is to be sought and received after conversion, was not so distinctly before my mind formerly as it has been lately. I am satisfied that this truth is abundantly taught in the Bible, and that the baptism of the Holy Spirit is the secret of the stability of Christian character. It is the water of life which Christ has promised, that if they drink it, "they shall never thirst, but that it shall be in them a well of water springing up into everlasting life." Converts should therefore have their attention definitely directed to what this blessing is, its nature, how it is to be obtained, to what extent and with what degree of permanency it may be expected. In short, they need to be baptized into the very death of Christ, and by this baptism to be slain, buried and planted, crucified and raised to a life of holiness in Christ. Anything short of this will leave the convert to inevitable backsliding, and to this attainment I am persuaded he may be led by suitable diligence on the part of his religious teachers.

To attain to this it is indispensable that he should be cut off from every kind and degree of unholy self-indulgence. His appetites and passions must be restrained and subdued, his body kept thoroughly under control; and his whole being must be honestly, fully, and sacredly set apart to the service of God.

Converts should be guarded, with great caution, against a self-righteous use of means, on the one hand, and an Antinomian neglect of them on the other. Antinomianism and Arminianism are two extremes between which they must learn to steer, or they will certainly make shipwreck of their faith. [2]

Converts should by all means be *kept* awake. If they are allowed to fall asleep, you might as well attempt to preach to the tombstones as to them. We may as well preach to dead men as to sleeping ones.

And now, beloved brethren, many of us have been and still are blessed with revivals of religion under our ministry. I pray you, let me inquire without offense, do we feel as we ought to feel the immense responsibility that has been passed on to us, in what an immensely important sense Christ has committed the keeping of His honor and the training of His little ones to us? Shall these converts backslide, through any neglect of ours? Shall the blessed work subside, react, and disgrace religion for lack of a deep sympathy in us with the heart of Christ? Shall the converts be watched over as the apple of our eye, and shall our souls continue "to travail in birth for them, till Christ be fully formed in them, the hope of glory"?

I wish to make some remarks on the treatment of particular classes of converts, but must defer them till my next letter.

Your brother in the bonds of the gospel,
Charles G. Finney

---

[2]Antinomianism teaches that the Christian is not obligated to keep the moral law. Arminianism is used here to describe the teaching that a person may repent and come to faith at any time apart from the influence of the Holy Spirit. See *Principles of Revival* (Minneapolis: Bethany House Publishers, 1987) and Andrew Murray and Charles G. Finney, *The Believer's Secret of Spiritual Power* (Minneapolis: Bethany House Publishers, 1987).

CHAPTER 14

To ministers of the Gospel of all denominations

May 20, 1840

Beloved Brethren:

In my last letter I intimated that I had several more suggestions to make in regard to the instruction needed by different classes of converts. The conviction in my mind is fully ripe that religious teachers cannot lay too much stress upon the indispensable necessity of the constantly indwelling presence and influence of the Holy Spirit to preserve the piety of Christians. [1] I want exceedingly to say much to my brethren on the necessity of *ministers* having the baptism of the Holy Spirit, and how utterly unable they will find themselves to be to give the requisite spiritual instruction without it. But what I wish to say at present is, that all our instructions should tend to this one great end, to promote the indwelling and influence of the Holy Spirit in the heart. Anything that quenches the Spirit will invariably destroy the convert's piety. Anything that will secure His indwelling and influences will confirm and perpetuate the convert's piety. Now the grand inquiry is, how shall converts be kept from grieving and quenching the Holy Spirit? How shall they be led in the fullest and most perfect and constant manner to abide in Him and He in them? It is very obvious that different classes of persons are exposed to different kinds and degrees of temptation, that their weights and besetting sins are as various as their circumstances, habits, education, modes of thinking, employments, health, constitutional temperament, etc.

---

[1] See Andrew Murray and Charles G. Finney, *The Believer's Secret of Spiritual Power*, (Minneapolis: Bethany House Publishers, 1987).

Now, beloved brethren, it has long appeared to me to be of the utmost importance, no, of indispensable necessity, that ministers should look upon themselves, and be regarded by others, as a class of persons set apart to watch for souls in a much higher sense than seems generally to have been understood, and that we should, so far as possible, in breaking the bread of life, give to each his portion in due season. This can only be done by looking closely into the circumstances of different individuals, and classes of individuals, in respect to their trials and temptations, that we may be able, as far as possible, to enter into the details of their Christian history and experience, so as to feed them with that knowledge which is indispensable to their growth in grace.

Male heads of families need instruction on many points pertaining to their relations and circumstances. They ought to feel, and we ought to feel, as if it were our business to inquire affectionately and particularly into all their habits in the relations they sustain to their families, to the Church, and to the world; to ascertain on what principles they conduct their business, in what manner and with what intentions, whether they are selfish or entirely benevolent in their business, what influence they are exerting over businessmen, what influence they are exerting to bring back the business transactions of the world to the standard of the law of God, what their political principles are in reference to party strifes and party questions, whether or not they are aspiring to office or whether they are cleaving to a party without regard to principle, in what manner they conduct themselves toward those who are in their employment, and how their clerks, apprentices, or laborers are regarded and treated by them. In short, it seems to me that we are to interest ourselves in whatever interests them, and interests Zion; and to watch over, warn, reprove, encourage, and instruct them in regard to everything that has a bearing upon their spiritual interests.

Female heads of families also need instruction, warning and reproof appropriate to themselves. Young men, young women and children all need specific instruction suited to all the circumstances in which they may be placed.

I know there is a difficulty in a minister's finding time to enter fully into the details of the history, circumstances and needs of the different individuals in his congregation, but might not much more of this be done than really is done? And if ministers were more particularly acquainted with the needs of all classes, would not their preaching be immensely more practical and influential than it is? If meetings of inquiry were held for different classes of professing Christians: male heads of families, female heads of families, young men, young women, merchants, lawyers, and in short whatever classes there are in a church, and an affectionate but searching inquiry instituted in respect to all that concerns their religious character and influence, and then a course of preaching instituted that should keep pace with the developed needs and circumstances of the Church, how immensely different would the results be from those that are commonly witnessed after a season of the outpouring of the Spirit. How much everyone needs to be watched over and warned in respect to the thousands of ways in which they may quench the Holy Spirit. And O, how jealous and eagle-eyed should a watchman be to guard every convert against everything that can quench the tender breathings of the Spirit in his soul.

See that young woman. O, how much she needs to have a plain, searching and personal conversation with her pastor. How much she needs to be told what will be the result of her pretension, showy dressing, tight-fitting apparel and the thousand other foolish and Spirit-grieving things in which young women are apt to indulge.

I cannot now enter farther into particulars. It is obvious that the old and the young, the middle-aged, the robust and infirm, the rich and the poor, the learned and the ignorant, the student and the laborer, all have peculiar besetments, trials and temptations, to which their attention needs to be particularly directed. And unless this be done by private interview, by letter, or in some other way, particularly and thoroughly done, they will inevitably disgrace religion and fall into temptation and the snare of the devil. It should be constantly insisted that they are expected to live wholly without sin, that this is demanded of them, that sufficient grace is proffered to them to secure them against every kind and degree of sin. The utmost stress should be laid upon this, and no sin should be made light of, but they should be taught constantly that it is "an evil and bitter thing to sin against the Lord," and so instructed as to feel as much shocked at the idea of sinning at all, as they would at the idea of theft or drunkenness or adultery. If they are allowed to suppose that a great deal of sin is naturally expected of them, under such instruction it is vain to expect them to grow in grace. Until ministers will lay immensely more stress than they do upon the principle of total abstinence from sin in their churches, they have no reason to be surprised that sin and moral desolation overspread the spiritual heritage of God. Where ministers, by their lives, their habits and their preaching leave the impression that as a matter of fact much sin is to be expected of them as long as they live; and indeed, where they do not lay themselves out with all their might to make the directly opposite impression from this, they may thank themselves for the results, when Christ is "crucified afresh among them, and put to an open shame."

Beloved brethren, it appears to me that the state of religion in the Church, as a whole, very nearly corresponds with the teachings of the ministry. By the teachings of the ministry, I mean, that which upon the whole they inculcate. Their teachings are made up of their public and private instructions, together with their daily walk, conversation and habits of life.

And now, brethren, permit me to ask, without offense, whether there is not as little backsliding, and upon the whole, as much piety in the Church as might be expected under the influence of such a ministry as we are. Suppose that in the cause of temperance, our instructions, both by precept and example in regard to total abstinence from alcoholic drinks, were just what they are in regard to total abstinence from sin in all its forms. What might be expected to be the standard of temperance principles and habits in our congregations? And who does not see that unless we give the whole weight and power of our preaching, private instructions, public and private example, to the cause of total abstinence from all sin, that the tide of iniquity will overflow its banks, and desolate the Church of God.

Your brother in the bonds of the gospel,
Charles G. Finney

CHAPTER 15

To ministers of the Gospel of all denominations

June 3, 1840

Beloved Brethren:

In my last letter, I observed that I had some things I wished to say to ministers on the necessity of their being baptized with the Holy Spirit. I begin by saying that to me it seems very obvious that the great difference in ministers in regard to their spiritual influence and usefulness does not lie so much in their literary and scientific attainments as in the measure of the Holy Spirit which they enjoy. The Apostles appear to have been entirely different men after the baptism of the Holy Spirit from what they were before. They had been converted and called to the ministry and enjoyed the personal instructions of Christ previous to His death, and yet they remained amazingly ignorant and ill-qualified for the work to which they were called until they were baptized by the Holy Spirit at the day of Pentecost. This baptism did not by any means respect principally the working of miracles as some seem to have supposed, for they possessed the power of working miracles before. But its main design and bearing was to fill them with light, love and power in preaching the gospel. And, as I said, after this baptism they appear to have been in almost every respect entirely different men from what they were before.

Now it seems that there are many ministers in the Church at the present time who have been converted, and perhaps called to the ministry, who have never received the baptism of the Holy Spirit, because they have never believed that any such thing was attainable, nor have they looked for or expected it. They have had the gospel, with but a slight measure of the Holy

Spirit, just as the Apostles had had the personal instruction of Christ, but with so little of the Spirit's influences as never to have understood and felt its power. They are, therefore, as much in the dark, and as poorly qualified for the work to which they are called, as the Apostles were previous to the day of Pentecost. Now the thing which they need and must have before they will have power with God or man is the baptism of the Holy Spirit. Without this, they will forever remain in the dark in regard to the spiritual needs of the Church. And however educated, philosophical, metaphysical, logical, or if you please "theological" their sermons may be, they will always be wide of the mark and never meet the needs of the Church until they are baptized with the Holy Spirit. They need to be set apart to the work by the anointing of God. They may have been called, but not anointed, because they have not sought the anointing. They are in some measure prepared intellectually, but scarcely at all spiritually for their work. Hence, they know not what to say to elevate the standard of piety among Christians. Many of them can produce conviction in the Church, but how few of them succeed in promoting the work of sanctification in the Church.

Beloved brethren, do not take it amiss that I speak so plainly. I speak in love, and, as I trust, in the tender affections of Jesus Christ. Do you, in fact, promote the spirituality of your churches?

A great deal is said about a thorough preparation for the ministry, at the present day. And certainly there cannot be too much said upon the importance of such preparation; but do permit me to ask, what in fact constitutes a thorough preparation for the ministry? Is it a mere college and theological education? By no means. These are important; but they are far from constituting the principal part of a thorough education. Indeed they are as nothing, when compared with the importance of the baptism of the Holy Spirit. The Apostles were for the most part unlearned in the world's accepted sense of that term, and yet, a more efficient class of ministers never existed. And what great numbers, both of ministers and laymen, unlearned in human science, have been among the most efficient and powerful ministers and laymen in the Church of God; while, for the most part, men that have been the most famed for human learning, have been in a great measure inefficient and useless in the Church of God. This by no means proves that human learning is unimportant; but it does prove, beyond all contradiction, the paramount importance of the baptism of the Holy Spirit. I would therefore repeat, with *great emphasis*, what

I said at first: the difference in the efficiency of ministers does not consist so much in the difference of intellectual attainments as in the measure of the Holy Spirit which they enjoy. And how abundantly do the facts that lie right upon the face of the Church's history demonstrate the truth of the assertion. I do not hesitate to say that whatever the age or the learning of a minister may be, he is a mere child in spiritual knowledge, experience, and qualifications for his office, without the baptism of the Holy Spirit. He certainly will, and must forever remain so, until he knows what it is to be "filled with the Spirit," "to be led by the Spirit," "to be endued with power from on high" to fulfill his high and responsible functions; he is a mere child, and by no means qualified to be a leader in the Church of God. [1]

A thousand times as much stress ought to be laid upon this part of a thorough preparation for the ministry as has been. Until it is felt, acknowledged and proclaimed upon the house-tops, rung through our halls of science, and sounded forth in our theological seminaries that this is altogether an indispensable part of the preparation for the work of the ministry, we talk in vain and at random when we talk of the necessity of a thorough preparation and course of training.

I must confess that I am alarmed, grieved, and distressed beyond expression, when so much stress is laid upon the necessity of mere human learning, and so little upon the necessity of the baptism of the Holy Spirit. What are we coming to? Of what use would ten thousand ministers be without being baptized with the Holy Spirit? Ten thousand times ten thousand of them would be instrumental neither in sanctifying the Church nor in converting the world. There is so little said, so little preached, so little thought upon this subject, that the Church is in a great measure in the dark in respect to what constitutes a thorough preparation for the ministry. Consequently, when they employ young men from our colleges and theological seminaries, they take it for granted that they have engaged a minister who has taken a thorough course and is well furnished for this work. But alas! How sadly and almost universally they are disappointed. They find after all, as a mat-

---

[1] See Charles G. Finney, *Principles of Prayer*, (Minneapolis: Bethany House Publishers, 1980) for understanding the relationship between prayer and being filled with the Holy Spirit. See also, Charles G. Finney, *Principles of Devotion*, (Minneapolis: Bethany House Publishers, 1987). And finally see, Andrew Murray and Charles G. Finney, *The Believer's Secret of Spiritual Power*, (Minneapolis: Bethany House Publishers, 1987).

ter of fact, that he is spiritually inefficient, in bondage to sin and lust, and is but a mere babe in Christian experience.

Now I am sure that I do not say this to rail, but in the grief and anguish of my heart. It is a solemn truth, to which the testimony of the great mass of the churches can unequivocally be given.

And now, dearly beloved, unless ministers will wake up to this subject, unless they will seek and obtain this baptism for themselves, unless they will preach it to the churches, unless this truth be insisted upon through the whole course of education, unless a thousand times greater stress be laid upon it, both in theory and in practice than has been, we multiply the number of ministers in vain. Numbers will but increase the discord, strife, sectarian zeal, darkness, and spiritual death of the Church of God. I might appeal to the experience of all the churches in the land to confirm what I say.

Your brother in the bonds of the gospel,
Charles G. Finney

PART 3
Letters to Parents

CHAPTER 16

To Parents

August 12, 1840

Dear Brethren and Sisters:

In compliance with a suggestion given some time ago that I should, God willing, address some letters to parents, I will now commence the series with the hope of promoting the interests of the rising generation. I shall begin with remarks upon Proverbs 6:22: "Train up a child in the way he should go; and when he is old, he will not depart from it," and shall develop my letters from this text, somewhat in the form of a sermon. In doing so, I shall endeavor to: show what is implied in training up children in the way they should go; notice several things to be avoided in training up children in the way they should go; mention several things to be attended to in the training of children; call attention to some of the difficulties in the way of training up children in the way they should go; observe that if the condition is fulfilled, that is, if a child is trained up in the way he should go, it is certain that when he is old he will not depart from it; and finally I will give some closing remarks.

What is implied in training up children in the way they should go? It implies such thorough instruction as to root and ground them in correct views of truth, and in right principles of action. If you consult the marginal reading of your Bible you will find the word rendered "train" in the text is, in the margin, rendered "catechize." The idea is that which I have suggested, to thoroughly instruct them in the great principles of righteousness.

It implies such thorough government as to root and ground them in correct *habits* in all respects, such as habits of cheerful

95

obedience to parents, correct habits in respect to early rising, early retiring to rest, correct habits in regard to taking their meals at stated hours, and in respect to the quantity and quality of their food, habits of exercise and rest, study and relaxation. In short, all their habits comprising their whole conduct.

It implies the training of them in a knowledge of and conformity to all the laws of their being, physical and moral. This is the way in which they should go, and it is in vain to expect to train them in the way they should go without giving them thorough instruction in respect to the laws of their bodies and minds, the laws of natural and spiritual life and health.

It implies not only giving them thorough instruction in these respects, but the thorough government of them and training them in all things to observe these laws.

Next, I will notice several things to be avoided in training up children in the way they should go. Avoid for yourself whatever would be injurious for them to copy, and do not suppose that you can yourself be guilty of pernicious practices, and by your precept prevent their falling into the same. Remember that your example will be more influential than your precept. I knew a father who himself used tobacco but warned his children against its use, and even commanded them not to use it, and yet every one of them did use it sooner or later. This was as might be expected. I knew a mother who used tea herself but warned her children against it as something unnecessary and injurious, especially to young people, but all her children naturally fell into the use of it. The fact is that her example was the most influential and impressive teaching.

Avoid all conversation in their presence upon topics that may mislead them and generate in them a hypercritical and wicked spirit, such as all sectarian conversation, unguarded conversation upon the doctrine of decrees and election, speaking of neighbors' faults, or speaking derogatorily of any human being; in short whatever may be a stumbling block to their infant minds.

Avoid all disagreement between the parents in regard to the government of the children.

Avoid all partiality or favoritism in the government of them.

Avoid whatever may lessen the respect of the children for either parent.

Avoid whatever may lessen the authority of either parent.

Avoid whatever may tend to create partiality for either parent.

Avoid begetting in them the love of money. Diligently remember that the love of money is the root of all evil.

Avoid the love of money yourself, for if you have a worldly spirit yourself, your whole life will most impressively inculcate the lesson that the world should be the great object of pursuit. A wealthy man once said to me, "I was brought up from my very infancy to love the world and make money my god." When we consider how impressively and constantly this lesson is taught by many parents, is it surprising that there is so much fraud, theft, robbery, piracy, and selfishness under every abominable form? Many parents seem to be engaged in little else, so far as their influence with their children is concerned, than making them as selfish and worldly as possible. Nearly their whole conversation at the table, and in all places where they are, the whole drift and bent of their lives, pursuits, and everything about them, are calculated to make the strongest impression upon their little minds, that their parents conceive the world to be the supreme good. Unless all this be avoided, it is impossible to train up a child in the way he should go.

Avoid begetting within them the spirit of ambition to be rich, great, learned, or anything else but good. If you foster a spirit of selfish ambition it will give birth, of course, to anger, pride, and a whole herd of devilish passions.

Avoid begetting or fostering the spirit of vanity in any way: in the purchase of clothing or any articles of apparel, in dressing them or by any expressions relating to their personal appearance. Be careful to say nothing about your own clothes, or the apparel of anybody else or of the personal attractions or beauty of yourself, your children, or of anybody else in such a way as to beget within them the spirit of ambition, pride and vanity.

Guard them against any injurious influence at home. Allow nobody to live in your family whose sentiments, habits, manners, or temper may corrupt your children. Guard the domestic influence as the apple of your eye. Have no person in your house that will tell them foolish stories, sing them foolish songs, talk to them about witches, or anything of any name or nature which ought not to come before their youthful minds.

Be careful under what influences you leave them when you go from home, and let not both parents take a journey at the same time, leaving their children at home, without apparent necessity.

Avoid every evil influence from outside the home. Let no children visit them whose conversation or manners may corrupt them. Let them associate with no children by going to visit where they will run the hazard of being in any way corrupted.

Avoid the cultivation of artificial appetites. Accustom them to no nonnutritious stimulants or condiments of any kind, for in so doing you will create a craving for stimulants that may result in beastly intemperance.

Avoid creating any artificial needs. The great majority of human needs are merely artificial, and children are often so brought up as to feel as if they needed multitudes of things, which they do not need, and which are really injurious to them, and if they ever become poor, their artificial needs will render them extremely miserable, if indeed they do not tempt them. Consider how simple and few the real needs of human beings are, and whatever your worldly circumstances may be, for your children's sake, for truth's sake, for righteousness' sake, and for Christ's sake, habituate them to being satisfied with the supply of their real needs.

Avoid by all means their being the subjects of evil communications. "Evil communications corrupt good manners." This is the testimony of God. If your domestics, your hired hands, your neighbors' children or anybody else, are allowed to communicate to them things which they ought not to know, they will be irrecoverably injured and perhaps forever ruined.

Avoid their reading books that contain pernicious sentiments, anything indecent, vulgar, or of ill report.

Avoid their reading romances, plays, and whatever may beget within them a romantic and feverish state of mind.

Avoid allowing gluttony or any sort of intemperance, eating at improper times, improper foodstuffs, improper quantities of food, and everything that shall work a violation of the laws of life and health.

Avoid all unnecessary occasion of excitement. Children are naturally enough excited. Pains should be taken to quiet and keep them calm rather than to increase their excitement. This is imperiously demanded both by their health and minds. Clubs are often started among children, and great pains taken to stir up an interest and excitement, insomuch that it is often attended with a loss of appetite and sleep, and a serious injury to their health and morals. Parents should be on their guard, against allowing their children to be drawn into such excitement or having any unnecessary connection with or knowledge of them.

This subject will be resumed.

Your brother in the bonds of the gospel,
Charles G. Finney

CHAPTER 17

To Parents

August 26, 1840

Dear Brethren and Sisters:

In pursuing this subject I will notice several other things to be avoided in the training of children.

Avoid everything that can be construed by them into insincerity on any subject, especially everything that may make the impression that your word is not to be depended upon.

Avoid every appearance of impatience or fretfulness in their presence.

Wholly abstain from scolding at them. If you have occasion to reprove them, let it be done with deliberation, and not in such haste and in such tones of voice as to have even the appearance of anger.

If you have occasion to punish them, first converse and pray with them, and avoid proceeding to severe measures until you have fully made the impression upon their minds that it is your solemn and imperative duty to do so.

Avoid in your conversation whatever might have a tendency to beget in them the spirit of slander and evil speaking. Never let them hear you speak evil of any man. But always, in their presence, as on all other occasions, "be gentle, showing all meekness to all men."

Avoid as far as possible whatever may be a temptation to them to indulge evil tempers. "Fathers, provoke not your children to anger," is both the counsel and the command of God. If you find your children naturally irritable and easily made angry, be sure to keep this verse always in your mind, that you may readily and certainly practice it whenever there is occasion to do so. If, therefore, you find your children inclined to the exercise of any evil temper whatever, be sure, as far as possible, to avoid all occasions that may prove too great a trial for them, and cause them to fall into their besetting sin.

Avoid unnecessarily exciting their fears upon any subject. Allow no one to make them afraid of the dark, or of Indians, or of witches, or of wild animals. Children are often very seriously injured by creating a morbid excitability upon such subjects, insomuch that from that time on they are afraid to be alone in the dark. And their foolish fears are often excited even at an older age, in view of things with which they were foolishly persecuted in their youth.

Never give them anything because they cry for it. If they find that they can get anything by crying for it, or that they are any more apt to get it because they cry for it, you will find yourselves continually annoyed by their crying. Children should be taught that if they cry for a thing, for that very reason they cannot have it.

I will now proceed to mention several things to be attended to in the training of children. First, be honest, and thorough, and correct in forming your own views and opinions on all subjects. This is of great importance. For if your children find you often mistaken in your views upon some important subjects, your opinions will soon cease to have much weight with them. It is immensely important that you be well instructed, and know how to answer their questions, especially on all moral subjects. Your opinions ought to carry great weight with them. It is for their own good. Your opinions will naturally carry great weight with them unless they find you in error. Be careful, then, as you wish to preserve your own influence over them for their good, and as you would not want to mislead them to their ruin, to be thorough and diligent in the use of means to obtain correct information on all moral questions.

Let your own habits be both right and regular: your rising in the morning, your retiring at night, the hours at which you take your meals, together with all your domestic arrangements. Let order pervade everything, and be sure to have a time and a place for every work, and everything around you. Have a place for every tool, and let every member of your family be constrained to keep everything in its place. And if they have occasion to use any tool, they ought to be sure to return it to its place before they put it out of their hands. By insisting upon this, you will soon save yourself and them a great deal of unnecessary trouble.

Be sure that they are up early in the morning, and retire early at night. This is imperiously demanded by their health, and almost universally by their morals. If children are allowed to be up late in the evening, they will not only lie in bed late in the morning, but almost always get into the habit of either making or receiving visits from neighboring children. This will bring in its train a host of evils.

See that your temper and spirit are right. "Let the peace of God that passeth all understanding dwell in your hearts, that you may possess your soul in patience." And never allow your angry feeling to come into collision with theirs.

Let the influence which you have over them be an ever present consideration with you. Do not forget it. Do not be unmindful of it, even for an hour or a moment. *In whatever you say and do in their presence, have an eye to its influence upon them.*

Your brother in the bonds of the gospel,
Charles G. Finney

CHAPTER 18

To Parents

September 9, 1840

Dear Brethren and Sisters:

In addressing you further on this subject of what is implied in training up children in the way they should go, I call to your attention that in training children, parents should remember their nature, and that their will is in the first instance influenced by senses, and not by moral considerations. Their bodily appetites come to have a strong influence over the will before moral truth can reach the heart through the conscience, unless their minds are enlightened by a supernatural divine agency.

Therefore, parents should remember that physical training must precede moral training. Pains should be taken to keep their bodily appetites in a perfectly natural state. And as far as possible, prevent the formation of artificial appetites, and do all that the nature of the case admits to restrain the influence of the appetites over the will.

Parents should remember that all artificial stimulants lead directly to intemperance; that tea, coffee, tobacco, spices, ginger and indeed the whole family of nonnutritious stimulants, lead directly and powerfully to the formation of intemperate habits, create a morbid hankering after more and more stimulants, until both body and soul are swallowed up in the terrible vortex of intemperance.

Parents should remember that the least stimulating kinds of diet are best suited to the formation of temperate habits in all respects. And just as far as they depart from a mild, bland, unstimulating diet, they are laying, for the perversion of the child's constitution, a foundation for any and every degree of intemperance.

Parents should remember that the temper of the child is in a great measure dependent upon and intimately connected with his physical habits. If, during the period of nursing, the mother makes a free use of nonnutritious stimulants, she is continually poisoning the infant at her breast, and rasping up its nervous system into a state of extreme irritability. The certain consequence sooner or later will be the development of an irritable temper, with many disagreeable and even disgusting traits of character. If, when the child is weaned from the breast, the irritating process is still kept up, if it is fed with much pastry, unripe fruits, at unseasonable hours and in improper quantities—nothing else can be expected than that it will be a *spoiled child*.

Parents should secure the earliest opportunity to get the mastery of the will. The very first time, at whatever age children manifest temper and set up their will, they should be calmly but firmly resisted. It matters not how young they are. If they manifest a disposition to obtain a thing by crying, or in any way insist upon having their will, the parent should at once adopt some method of steadily and perseveringly opposing their will in that particular. To press the hand upon them and hold them still when they are struggling and screaming to get up, or even to let them lie and scream is vastly better than to yield any point to them when their spirit is stirred and their will is stubborn.

Parents should begin at the outset to get the mastery over the will and then keep it. The most steadfast and uniform perseverance is essential to retaining the mastery of their will. I have always observed that persons whose will has not been early subdued and kept under, are either never converted, or if hopefully converted, make but little progress in piety. I have had so much opportunity of making observation in this respect that if I find a person lingering under conviction and finding it very difficult to submit to God, if I find him grieving and quenching the Holy Spirit, and if converted, given to perpetual backsliding, I often make inquiry, and with scarcely a solitary exception, find that parental authority has never had a thorough influence over him: his will was not early subdued, and ever after, while still a minor, he was not kept in a state of unqualified submission and obedience.

Parents should lay great stress upon the unconditional submission and obedience of their children. Some parents seem to have adopted the principle of not subduing the will of their children until they are old enough to be reasoned with, when they expect to govern them by reason, and moral suasion as they say. Now it should be understood that anything is moral suasion that acts as a motive, that the rod is one of the most powerful and even indispensable forms of moral suasion. It acts as a most commanding motive when the mind is very insensible to the voice of reason. It is no doubt the duty of parents to teach their children in the outset that it is their right and their duty to insist upon unconditional submission to their will, to make the child understand from the very first, that the will of the parent is a good and sufficient reason for the child's pursuing a required course of conduct. If the child is not taught that this is a good and sufficient reason, if he is left to demand other reasons, and if the parent only succeeds in gaining the child over to any course of conduct in proportion as he satisfies or fails to satisfy the child with the proffered reasons, the child is inevitably ruined. For in such cases, if the reason satisfies the child, and he yields obedience, it is not filial obedience, it is not rendered out of respect for the authority of the parent. It is no recognition of the parent's right to govern or of the child's duty to obey the parent. It is simply yielding to the offered reasons, and not to parental authority. Parents must, therefore, commence the government of the child, and perfect their influence over its will, if they ever expect to do so, long before the child can be reasoned with. In this respect the parent stands to the child in the place of God, lays his influence upon the will, and holds it in a state of submission to parental authority until the higher claims of God can come in, until moral considerations can be thrown in upon the mind as the regulator of the will. And ordinarily moral truth will have greater or lesser influence with the will just in proportion to the perfection or imperfection with which parental authority has influenced the will.

Your brother in the bonds of the gospel,
Charles G. Finney

CHAPTER 19

To Parents

October 7, 1840

Dear Brethren and Sisters:

In continuing my remarks upon what to attend to in the training of children, let me emphasize that you must keep them, as much as possible, with yourself and under your own eye. Make yourself, as far as possible, the companion of your own children. There is perhaps no greater error among parents than to allow the children of a neighborhood to mingle with each other, and without restraint find their own sports and employ themselves as they please. There is scarcely a neighborhood in which there are not, more or less, children who have heard various degrees of filthy conversation, vulgar, hateful, polluting, immoral, and perhaps profane and blasphemous things; and whose minds have become deeply imbued, perhaps, with the spirit of the pit or some other abomination, which, if left without restraint, will corrupt all the children in the neighborhood. Thus, one wicked child, if left to mingle freely with the whole neighborhood of playful, confiding and unsuspecting children, will defile and ruin them all. Therefore, beloved, keep your children at home. Allow no children of your neighbors to come within your yard, or upon their playground, without your consent. And be careful not to give your consent, unless you or some responsible adult member of your family can be with them. Be sure that you do not trust in the purity of a neighbor's children just because their parents are good people, nor assume that the minister's or the deacon's children may be left to mingle with your children safely. You should remember that the best of parents may have their children corrupted by contact with other wicked children, and you cannot be sure that they have not been. Therefore, be on your guard, or perhaps from the children of pious parents an influence may flow in upon your family that will deeply corrupt and finally destroy your children.

"But," most parents are apt to object, "we cannot give up our time to our children. We are obliged to attend to other matters." To this I reply that very seldom is this necessarily so. If the parents would satisfy themselves with a moderate supply of this world's goods, and abandon their fastidious and fashionable ways of living, they would, in almost all cases, have abundant time for companionship with their children.

But again it is objected, "Our children need the society of each other. The children of a neighborhood are benefited by contact with each other. Without this contact, they are apt to be selfish, proud, and to lack interest in others besides themselves." To this I answer, to be sure children need society. They need contact with other minds. They need to be so associated with other human beings as to take an interest in them, to witness the developments of character, and to develop their own characters. But it is believed, at least by me, that children are vastly more benefited by contact with adult minds than with the minds of children. I mean of course, those adults whose spirit, conversation and conduct are what they ought to be. And, to be sure, it ought to be contact with those who take an interest in them. The example of adults has more influence with children than that of children with each other. And I honestly say, I would not care to have my children ever see any other children, could they be favored with the right kind of adult contact.

Provide means for engaging their attention at home. Children must have amusement. They must and will be involved in activities. They must have a room and grounds to play in. They must have means and things with which to occupy themselves. And parents can never make a more just and appropriate use of their money than providing with it the means of occupying, employing and educating their children. It is a vast mistake in parents to consider their money thrown away or misapplied when it is expended in the purchase of hobbyhorses, little carts, wagons, sleds, dolls, sets of furniture for their playhouses, needles, thimbles, scissors, boards, hammers, saws, augers, and tools with which their children may busy themselves, and with which to begin to design for themselves the structures which they see around them.

It should be remembered, however, that children love variety; they are never satisfied long with any one thing. They should not, therefore, be provided with too many things at once. For should you purchase many things at a time, you will soon find it impossible to provide novelties for them. Generally, a single new item at a time is sufficient to occupy their attention. A child will find a great many things to do with a gimlet.[1] When he has busied himself with this, and finally lays it aside, add a pocketknife. With his gimlet and knife he can peg pieces of wood together. If to these you add, after a time, a hammer, then a little saw, and thus proceed carefully, but with due attention to just what is needed to sustain their attention, you will render them content at home without occupying much of your own time.

You will find it very important to let your children each have some place for his tools; and let it be an invariable rule, that whenever he has finished using them, they are to be put every one in its place. Let the child be made to feel that it is of great importance that nothing should be lost or mislaid. Thus you will cultivate a habit that will be of vast service to him through life. If he has little carts or wagons, be sure that he never leaves them out in the rain or dew, but has them securely housed; and the reasons why tools should not be exposed to the weather should be made familiar to his mind. If you have but one child, he will be lonesome, unless you take a little trouble in teaching him how to amuse himself. You must play with him, take him with you when it is convenient, go into his playroom or playground, show him how to use his little blocks, his little tools, his hobbyhorse, and try to give his little mind a start in the direction of inventing his own activities.

If you have several children, endeavor to make them satisfied with each other's companionship, without feeling a disposition either to go away from home for companions, or to invite those from outside to come to them. They must be restrained and kept from doing these things or they are certainly undone. This, then, must be a subject of study, of prayer, of much consideration on your part, how you may make your children love each other, be willing to stay at home, and be satisfied with their books, playthings, home, and siblings without roving the neighborhood for their amusements and activities.

Cultivate in them a taste for reading. To this end you must read to them yourself, or employ some judicious and excellent reader to read to them. You should yourself continue, from time to time, to search out and purchase such books as will interest and edify them, from which you can read to them from time to time such stories and things as will interest them and make a

---

[1] A small, hand-held, wood-boring tool.

deep and right impression on their minds. But, beloved, be sure to be judicious in the selection of books and stories. Read nothing to them which you have not read over yourself. Consider what your children are, and ponder well what will be the natural influence of the material which you intend to read or to have read to them. And in all your selections have the moral bearings of whatever you in any way communicate to them strongly before your mind. Be sure to let no one at any time give your children books, tell stories, read things, or sing songs, or in any way make communications to them, the moral tendency of which is injurious.

Encourage them in employing themselves usefully; that is, in doing whatever may be beneficial to themselves or others. In the summer they may keep a little garden. At all times they may be involved in imitating the mechanical arts, making any pieces of machinery or tools for their own use, little tables, chairs, bedsteads, and in doing, in short, whatever can contribute to the well-being of their species.

Make your children your confidential friends. In other words, you be the *confidential* friends and companions of your children. Accustom them to confide to you all their secrets and everything that passes in their minds. On multitudes of occasions, they have thought, and not infrequently you will find obvious suggestions from Satan, which, if known to you, might enable you to do them immense good. Now, if you accustom them to throw their little minds open to you, and to feel that you, in everything sympathize with them, they may have the most perfect confidence in you; you will naturally come to be, as you ought to be, their confidant and their counselor. But if you will not give your time to this, if you turn them off and say, "Oh, I cannot attend to you," or if you treat them harshly, or sarcastically; if you humiliate, embarrass, and treat them with unkindness, if you manifest no sympathy with and for them after repeated attempts to get at your heart, finding themselves baffled, they will turn sadly away, and by degrees seek sympathy and counsel from others. Thus you will lose your own influence over them and give them over to other influences that may ruin them. How amazingly do parents err in these respects. Father, Mother, how sadly do you err, how grievously do you injure your children; no, how almost certainly you will ruin them, if you drive them, by your own wickedness, or leave them to seek for confidential companionship away from home.

Your brother in the bonds of the gospel,
Charles G. Finney

CHAPTER 20

To Parents

October 21, 1840

Dear Brethren and Sisters:

I will continue my remarks on what to attend to in the training of children by urging you to cultivate natural affection among your children. Remember, natural affection is natural in no other sense than that it is natural for children to love those who love them. Therefore, what is generally called natural affection is *cultivated affection*. Therefore, great pains should be taken by parents to cultivate among children not only an affection for themselves, but for each other. Many parents, and fathers especially, treat their children in such a manner that their children have very little affection for them, and in many instances, it is to be feared that they have none at all. And then, perhaps, the children are reproved for the lack of natural affection. But parents should have consideration enough not to wonder at the absence of natural affection, as they call it, in their children, when they take little or no pains to be worthy of or to cultivate their affection.

Again, encourage inquiry on the part of your children. They come into a world of novelties. Before they are a week old, they may be seen staring around the room, as if they would inquire who, and what, and where they are. As soon as they are able to talk, they display the most intense desire to be instructed in regard to everything around them. Now parents, and all others who have the care of children, should encourage their inquiries and as far as is possible, or proper, give them satisfaction on every subject of inquiry. Give them reasons, discerningly detailed, as shall satisfy their little minds.

Parents will find their children inquisitive on those subjects that are by many supposed to be of too delicate a nature to be conversed upon by children. For example, what constitutes a breach of the seventh commandment, and things of this nature. At a very early age, it is no doubt proper to inform children that they are yet too young to be instructed upon such subjects; but that, at a suitable time, you will give them the necessary information, requesting them at the same time not to converse with others than their parents about such things as these. But prior to the age of puberty, and before an explanation of such things will excite improper feelings, parents should, beyond all question, give their children necessary instruction and caution upon all such subjects. When instruction is given, caution and admonition should be frequently repeated, accompanied with solemn prayer and instructions from the Word of God, so as to make a deep impression on the mind, and thoroughly to sensitize and awaken the conscience. Parents cannot neglect to do this without guilt in as much as this is a responsibility plainly enjoined upon parents by the authority of God, to teach their children the law and commandments of God. "And thou shalt teach them diligently unto thy children, and shalt talk of them when thou sittest in thine house, and when thou walkest by the way, and when thou liest down, and when thou risest up."

Parents, and the guardians of children, should never allow themselves to evade the inquiries of children by falsehood. For example, when an infant is born in the family, telling them the physician brought it, *or* that it was found in a hollow tree, or, in short, telling them anything false about it. There is nothing improper, unnatural, or indecent, in letting them know so much upon the subject, as that it was born of their mother.

To tell children falsehoods about such things is only still further to excite their curiosity, and create the necessity either of telling them the truth or still more falsehoods.

Be especially careful of the influences that act upon your children at public schools. It often seems to me that parents hardly dream of the amount of corruption, filthy language and conduct often witnessed in public schools. Little children of the same, as well as of opposite sexes, deeply corrupting and defiling each other. These things are often practiced to a most shocking extent, without parents seeming even so much as to know of it. I would rather pay any price at all within my means, or even to satisfy myself with one meal a day, to enable me to educate my children at home sooner than give them over to the influence of public schools as they are often arranged and conducted.

Remember that your children *will be educated*, either by yourself or by someone else. Either truth or error must possess their minds. They will have instruction, and if you do not secure to them right instruction, they will have that which is false.

Prove yourselves in all respects worthy of the confidence of your children. Let them always witness in you the utmost integrity of character. Let them, in no instance, see in you the appearance of deceit, falsehood, or unkindness. Let your whole heart stand open to them; and in return, you will find that their little hearts will stand open to you. If you show yourselves worthy of their confidence, you can depend on having it.

Deal thoroughly with their consciences. As soon as they are able to be instructed on moral questions, give yourself to a thorough enlightening of their minds upon every precept of the law of God. Put their minds as fully as possible in possession of those truths that will make their consciences quick and as sharp as a two-edged sword.

Guard against the cultivation of so legal a spirit, as to drive them to despair when they have sinned. While you cultivate the most discriminating conscience, be sure also to instruct the little one thoroughly in respect to the plan of salvation by faith in Jesus Christ.

Add physical discipline to moral instruction. I have referred to this subject before, but wish to say in addition that it is doubtless one of the greatest errors in the education of children to overlook the fact that at that early age the discipline of the rod will often present to them a more powerful motive than can be brought to bear upon them by moral truth presented to their uninformed minds. The rod cannot safely be laid aside until the powers of the mind are so fully developed and the mind so thoroughly instructed that the whole range of moral truth may be brought to exert its appropriate influence upon the mind without the infliction of pain. It seems to me that some parents presume to be wiser than God, taking it upon themselves to decide that it is not wise to use the rod upon children. Remember Proverbs 19:18 and 23:13,14: "Chasten thy son while there is hope, and let not thy soul spare for his crying." "Withhold not correction from the child: for if thou beatest [1] him with the rod, he shall not die. Thou shalt beat him with the rod, and shalt deliver his soul from hell."

---

[1]The word "beat" is better translated in modern English as "spank." The intention of the word is striking to inflict pain for the purpose of correction, not striking to abuse, harm, or injure.

Let them see that your religion is your life—that it is your joy and rejoicing from day to day, and not that it fills you with gloom and melancholy. Many professing Christians have such a kind of religion as to render them miserable rather than happy. They are almost constantly in bondage to sin, and consequently under a sense of condemnation. They are wretched, and exhibit this wretchedness daily before their children. This creates the impression on their little minds that religion is a gloomy thing, fit only for funerals and deathbeds; and only to be thought of on a near prospect of death. Now this is making the most false and injurious impression upon their minds that can be conceived. It is a libel upon the religion of Christ. But shocking to say, it is almost as common as it is false. Your children should see that you are religious in everything, and that in all things you are not reluctantly but joyfully acquiescent in the will of God.

By all means let them daily see that you are not creatures of appetite—that you are not given up to the pursuit of wealth, or to the pursuit of fashion, not seeking worldly reputation or favor, that neither good eating, nor good drinking, nor good living, in any other sense than *holy* living, is the object at which you aim. Let them see that you are cheerful and contented with plain, simple food, that you are strictly temperate in all things, in respect to the quality and quantity of whatever you eat, drink, do, or say. In short, let your whole life inculcate the impressive lesson that a state of entire consecration to God is at once the duty and the highest privilege of every human being.

Be sure to pray much with and for them. Never punish them without praying with them. Whenever you give them serious admonition pray with them. Pray with them when they lie down and when they rise up. And enforce the lesson by your own example, that they are never to do anything without prayer.

Lay hold on the promises of God for them. Search the Bible for promises. Lay your Bible open before you. Kneel over it, and spread out the case of your children before God. Begin with the covenant of Abraham, and understand that God made the covenant as well with the children as with the parents. And remember that an inspired Apostle has said, "The promise is unto you, and to your children, and to all that are afar off, even as many as the Lord our God shall call." Take the promise in Isaiah 44:3–5: "I will pour water upon him that is thirsty, and floods upon the dry ground: I will pour my spirit upon thy seed, and my blessing upon thine offspring: and they shall spring up as among the grass, as willows by the water courses. One shall say, I am the Lord's; and another shall call himself by the name of Jacob; and another shall subscribe with his hand unto the Lord, and surname himself by the name of Israel." Remember, that this promise was made more especially to the Church under the Christian dispensation, and respects the children of Jewish parents. Throw your souls into these promises, and wrestle until you prevail.

Your brother in the bonds of the gospel,
Charles G. Finney

CHAPTER 21

To Parents

November 4, 1840

Dear Brethren and Sisters:

I will now call your attention to some of the difficulties in the way of training up children in the way they should go.

One difficulty is a lack of the requisite information on the part of parents, and especially on the part of mothers, to whose care and management they are principally committed. Thus far, as a general fact, female education has been so much neglected that only a few women have the necessary information for the proper training of children. There is a most sad deficiency in this respect, in the training of young women in reference to their being future mothers. Why, the education of daughters is one of the most important things in the world. That women should be educated is wholly indispensable to the salvation of the world. An enlightened and sanctified generation of mothers would exert the greatest influence upon future generations that ever was exerted upon human beings. It is one of "guilt's blunders," to educate the sons and allow the daughters to go with little or no education.

Another difficulty is the frequent lack of education, and still more frequently of consideration, on the part of fathers. Most fathers seem to be so much engaged in business, politics, or personal pleasure and recreation as to leave very little time for deep consideration in respect to their responsibility and influence with their children. This is all wrong; for if there is anything that demands the attention and time of the father, it is those things that concern the well-being of his children. If he neglect his own household, whatever else he does he virtually "denies the faith, and is worse than an infidel."

A lack of a sense of responsibility in both parents often prevents their training up their children in the way they should go. Without a keen and efficient sense of responsibility, parents will never do their duty to their children, however much they may love them.

A lack of agreement between the parents in regard to training their children becomes another difficulty; for if the parents do not agree upon the course to be pursued, if they do not lend to each other the whole weight of their influence, children will soon see it and parental influence will soon lose its power over them.

Also to be noted is the ruinous notions that are prevalent among parents in regard to training up children. Many parents have given themselves so little to consideration upon this subject that their opinions are little more than dreams and old wives' tales upon the subject of training children.

There is often a great difficulty on account of the irrational thinking and habits of neighborhoods in regard to their children. If a parent who is anxious to preserve the morals of his children makes up his mind to keep them at home, it is often unjustly thought and said that it is because he thinks his children better than the neighbors' children. Or, if he keeps his children at home, the neighbors' children are allowed to come in throngs to visit them. In this case they must be either sent home, at which their parents are often offended; or they must be allowed to remain, introducing the hazard of all those evils that arise from permitting children to mingle together without restraint. Or, to avoid this, the time of the father or mother, or of some adult member of the family, must be given up to superintend and accompany them in their play. It should be always understood by parents that they have no right to allow their children to go to a neighbor's house to play with his children without first obtaining the consent of the parents of such children. And, if they do, they ought to be willing to have them sent home at the discretion of those whose children they visit. Certainly no man has a right to inflict on me or my family the visit of his children without my knowledge or consent. Nor have I any right to do so to him. And I would much prefer my neighbor to turn his horse into my yard to feed without my consent, than to turn his children into my yard to play with my children without my consent. I say *much prefer*. I might say, almost *infinitely prefer*, as the horse would only devour the feed; but who can calculate the evil that may result from one hour's unrestrained and unobserved interaction of children with each other.

Another great evil is the recklessness of parents in respect to training their children. Many parents seem to allow their children to run here and there, to wander like a wild ass's colt. As long as their children are out of the way, it matters little to these parents where they are, or with whom they are keeping company. Now if there is anything in the universe that deserves the severest reprehension, and I must add, the deepest damnation, it is such a reckless spirit in parents. It is tempting God. No language can describe its guilt.

A great lack of firmness on the part of parents in training their children is another great evil. By firmness I refer to: the government and discipline of their children; guarding them against evil influences from outside the home; resisting the commonly accepted practices of society that would subject their children to the kind and degree of contact with other children which will positively ruin them; and, deciding against those fashions, in regard to dress and many other things, that tend to carry their children away from God.

Another difficulty in the way is a lack of faith and deep piety in parents. Many parents seem to have no practical confidence in the promises of the Bible in respect to their children. They have very little piety; and many of them seem not to know that there are such multitudes of exceeding great and precious promises upon which they may rely.

Another difficulty is a lack of a sense of responsibility to the neighborhood, in parents. An ill-managed family is the greatest nuisance that can infest any neighborhood. No man has a right to neglect the proper training of his children, and thereby render them a pest to society, any more than he has a right to build a mill dam that will flood a timbered country and thereby destroy the lives of the people. Now the former is a sin of an infinitely greater degree than the latter. And if a man deserves to be indicted for building such a mill dam, as is often the case, how much more does he deserve to be indicted for a common nuisance in allowing an uninstructed and unmanaged family to pour their abominations over the neighboring children. Such a family ought to be regarded as a public nuisance. Such fathers and mothers ought to be worked with, advised, admonished, and if need be, rebuked and even indicted. And the influence of such families should be as strictly and religiously guarded against as we would guard against the influence of the devil.

Another great difficulty is the influence of the flesh in the present state of the human constitution. The bodies of infants generally come into the world saturated with tea, coffee, and often with alcohol. They are born of mothers who have lived on the most stimulating kinds of diet, and from their very birth nurtured upon whatever is calculated to pamper their appetites and rasp their nervous system into a state of the utmost excitability. This promotes a precocious development of all their organs, and gives great power to their animal propensities. It is almost sure to deliver them over, at a very early age, to the dominion of appetite and lust.[1]

Your brother in the bonds of the gospel,
Charles G. Finney

---

[1]With all of the recent concern about Fetal Alcohol Syndrome, and the alarm at how many children are born with drug addiction due to their mother's addiction and use of drugs while pregnant, Finney's Christian common sense makes him seem far ahead of his time instead of an antiquated backwoods preacher.

CHAPTER 22

To Parents

November 18, 1840

Dear Brethren and Sisters:

I now come to my fifth observation on Proverbs 6:22: If the condition is fulfilled, that is, if a child is trained up in the way he should go, it is certain that when he is old, he will not depart from it.

First of all, because God has said it.

Secondly, because He has laid the foundation of this certainty in the very nature of human beings. It is a fact, well known to everybody, that human beings form habits by the repetition of any given course of conduct, or feeling, until their habits become too confirmed to be counteracted and put down by anything but Almighty Power. It is the law of habit that lies at the foundation of the difficulty of bringing sinners to abandon their sins. A long indulged and confirmed habit is, in the Bible, compared to the strength and stability of nature itself. God says, "Can the Ethiopian change his skin, or the leopard his spot? Then can ye, who are ACCUSTOMED to do evil learn to do well." Here the law of habit is compared to the strength and permanency of nature itself. Now if a child be trained up in the way he should go, the uprightness of his future conduct is secured, not only by the promise and grace of God, but by this law of habit, which is laid deep in the foundation of his constitution.

Thus God has put the destiny of the child into the hand of the parent, who naturally loves it more than any other human being.

But again, God has established the law of parental affection for the benefit of the child, and so far as possible, to secure the training up of the child in the way it should go. I might quote a great many passages of scripture in confirmation of this doctrine; but if the text itself does not satisfy your mind, no multiplication of texts would do so.

Here I must notice an objection to the view of the subject I have taken. There is one common and grand difficulty, which has seemed to stumble Christians, in respect to their laying hold on the promises in regard to their children, and counting upon their being converted, sanctified, and saved with any sort of certainty. It is this: Many good men have, in all ages, had shameless and reprobate children. To answer this, I point out that good men are not always perfect in judgment, and therefore may be, and sometimes doubtless have been guilty of some primary error in training their children.

A great many good men have been so occupied with the concerns of the Church and the world as to pay comparatively little attention to the training of their own children. Their children have been neglected and therefore almost certainly lost. Whatever the case, when they have been neglected, they have not been trained up in the way they should go. So, the condition has not been fulfilled.

Many good men have lived in bad neighborhoods, and found it nearly or quite impossible to train up their children in the way they should go without changing their locations. And although they saw the daily contact of their children was calculated to ruin them, and did, as a matter of fact, prevent their training them up in the way they should go, yet they have, probably from a sense of duty, remained where they were, to the destruction of their children. In such cases, the ruin of their children may be chargeable to their neighbors, because the influence of their neighbor's children prevented their bringing them up in the way they should go.

A few remarks must conclude what I have to say to parents at this time. You see the great importance of mothers' organizations. Mothers must make the training of their children the subject of much consideration, study and prayer. If any mind should be well stored with knowledge, it is the mind of a mother. If anyone needs to understand philosophy—mental, natural, and moral—it is a mother. If anyone needs the wisdom of a serpent and the harmlessness of a dove, it is a mother. It is, therefore, all important that mothers should meet together, exchange views and books, and converse, pray, and devise every measure for training up their children in the way they should go.

There should also be fathers' organizations. If there is anything important to the interests of this world, it is that children should be universally trained up rightly. And how amazing it is that fathers are so slow to perceive the necessity of deep study and research, prayer, discussion, reading, and conversation on the subject of training their children. There are organizations among men for almost everything else, and yet, I hesitate not to say that organizations for this end are as necessary and important as for any other object whatever. Pious mothers are often at their wits' end to know what to do to secure the salvation of their children. They are greatly at a loss to know what course of training will most likely result in their sanctification. They go to their husbands; but their minds are engaged in everything else. They have paid very little or no attention to the subject of training their children. And, as a general thing, if a father governs his family at all, it is only by a legal system, more or less rigid, according to his natural temper, habits, and way of doing things. And, notwithstanding, the wife needs the counsel of her husband, and the father of her children; fathers are, as a general thing, little prepared to give them counsel. There should be a great deal of consultation between the father and mother of every family in relation to training the children, and a great deal of consideration and forethought.

But another thing that renders both fathers' and mothers' organizations of the utmost importance is that there may be cooperation and unanimity in the neighborhood on the subject of training children. If possible, every father and every mother should be enlisted in these organizations, so as to secure the right training of all the children in the neighborhood. For, as I have said in a former letter, one unmanaged family will often, in spite of all that can be done, corrupt a whole neighborhood. Parents, therefore, ought to be instructed throughout whole neighborhoods in respect to training their children. For if some families of children are allowed to run about and visit, both by day and by night, it will be difficult to restrain other children; and just as moral influences reveal themselves quickly, so the results will spread as naturally and as certainly as a contagious disease. It is, therefore, of the utmost importance to secure the attention and hearty cooperation of every parent in the neighborhood.

Permit me here again to revert to a topic, which I have mentioned in a former letter, and say again, that it is of the utmost importance that care should be taken to secure the right kind of domestic help. As you value the souls of your children, do not receive into your family any filthy girl or young man, or old man, that will tell falsehoods to your children, tell them vile stories, use vulgar language, or in any way corrupt their morals or their manners. I would sooner have the plague in my family than to have such influences as these. I would not allow the nearest relative I have on earth to remain in my family, unless he would refrain from corrupting my children.

Again, see the great importance of selecting the right kind of Sunday school teachers.

You see the great importance of selecting the right kind of books and periodical literature for your children. There are many books and periodicals, and those too that are extensively circulated, that I regard as of a very pernicious and highly dangerous tendency. They are calculated to form anything but right thinking and character among children.

All the domestic arrangements of every family should have a special regard to the training of their children. The right training of them should be a prime objective, and every other interest of the family should be made to bend to this. The hours of retiring in the evening and rising in the morning, the hours at which meals are taken, kinds of food, and in short all the habits of the family should have a direct reference to the right training of the children. Nothing should be allowed to enter into the family arrangements that has a tendency to injure their health, their intellect or their heart. No company should at any time be received and entertained whose conduct may endanger the manners or morals of the children.

Mothers should never, under any pretense whatever, neglect their own children for the purpose of attending to other matters. Mother, remember that nothing can compensate for the neglect of your duty to your children. This is your first great indispensable duty, to train your children in the way they should go. Attend to this then, whatever else you neglect.

Do not suppose that you can attend to this without being yourself devotedly pious. No mother has begun to do her duty to her children, who is not supremely devoted to God, and is not endeavoring to train them up for God. Some mothers will neglect their children under the pretense of going to meetings and especially attending seminary, leaving it, as they say, "with God," to take care of their children while they do His work. They seem to think the time spent in taking care of their children is almost thrown away. And even some seem unwilling to have children because they shall have to "throw away" so much time in taking care of them. Now woman, you ought to know that a leading objective of your life is to bear and train up children for God—time which you spend in this employment is as far as possible from lost.

Other women, instead of neglecting their children to attend to their devotions, are neglecting their devotions almost altogether, and pretending to discharge their duty to their children while they are neglecting God and religion. Now this is equally erroneous in the other direction. No parent can train up children in the way they should go, without maintaining a spirit of deep devotion to God on the one hand, and on the other hand, without paying the most rigorous and unremitted attention to their personal training—physical, intellectual, and moral. Mothers should be emphatically "keepers at home." While the children are yet minors, mothers should consider it their business to train them up in the way they should go.

But in doing this they should consult God at every step, and should not imagine that they begin to do their duty any further than they consult the Word of God and live under the constant guidance of the Holy Spirit.

If you would train your children in the way they should go, be invincibly firm in training your own family, let other families do as they may.

Remember that if you resist the true light, or neglect your duty to your children, God "will visit the iniquities of the fathers upon the children, and upon the children's children, unto the third and fourth generations."

Your brother in the bonds of the gospel,
Charles G. Finney

PART 4

Letters to Christians

CHAPTER 23

Professor Finney's Letters to Christians

December 23, 1846

Dear Bro. Cowles[1]:

Will you permit me through the columns of the *Oberlin Evangelist* to address a few lines to Christians on several highly practical and important subjects? I will begin with the inquiry, WHAT IS SIN?

Sin is the transgression of the law of God. The law of God requires supreme and perfect love to God, and equal love to man. In other words, the law of God requires disinterested, perfect, universal benevolence or good will to all that exists. The law of God requires consecration of all we are and have to the promotion of His glory and the highest good of His kingdom. Therefore, "whether we eat or drink or whatever we do, we should do all for the glory of God." We should have a *good reason* for all we do or omit. This reason should be that, in our estimation, the glory of God and the highest good of being demands it.

Sin is the opposite of all this. It is consecration to self-interest and self-gratification. It is self-seeking instead of seeking the the good of universal being. It consists in choosing the wrong end and preferring our own interests and gratification to the infinitely higher interests of God and the universe. Sin is a *choice*, a state of mind, and does not consist in outward action. It is manifested by outward acts, but does not consist in them. Sin consists in willing and acting without *good reasons* or in a manner not demanded or approved by reason. Holiness

---

[1]Brother Cowles, (Henry Cowles) was the editor of the *Oberlin Evangelist*.

is obedience to the demands of the reason or to the law of God as it lies revealed in the reason. Sin is obeying the law of the sensibility (or feelings and emotions). That is, sin consists in surrendering the will to seeking the gratification of the desires, appetites, passions, and propensities (or natural tendencies).

Every moral agent *knows* and really assumes, in spite of himself, that he ought not to be *selfish*, that he ought to obey *reason* and not *appetite*. This knowledge he has and cannot avoid having from the laws of his nature. Selfishness then is sin in him, whether he thinks of it as such or not. Selfishness is obeying the desires, appetites, propensities, as I have said. When we act simply in obedience to appetites or passions, we sin, whether we think of it in that light or not.

Sometimes, indeed, reason sanctions and demands the appeasing of appetites. Under certain circumstances this *is* for the glory of God, and for our highest good and for the highest good of His kingdom. In such cases the gratification is not strictly in obedience to the appetites, but obedience to reason which says, seek the object and appease the appetites. But unless the reason approves the gratification, it is sin.

Let it be understood then, that self-gratification is always a sin, unless it be sanctioned and demanded by the law of the intelligence, or by the law of God, which is the same thing. Unless the law of benevolence demands it, and unless we do it for that reason, or in obedience to that law, we sin. We must have a *good*, that is, a *benevolent* reason for all we do. The questions, always to be asked, are: "Does the glory of God and the highest good of being demand this? Have I a good reason for this course, such a reason that I am confident God will approve?"

I fear that many professed Christians have very loose ideas on the subject of sin, and are living in daily and constant sin without seriously inquiring into the nature of sin. This is infinitely dangerous, and my spirit is often stirred within me when I consider the conduct of many professing Christians, and the fact that without being at all aware of it, they are certainly in sin and in the way leading to hell. I propose with your permission to address to them, as frequently as I can get time to write, some serious and searching questions in regard to some of their habits and practices. And may the Lord search us all out.

Your brother,
Charles G. Finney.

CHAPTER 24

Professor Finney's Letters to Christians

January 6, 1847

WHY DO YOU USE TOBACCO?

The practice of using tobacco is very general even among professing Christians. Have they any *good reason* for it? Now, my Brother, my Sister, if you are in the habit of using tobacco in any way, will you consider yourself as *personally* addressed by me upon this subject? Please consider what I now write as written explicitly to and for you.

Why do you use tobacco? In my last letter I showed that everything is sin in a moral agent, whether he considers it as such or not, for which he has not in his mind a good, that is, a benevolent reason; unless in his honest view it is demanded by the great law of love to God and man. My Brother, what reasons may I suppose you to have for this practice? In many instances when I have spoken to professing Christians and others, on the subject of their using tobacco, they have promptly replied, I do not consider it sinful. Now the question is not whether you so *consider it*, but whether it is sinful in fact. Sin is self-indulgence, and is so whether the sinfulness of self-indulgence is *considered* or not.

Suppose I ask you in reply, Do you consider the use of tobacco a solemn duty you owe to God and your neighbors? You are a moral agent; whatever you do intelligently must have some moral character. It must be either sinful or holy. It must be done for God, or for the gratification of self. Do you consider it as a duty to God and your neighbor, and do you do it for the sake of promoting the honor of God and the good of the world? Do you think that God would be displeased with you if you

126

should neglect it? If you do not do it as a work of love to God and your neighbor; if you do not act from a regard to the highest good of all that is in such a sense as to have the solemn conviction upon your mind that it would be sin and displeasing to God for you to neglect it, you sin in using it. *Remember this, my brother!* You cannot but be aware that tobacco is one of the most deadly and destructive poisons that exists in the whole vegetable kingdom. Do you think it a solemn duty to take poison habitually? Do you think it your duty to promote by your own example the practice of using tobacco? If you are a Christian you not only ought to but you actually do live for the good of the world. Now do you think the use of tobacco to be so important to the rising generation as to feel called upon to use all the influence you possess to extend and perpetuate its use and to render its use universal among men? Do you desire to live and to die and go down to the grave with the reflection that you have exerted the highest influence in your power to pass this practice on to all future generations? Do you think that future generations will rise up and call you blessed should they read on your tombstone, "Here lies a man who lived and died in the use of tobacco and did what he could to pass on its use to all future generations?" Will they say of you, "Blessed man, how much the world is indebted to him for *his self-denying labor of love* in doing so much by his self-denying use of tobacco to pass on this most blessed and indispensable practice to all generations?"

Your brother,
Charles G. Finney

CHAPTER 25

Professor Finney's Letters to Christians

January 20, 1847

EXAMPLE IS THE HIGHEST MORAL INFLUENCE THAT CAN BE EXERTED.

A father, who used tobacco, said, "I do not know how it can be. I have told my boys again and again not to use tobacco, but in spite of all my advice, every one of them has got into the practice." "Yes, father," said one of them, "example is more forcible than precept. By precept you taught us not to use it, and by example you taught us to use it. We follow your example because it has more weight than precept."

In my last letter, I inquired of professing Christians—tobacco users—whether they deliberately intend to promote the use of tobacco among all classes, and especially among the rising generation, to the utmost of their ability. Now, Brother, to this inquiry I presume you will answer, no. This, you say, is not the reason why you use it. You do not use it for the purpose of promoting its use. But why do you use it? "Whatsoever ye do, whether ye eat or drink, do all to the glory of God." Do you do it for the glory of God? If you do not, the use of it by you is sin. Of this you may rest assured. If you habitually use it for any lower reason than as a duty to God, you live in habitual sin. But you say, I do not mean to sin. The thing at which you aim is not sin. You do not use tobacco *because* it is sinful, but nevertheless it is so. So with the intemperate man in any thing else. The drinker of strong drink, for example, does not drink *because* it is sinful, but nevertheless it is so. But, you say, I don't think it is sinful to use tobacco. But remember that all self-indulgence, not demanded and approved by the law of love

128

to God and man, is sin, whether you consider it so or not. But, you say, I do not think it sin in *me* to use it. Why not? "Because I have become so habituated to it that I cannot give it up." Then this form of self-indulgence is your master. You have become so accustomed to this indulgence that you cannot live without it. Now if this is your excuse, remember and *mark what I say.* If you can't mortify this appetite, you can't possibly be saved. "If ye live after the flesh ye shall die. But if through the Spirit ye do mortify the deeds of the body, ye shall live." If you allow any appetite, passion, or propensity whatever to have dominion over you, you cannot possibly be saved. Cleaving to any one form of self-indulgence is just as fatal to your salvation as if you wallowed in all filth. If you only clearly realized what sin is, you would see that indulging in the use of tobacco for the sake of the gratification, or because you have so long been accustomed to it, is just as really sinful as for the alcoholic to do the same. His habit is no more actually and truly self-indulgence than yours, and he has the same excuse for it, namely, that he can't break the habit. But you say, perhaps, I am sure that my tobacco does me good. I feel decidedly better when I use it than when I do not use it. I have tried this experiment and find that I can perform more labor, think better, and even pray better when I have my tobacco. Yes, and the drunkard might with equal truth say the same. It may be true that both you and the drunkard *feel* decidedly better when you have your accustomed stimulants, but does that prove that either of you receive any real benefit from your indulgence? It gives you present relief at the cost of obvious and lasting injury to your body, and if you persist for such a reason, it will ruin your soul. But you say I was directed to use it by a physician. If so, surely "he was a physician of no value." "I take it for the toothache, or for a cold, or acid stomach, or some ailment for which my physician prescribed the use of tobacco." Now you ought to know that all such advice is mere quackery and nonsense. There is not one of those or any other form of disease that is not aggravated by the use of tobacco. Tobacco like alcohol may appear to afford relief by rallying the vital powers to resist its action. But it rapidly exhausts the vitality of the system upon which life and health depend, and thus in the end only aggravates instead of curing the disease. But suppose it really was a benefit to *you.* Is this a sufficient reason why you should use it? Everybody will not know why you use it. You do not believe it is well for all persons to use it. Even though it *might* be useful to you, why run the risk of passing on the curse of its use to others by your example on those to whom the use will be a greater injury than it is to you a benefit? If you might injure others by the use of it, ought you not to deny yourself even if it be a real sacrifice?

You recollect that when the temperance reformation began, the pledge was to abstain from ardent spirits, except as a medicine. A worthy brother in New York, said, "The use of spirits is a great evil in the land—While I use a little as a medicine, others will use it as an indulgence; therefore, I will sacrifice my life, if die I must, without it, before I will use it even as a medicine." This was noble. The fact is, you do not need it for your health. Just set down your foot that you will not use it come what may, and look to God for help against the temptation, and in a few months you will see that you are much better off even in the very respect for which you took it, than you were when taking it. But even if you think you need it, yet for the sake of doing good or of preventing evil, deny yourself. Do you think that you would or could be the worse by it? I tell you, no. Your life is the Lord's. It is good for nothing only as it can be used to promote the glory of God and the good of man. Why should you try to prolong it if it can be done only by means that will tend only to the injury of others? Will you strive to live by means that are deeply injurious to your fellowmen? What right have you to live if you must live by such means? But that you cannot live without it is all a mistake. Go to the records of the state prison and learn that the total abandonment of the use of tobacco by the tobacco takers that go there is found in no case to be an injury to them, but on the contrary invariably a benefit. My Brother, you do not really need it. But if you did, can you not at once abandon it, rather than be so powerfully instrumental in passing it on to all succeeding generations?

Your brother,
Charles G. Finney

———————

Finney's letters end here. Evidently he planned to write more letters, but 1847 was the year he completed Volume II of his *Systematic Theology* (he never completed his projected Volume I or Volume IV). Also in the same year, he became quite ill and almost died. His wife also became ill, and did die in December of 1847. For an account of his illness, written by his wife, see Charles G. Finney, *Answers to Prayer*, (Minneapolis: Bethany

House Publishers, 1983). Finney continued to publish lectures and sermons in the *Oberlin Evangelist* until it ceased publication in 1862. The following letters in this book consider the topic of sanctification, especially his lectures found in *Principles of Sanctification*, (Minneapolis: Bethany House Publishers, 1986). Finney's letters clarify this book by answering questions posed to him, and by replying to his critics.

PART 5

Letters on Sanctification

Chapter 26

To Believers in the Doctrine of Entire and Continued Sanctification in this Life

November 4, 1840

Beloved in the Lord:

The present is a time of trial with you, and I feel as if it was of the utmost importance that in these days you should "possess your souls in patience," that "patience should have its perfect work, that ye may be perfect and entire, wanting nothing." As I have heard much of your trials in some places, and know, in some measure, how many of you are situated in respect to your church relations, will you permit me, in the tender affections of Jesus Christ, to give you a little fraternal advice.

I have often thought that the early history of Methodism, were it known to churches of other denominations generally, might, in many respects, be very useful at the present day. Wesley, as you probably know, belonged till the day of his death to the High Episcopal Church of England. And during his day, the Methodists continued in the Episcopal and National Church. I have often been struck with his admirable meekness, patience, disinterestedness, and fear of God in sustaining the opposition and persecution which he did without either withdrawing or being driven from the Episcopal Church. He visited various parts of England, together with his brother and other churchmen, and preached a full salvation from sin. He formed what were called "Bands," in the different churches, composed of those members that were seeking after holiness of heart and salvation from all sin. These "Bands" had their regular prayer and conference meetings by themselves, at such times and places as were convenient, for prayer, conference, and mutual edification. Only those who were seekers for the great blessing were admitted as members, the blessing after which the "Bands" were pressing. These "Bands" were under the supervision of one of the preachers or of a layman who was fitted to take charge of them. But my memory is not very definite in respect to the particulars, I have referred to them principally for the purpose of saying that those "Bands," or "Methodists," as they soon called themselves in the different churches to which they belonged, were extensively and bitterly opposed by the churches of which they were members. They were said to consider themselves better than others. They were called sanctimonious, hypocritical, perfectionists, and almost anything and everything, that prejudice, irreligion, pride, and ignorance of God, could heap upon them.

Now, instead of withdrawing disgusted or from any conscientious objection from the bosom of the churches to which they belonged, they remained as quietly as possible in them. And by their admirable meekness, sweetness, and charity, extended their influence and promoted holiness in those churches to an astonishing extent. They, no doubt, did a hundred times more good as they could have done by withdrawing from the churches, setting up separate meetings on the Sabbath, forming themselves into distinct churches, and thus outfitting themselves in the attitude of a distinct denomination.

After Wesley's death, they had become so very numerous that they withdrew from the Episcopal Church and organized themselves into a distinct denomination. As to the wisdom of this measure, I have nothing to say, as I am not sufficiently informed in respect to the particulars to have any opinion about it. But I have been greatly affected, edified, and I may say, blessed in contemplating the spirit, movements, and success of the early Methodists in England.

And another thing is worthy of remark. In spite of the carnal state of the Episcopal Church in general at that time, the Methodists were by no means hunted from their churches, as such heretics as not to be worthy of communion. Much has been said about the High Church, and the high-handed notions of that church, in respect to church organization, and ecclesiastical domination; yet the Methodists were allowed to remain in their communion without excommunication or suspension. Their ministers were allowed to preach the doctrine of entire and continued sanctification in this life. They were allowed to visit the churches through the length and breadth of the land, and as it were to form churches within churches; or, in other words, establish their "Bands," and promote the work of God in their own way without being denied or cut off from the churches. This was Episcopacy in the days of its strength and at a time when it possessed its most unbroken power. How all this will compare with the movements of some of our Congregational and Presbyterian churches and ecclesiastical bodies at the present day I need not say.

The things which I wish to say to you, particularly at the present time, are as follows: I advise and beseech you to be filled with the love of Jesus Christ, and on all occasions to exhibit entire patience, kindness, and forbearance toward those who differ from you and who oppose you.

Do not allow yourselves to talk about the opposition you meet with from ministers and Christians. Do not pray for yourselves or for others as if you or they were persecuted. Especially, do not do this in public; nor allow your minds to dwell upon the opposition you meet with, lest you should be "overcome of evil."

If you are accused of things of which you are not guilty, if slanderous and unfounded reports are circulated about you, if they come to your ears, I beg of you not to open your mouths in reply, lest you should speak unadvisedly with your lips. Preserve entire silence, and go aside and pray, feel, know, that your reputation is of no value, except as it can promote the interests of the Kingdom of Christ. Leave your reputation, then, entirely with God, and possess your souls in entire patience.

I advise and beseech you, to be exceedingly careful what you say of your minister, or of ministers in general. Be careful to "speak evil of no man," but be "gentle, showing all meekness unto all men." Be especially careful of the reputation of ministers. Treat them with great kindness, respect and love, for their office and their work's sake. Avoid hypercriticism as you would avoid a serpent, and I implore you not only to watch over yourselves in this respect, but watch especially over your brethren and sisters who believe as you do. Admonish, warn or reprove them, as circumstances may require, on the first appearance of hypercriticism in them.

Learn to account in the most charitable manner for all the opposition you meet with. Consider that in many things you may be mistaken and wrong, and also that much of the opposition you meet with originates in mistakes and misapprehension on the part of your opposers, rather than in any ill-will to you or opposition to what they understand to be the truth. Consider, also, how long you yourselves have been in bondage to sin, the slaves of prejudice; how long you possessed more or less of a sectarian and persecuting spirit; and how long it took you to rise above your prejudices and get away from under the influence of your stereotyped errors of opinion so as to understand the liberty of the gospel. Consider the longsuffering and compassion of God toward you, and how much pains He took to kindly undermine your prejudices, to correct your opinions, and draw you over to the belief and the practice of the truth.

I advise and beseech you by no means to withdraw from the churches to which you respectively belong. Why, dearly beloved, there is the very place for you to hold up your light. Do not, therefore, withdraw and separate yourselves from those who are yet in the dark in respect to this glorious doctrine. Did the Apostles, when their eyes were opened on the day of Pentecost, withdraw at once, disgusted and disheartened, from their Jewish brethren, as either too unholy or too hopelessly hardened to be associated with or won over to the truth as it is in Jesus? You will, no doubt, do a hundred times more good, if you take the right course *in your own churches*, as you will by withdrawing from them. At first, perhaps, many of you will feel yourselves shut in, and your influence for a time may be greatly curtailed or even destroyed; but this state of things will not, cannot long continue. If you really possess and everywhere manifest the spirit of Christ, if your tender heart of compassion yearns over your brethren, if you are meek, kind, forbearing and loving, if you are really holy in your walk and behavior, it will be seen, felt and acknowledged sooner or later by your brethren and ministers; and your influence and character will be felt and appreciated at some time, if you will simply continue among them and seek their purity and edification. I have been greatly grieved to learn that some who believe in this glorious doctrine have felt it to be their duty to withdraw from the communion of the churches to which they belong. I fear they have committed a great error, and shut themselves out in a great measure from doing the good which they otherwise might have done.

Some of you have been excommunicated, as I am told, and many more of you probably may be. I fear that some of you have placed yourselves in such an attitude as to compel the churches to excommunicate you, and that they have not done it so much because you hold the doctrine of entire sanctification in this life as because you declined communion with the church and perhaps treated the minister and the church in a manner that made them feel called upon to excommunicate you.

Now, dearly beloved, if any of you have been guilty of any

errors, in theory or practice, that have compelled the churches to excommunicate you, I would beseech you, on my knees, to confess. Make all the restitution in your power, request to be taken back into the communion of the church, and take away every reason for their not receiving you, except the fact that you hold the doctrine of entire sanctification in this life. This will throw the responsibility upon them to decide whether for this "error," as they call it, they will cut you off from their communion. I trust that not many churches of any denomination in the land will go so far as to excommunicate a member for the belief of this doctrine. In any event, I cannot think that the Congregational or what are denominated the New School Presbyterian Churches will do any such thing, standing as they do, removed from the Presbyterian Church, for supposed errors in doctrine. For to me it seems impossible that for this one point of difference between you and them, they should excommunicate you and at the same time complain of the removing act of the Old School (Presbyterian) General Assembly, from whom they differ in very many material points of doctrine. That they should complain of being rejected from the Presbyterian Church, when, as a matter of fact, they differ so extensively and on many points of doctrine from them, and at the same time reject you for differing only on one point, and that too a point always held by the Methodists, who are acknowledged by them as evangelical, I cannot believe.

Before I close this letter, do let me again beseech you, whatever may occur, whether the churches tolerate you or reject you, to preserve a spirit of entire patience, sweetness, meekness and charity. You can in no way do so much mischief, as to profess to believe the doctrine of entire sanctification in this life, and at the same time exhibit a wicked spirit. All the opposition that is or can be made against this sentiment by its opposers can hardly begin to be so injurious to the cause of truth as a wicked, hypercritical, sarcastic, denunciatory, pharisaical spirit and behavior in those who profess to believe it. I beseech you, by the mercies of God; no, beloved I adjure you, by your love of truth, by your attachment to Christ, by all that is sacred and lovely and of good report; keep yourselves pure; exercise the utmost patience, forbearance and kindness, and do not let your holiness be a holiness in theory only. But let it be the very light, temper, spirit, and life of the blessed Son of God. Remain as quietly as possible in the churches to which you belong. Possess and exhibit an anti-sectarian spirit on all occasions. And if you are reviled, be sure not to revile again. And if you are persecuted, threaten not. And do not let those who misapprehend your views or misrepresent your practices have occasion to triumph over you, as those who, while they profess holiness, exhibit a spirit that is earthly, sensual, devilish. I may soon address you on this subject again.

Your brother in the love and fellowship of the blessed gospel,
Charles G. Finney

CHAPTER 27

To Believers in the Doctrine of Entire and Continued Sanctification in This Life

November 18, 1840

Beloved in the Lord:

In my last letter I expressed the hope, if not the opinion, that no Christian church would excommunicate you simply for believing the doctrine of entire and permanent sanctification in this life. Since writing that letter, I have learned with surprise and grief that at least a portion of the Christian Church has resolved to put away from its communion believers in this blessed doctrine, either by excommunication or by desiring or permitting you to withdraw from their communion.

Now, beloved, will you permit me in this letter to suggest a few thoughts upon this subject for your consideration. I have supposed, and never until recently did I know that a different opinion was entertained by any minister of the gospel (especially of the Presbyterian or Congregational order), that persons who had once entered into solemn covenant with God and with His Church on earth could never revoke that covenant, or by any possibility get out of the Church so as not to be subject to its discipline, or so as not to have a right to the enjoyment of its ordinances, except by death, regular dismissal from one church to join another, or by excommunication.

And now permit me to observe that you who are members of churches are in solemn covenant with God and with the church, and you cannot withdraw from the communion of a church, unless with the express design of joining the communion of another church. I suppose you have a right, in case a regular dismissal and recommendation should be denied you by the church to which you may belong, to withdraw from the watch, discipline and communion of one church for the purpose of uniting with another under certain circumstances, for this is not withdrawing from the Church, neglecting its ordinances or refusing its discipline. But you have no right in any case whatever to withdraw from the Church militant, to neglect its ordinances or its discipline. This would be a direct and palpable breach of covenant.

No church has a right to ask you to withdraw from their communion, or to permit you to do so should you request it, except as you request it and they grant it for the purpose of your uniting with some other church.

If the members of the church to which you belong desire you to be out of their communion, they must suppose themselves to have some good reason for it; and if there is some good reason why you should not belong to their communion, they should by no means permit you to withdraw, but should take the responsibility of excommunicating you, and thus bear a public testimony against your errors or your sins. To me it is a novel idea that if churches wish to get rid of the influence of any of their members, they do well to give them leave, or even request them to withdraw from the church, and thus break their covenant with God and with His Church. Have churches a right to so dispose of the covenant obligations of their members? If this is so, I have been, and still am mistaken. By what authority, I would ask, do churches suppose themselves to act when they take it upon themselves to give their members advice or leave to withdraw from the communion and discipline of the Church of God?

Permit me to inquire in the tenderest manner, whether you who have withdrawn from the communion of the churches to which you belong have well considered and understood what has become of your covenant engagements? Do you complain that you were ill treated in the churches to which you belong? But is this a good reason why you should break your covenant with God and with His Church?

Do you say you were not edified and built up in the faith under the influence of the churches to which you belonged? But is this a good reason why you should break your covenant with God?

But do you say that your usefulness was destroyed, and that you could do no good by remaining in those churches? But again I ask, what became of your covenant engagements? How do you know how much good you might have done had you persevered in your endeavors to do them good?

But do you say that you could not fellowship with them because they rejected the glorious doctrine of entire sanctification? And is this a reason why you should withdraw from them, and virtually excommunicate them? Do you hold and believe that none can be Christians who do not receive this doctrine? Do you believe that you had never been converted until you became acquainted with it? If you withdraw from their communion because they do not believe this doctrine, do you not thereby maintain that the difference between you and them is so great as to render it impossible or improper for you to walk together? In this case certainly you should not complain of those churches that excommunicate persons of your belief, because the difference between them and the Church is too great to be tolerated.

But have you withdrawn because of the supposed insincerity and hypocrisy of the churches to which you belonged? But is this a good reason for breaking your covenant with God? Was there not a Judas in the first Christian Church? Have there not always been tares among the wheat? Suppose there are many hypocrites in the Church? Is it not your business to reform the Church instead of attempting to withdraw from it, and thereby violating your solemn covenant engagements and dishonoring Christ?

If the churches to which you belong ask you to withdraw, I beseech you to remind them in the spirit of perfect meekness that your covenant cannot thus be disposed of, and that if they wish you to be out of their communion they must take the responsibility of excommunicating you.

Let me also beseech you to be very temperate in all your language and deportment under the trials to which you are called. Remember, "a soft answer turneth away wrath, but grievous words stir up anger." I have of late seen one or two letters in which there were some expressions that appeared intemperate, and to savor somewhat of a bitter and accusing zeal. I am pained and alarmed whenever a thing of this kind comes to my knowledge. Dearly beloved, it may be impossible that offenses of this kind will not come. But let me beseech you, by the meekness and gentleness of Christ, that you leave wholly and forever to your opposers the use of harsh, bitter, accusing language. If such language must be used, leave the use of it altogether to them. If such feelings as are expressed by this language must be exercised, leave the exercise and manifestation of them wholly to your opposers. And be ye "rooted and grounded in love." "Let the law of kindness dwell upon your lips, and the peace of God rule in your hearts."

It is no doubt the policy of Satan to stir up within you a bad spirit. If he can only by any possible means, "provoke you to wrath" and lead you to contend for the truth in a bitter, rasping, judgmental spirit, he will effectually secure his object. Let it be remembered, and I beseech you to bear it perpetually in mind, that the truth of the doctrine of entire and permanent sanctification must be illustrated and confirmed by the lives of those who profess to believe it, or it will not to any considerable extent be received by the Church.

If the churches to which you belong refuse to learn anything upon the subject, if they will not read, if they misunderstand and pervert when they do read, if they will not hear you converse or pray upon the subject, you still have the most forcible possible way of communicating the truth. Remember that example is the highest possible moral influence. Let your life, temper, spirit, and daily, and hourly deportment, read them continual lectures and declare as from the housetops the glorious gospel which you profess. They cannot silence your example. Nor can they resist for any length of time the power of its influence. If you are really whole-hearted, full of faith and of the Holy Spirit and let your works shine among men as you ought, this is the loudest possible preaching. It is worth more and will be more influential, indeed a hundred times more powerful, than if you were allowed and encouraged to talk, pray, preach, and write in favor of the doctrine, continually, while your life contradicts it.

Remember that the whole of religion is love, not the love of a party, not contented satisfaction in those of a particular name, not a fondness for those and those only who particularly coincide with you in opinion. But religion is benevolence. It is good will to mankind in general. Contented satisfaction with the virtuous is only one of the modifications of benevolence.

Beloved, let me recommend to your frequent and prayerful consideration the thirteenth chapter of I Corinthians. Will you read it often? Will you read it on your knees with much prayer? Will you deeply consider it, and let it be copied into all your lives?

Do not be discouraged or at all disheartened, beloved brothers and sisters, by any removing measures of any of the churches to which you belong. If they cut you off from their communion, be sure to pray for them and not against them. And remember, these days of rebuke and of removing will not last always, and the more violent it is the sooner will the storm blow over. But still I cannot but hope, that the Church of the blessed God is to be spared the disgrace of the violent and anti-Christian movements which at present seem to be meditated. However, if it must be so, if you or I must be removed from the Church of God for a belief of what we understand to be the glorious gospel of the blessed God, let come what may, we will rejoice and be glad. We will, by the grace of God, be quiet as a weaned child, and not allow ourselves "to be overcome of evil." But let us, beloved, "overcome evil with good."

You may probably hear from me again upon this subject soon.

Your brother in the love and fellowship of the blessed gospel,
Charles G. Finney

CHAPTER 28

To Believers in the Doctrine of Entire and
Continued Sanctification in This Life

December 2, 1840

Beloved in the Lord:

In my last letter I made some remarks upon the impropriety of your withdrawing from the churches to which you belong, either upon your own suggestion, or upon the suggestion of the churches themselves, unless for the purpose of uniting with some other evangelical church. Permit me now to make the following additional suggestions in respect to our present circumstances.

I have always observed that where the fear and love of God do not prevent or rebuke a spirit of persecution or ecclesiastical violence, that public sentiment will effectually do it whenever the crisis is sufficiently formed. Now there can be no doubt that if you possess your souls in patience, and observe several conditions which I wish to mention to you, that should the churches to which you belong, or the ecclesiastical bodies of which you may be members proceed to any uncharitable and removing measures, public sentiment will severely and effectually rebuke them and compel them to desist from such proceedings.

The first condition upon which you may expect this to be done is, to keep yourselves *quiet*, that you avoid becoming excited, and getting into a vociferous and scolding manner of speaking, praying or preaching upon the subject of your peculiar views. And especially in reference to the opposition that is made to them. Be sure to preserve a collected state of mind. Be sure to walk softly before the Lord. Commune with your own heart and with God and be still.

In order to do this do not allow yourself to dwell in your thoughts and meditations upon the opposition you meet with, nor upon the unreasonableness of your opposers. Avoid such contemplations, or they will probably be too great a temptation to you and you will be "overcome of evil."

Give up your mind to the contemplation of the love of God, of the patience and meekness and gentleness of Christ. Dwell upon the exceeding great and precious promises, and enrich your mind and inflame the love of your hearts by a continued perusal, with much prayer and supplication, of the blessed oracles of God.

Do not cry *persecution*, and self-satisfiedly hold out the idea that you are persecuted for righteousness' sake. If this be really the fact, let others see and say it rather than yourselves.

Do not give up your time and thoughts to defending your own reputation or character. Concern yourself only to promote the glory and honor of God, and leave your reputation to be taken care of by Him. If you attempt to defend your own reputation, you may expect that God will leave you to the defense of it without defending it himself. But if He sees that you are concerned only to promote His reputation, He is then concerned to defend your reputation as the means of promoting His own. Some of you are aware that in the providence of God, I have had some experience in respect to the influence of slanderous reports and injurious treatment upon Christian character and usefulness. In view of all the experience I have had, and the observation I have been able to make, I do not recollect ever to have seen a minister or private Christian become excited about, and give himself up to the defense of his character, without manifestly losing the Spirit of God, and eventually suffering a severe and permanent loss in respect to his own reputation. Nor do I on the other hand recollect ever to have seen an instance in which a minister or private Christian kept calm, unexcited, about his own reputation, and gave himself up to promoting the honor and glory of God, by laboring for the salvation and sanctification of souls, in which God did not sooner or later appear for his defense and "make even his enemies to be at peace with him," and "bring forth his righteousness as the light, and his judgment as the noon-day."

Be sure that your labors are as abundant, and as extensive as the providence of God will permit, for the conversion and sanctification of sinners. Do not let it be said of you, at least with any degree of truth, that your religion is of an antinomian character. But let your belief and love of the truth lead you to imitate Christ, laying your whole being upon the altar of prayer and laboring for the salvation of souls.

Avoid controversy. Few persons can engage extensively even in discussions that assume the form of controversy without sooner or later getting into a bad spirit.

Be sure that you are not uncharitable in the opinions you form and express in relation to the piety of those who differ from you in their views. Most minds are very apt, by dwelling a great deal upon some one doctrine of the Bible, so to magnify that particular point as to make it seem as of fundamental importance in the scheme of religious truth. They consequently come to the conclusion that none can be Christians who do not embrace and magnify that particular topic as they themselves do. I have had an opportunity to witness with pain the developments of this principle of the mind for many years. To this principle may be traced almost all the sectarian zeal in our land and in the Church of God. One man dwells upon the *mode* of baptism until it assumes such an importance in his mind that he seriously and sincerely doubts whether any can be Christians who do not view it as he does. He feels as if he could give up his life to extending his particular views upon that subject. Another gives up his mind to the contemplation of the subject of infant baptism until he comes to conclusions either in favor of or against it, and until his mind becomes so absorbed in it, to the exclusion of almost everything else, that it will be to him the great and important point in the gospel. The millenium can never come until the Church is set right upon that subject. Hence he seriously doubts whether there is any religion any farther than there are right views upon this subject, and is ready to launch forth as an apostle for the extension and defense of his particular views. Now who has not been pained and grieved by witnessing the development of this principle of the human mind, on almost every topic that agitates and has agitated the Church of God.

And now beloved, let me say that as great and momentous, and as glorious and blessed, as the doctrine of entire sanctification in this life is, it may no doubt be looked at in such relations, and by certain ardent minds in such a manner as to lead to the conclusion that none are Christians except those who embrace it. Be therefore, I beseech you, on your guard, lest before you are aware you find yourself forming uncharitable conclusions and expressing uncharitable opinions in respect to your brethren who differ from you. Remember also, I beseech you, that the way to convince them of the truth of this doctrine is not to denounce them as hypocrites, heretics or cold-hearted, but treat them with great candor and forbearance and, as you have opportunity, make such suggestions and present such passages of scripture and considerations as may tend to bring them into the light upon this subject. And do this in such a spirit of kindness as to win them rather than repel them. Let it be borne continually in mind that your spirit and life, rather than your arguments, are to carry conviction to the minds of the opposers of this doctrine. I know it has been singularly said in some instances by those who oppose this doctrine that the spirit of those who believe it is both commendable and excellent, but that the doctrine itself is detestable. But the common sense of mankind will soon correct such loose statements as these. Such a sentiment as this cannot often be bandied about without meeting the rebuke of common sense. What, the spirit of the Christian religion excellent, but its doctrines pernicious! This is strange logic. A doctrine is pernicious, but the spirit and temper of mind produced by it excellent! "By their fruits shall ye know them. Do men gather grapes from thorns or figs from thistles?" This applies as much to doctrines as to men. The natural tendency or fruit of a particular doctrine or system of doctrines is not only a legitimate evidence, but one of the most conclusive evidences of its truth or falsehood. Therefore, beloved, let me repeat that if you exemplify in your daily deportment, temper and manner of life, the spirit of entire consecration to God, the Church will sooner or later receive this testimony and declare itself in favor of this blessed doctrine to which your life bears most emphatic testimony.

But I must close. You may expect, the Lord willing, to hear from me again soon upon this subject.

Your brother in the love and fellowship of the blessed gospel,
Charles G. Finney

CHAPTER 29

To Believers in the Doctrine of Entire and Continued Sanctification in This Life

December 16, 1840

Beloved in the Lord:

Since my last letter, it has been suggested to me that some of you have thought yourselves warranted in withdrawing from the particular churches to which you belong because they lived in the open violation of their covenant engagements; and even account it heresy in you to profess to live in accordance with your covenant engagements, or even to believe that anyone ever did or will live up to their covenant engagements in this life.

Now, beloved, permit me to say that although the churches to which you belong may have violated their covenant engagements everyday of their lives in neglecting to watch over you, to promote your purity, peace, and edification, or in anything else that falls short of a rejection of the fundamental truths of Christianity; yet this cannot justify a disregard of the covenant on your part. The covenant was made by all, with God and with each other. If any of your brethren have violated the terms of the covenant, your business is to labor with them, patiently and perseveringly, in order to bring them to repentance; but not to consider yourselves at liberty to abandon or break the covenant because they do. You ought not to suppose yourselves discharged from your covenant obligations to them, because they neglect to fulfill their covenant obligations to you. Can it be that a breach of a church covenant, on the part of any of its members, can discharge the other members from their covenant obligations, and thus set aside, as it respects all obligation to him who has violated it? If so, there is probably not a church in the land whose covenant is not, long ago, nullified and no longer binding on its members. The truth is, church covenants can never be disposed of in this manner. If your brethren have neglected to fulfill their covenant obligations to you, this is no good reason why you should do the same to them. Remember, the covenant was primarily made with God. With Him you covenanted to watch over your brethren, to seek the purity, peace, and edification of the church. And shall sin, on the part of the church, render this covenant null and void, and discharge you from obligation to fulfill it? Certainly not!

Permit me, beloved, to beseech you in these days of rebuke, misunderstanding and misrepresentation, to beware of controversy, and remember that you will find it very difficult to indulge in the form without imbibing the spirit of controversy. The Lord is undoubtedly designing an appropriate trial of your faith, and to bring your patience into perfect exercise. If those religious papers fall into your hands, which are professedly opposing the doctrine of entire sanctification in this life, you will need great patience, love, forbearance, and candor to possess your souls in such a sweet and heavenly frame, as not to quench the Holy Spirit and fall into bondage. The amazing amount of misapprehension, misstatement, false logic, false philosophy, and erroneous interpretation of Scripture; together with so much apparent lack of candor, as you will witness in some instances, at least will greatly try your feelings. And let me advise you, often to recall the states of mind through which, probably, most of you passed in respect to this doctrine before you embraced it. You will do well to reflect upon your great misapprehension of it at first—the prejudice of education that so long surrounded and enslaved you—the amount of influence which a regard for your own reputation had, for some time, in keeping you back from either seeing or embracing the truth—what erroneous definitions you gave of Christian Perfection, or entire sanctification—and how inappropriate many of the prooftexts and arguments in favor of this doctrine appeared to you, and while under the influence of your erroneous definitions. In short, I beg of you to reflect upon the whole process through which your mind was led, and the exceeding patience and forbearance of God in conducting you to your present conclusions. You are no doubt now often tempted to be impatient with your brethren, and to accuse them, either of great stupidity or dishonesty in treating this subject as they do. Now, it is true that many of them may be guilty of both. But you would do well to reflect, that you have also, in all probability, been as stupid, dishonest, blind and hateful as most of them. Now copy the example of God. Be as patient with them as He was with you. Be as persevering and kind in endeavoring to guide and instruct them, as He was with you. Do not speak bitterly, nor fret, nor be discouraged in your efforts to do them good. But in these respects copy the example of God.

Remember that the excitement upon this subject must form a crisis. It is a great and solemn question. It deeply concerns the vital interests of the Church. It is one over which the Calvinistic churches have long and wickedly slumbered, and which has been, as yet, but very imperfectly agitated, discussed, and understood by any branch of the Christian Church, at least for centuries. The light is now dawning upon this question. For some time, it was looked upon by the great mass of the Church as a kind of weakness, if I may so express it, in our Methodist brethren, and worthy of, and likely to excite but very little attention. But God is evidently, by His providence and His Spirit, pressing the subject upon the general attention of Christians of all denominations and to a greater or lesser extent in all truly Christian countries. The question is now likely to undergo a thorough investigation; and the truth upon this subject must and will be known. That any of us have yet exactly arrived at the whole truth upon this subject, may be questionable. At least, some or many of the statements of our views, as well as our views themselves, may be seen, in the course of the discussion, to need correction and amendment. And one thing is of the greatest importance; that is, we should every one be sure to gain and maintain an entirely honest, candid, firm state of mind in relation to the whole question, holding our minds continually open to the influence of new light, and be willing to candidly weigh the arguments on all sides of this question, and make up our minds and frankly and meekly avow our sentiments, as we have opportunity, without disguise and without the fear of man.

Let us, brethren, be especially on our guard against feeling ourselves so committed to any opinion upon this subject, as to feel called upon to defend our opinion for consistency sake. Let our love of consistency be entirely subordinate to our love of truth; and let us come to a critical and honest examination of the Bible, with the fixed determination to follow its teachings wherever they may lead.

Beloved, we must expect that there will be a great deal of excitement upon this question, a vast deal of misapprehension, misstatement, lack of candor, and multitudes of grievous things. For the state of the Christian Church is such that it were entirely unreasonable to expect any other result; when the entire and universal and eternal abandonment of all sin, lust and selfishness is pressed upon them as their immediate and practicable duty. It will not surprise me, if this question should produce a greater amount of excitement, and a greater commotion in the theological world, than has been witnessed upon any one subject, since the days of the Reformation. As I said, upon this subject, there must be a crisis formed, a rallying of all the powers and elements of mind, and a coming up from one motive or another to an examination of this question. No doubt many grievous and unreasonable things will be said and done; but, "possess ye your souls in patience," and "fret not yourselves because of evil doers," but "let us patiently gird up the loins of our minds," and meekly address ourselves with all perseverance and love to the thorough investigation of this glorious truth of the blessed gospel of God.

Your brother in the love and fellowship of the blessed gospel of God,
Charles G. Finney

CHAPTER 30

To the Editor of The Oberlin Evangelist

January 6, 1841

Dear Brother:

In my lectures on entire sanctification, in the last volume of your paper, I gave an intimation that I might notice and reply to any objection that might be seriously felt by myself or others to the view I then presented. There are two objections that seem to have been felt by a number of minds to some things which I presented upon which I beg leave to make a few remarks; not by way of controversy, but for the purpose of calling the attention of the brethren to what seems to me to be a full answer to the objections mentioned.

I have recently received from a very esteemed brother a communication in respect to two positions taken by me in my lectures upon sanctification, from which I now quote the first of his two objections.

"What you teach about consciousness as evidence of a state of entire sanctification, I consider as leading to serious error. The sum of what you say is, That consciousness, with the law of God before us as the standard, is the highest and best evidence of a state of entire sanctification, whose testimony we cannot doubt. This I admit, supposing the mind not ignorant, but perfectly acquainted with the claims of the law upon it and with perfect accuracy to recognize its own states and operations. But, my dear brother, how can this be, *'with all the ignorance and debility of body and mind* caused by intemperance and abuse of the human constitution, through so many generations?'* Can we, in these circumstances, have a consciousness so perfectly enlightened and accurate? Is it not a contradiction?

See what our consciousness, with all our ignorance and debility of body and mind, must do. First, it must determine, with unerring accuracy, what all the ignorance and debility which belong to the particular person amounts to, that it may decide how much the law requires of him; for this it must exactly determine, or it cannot tell when he will be conformed to the standard; and then *it must know*, with the most perfect accuracy, every state of the mind, every feeling, motive and volition, or it cannot testify to the entire sanctification of the person. And I ask, if this is not the work rather of a mind perfect in its powers, and infallible in its knowledge of its own operations, than of a mind ignorant and debilitated in consequence of folly and sin."

I will make a few brief remarks upon this extract for the purpose not merely of answering the esteemed writer, but also with a design to anticipate the difficulties to which he alludes, as they seem to lie in other minds besides his. In the volume I have just published upon this subject, which is just through the press, I trust I have made this subject sufficiently plain.[1] But as it is not yet bound, and will not be in circulation for some weeks, I will in the mean time make the following remarks.

The difficulties felt by my brother upon this subject seem to be founded in the assumption that man can by no possibility know his own *present character*; or, if he can know it, he can only know it in some other way than by his own consciousness.

Upon the first of these assumptions I remark: if man is not naturally able to know his own character, he is not bound to know it. If a man, through his own fault, had become delirious, or an idiot, his blame lies altogether in that act or those acts that deprived him of the use of his reason. And that, being an idiot or lunatic, he is no longer a moral agent, and is no longer under moral obligation, while his idiocy or lunacy remains.

Furthermore, if man is not naturally able to know himself, God has no right to require him to know himself. But since God does require him to know himself, as in 2 Corinthians 13:5, the presumption is inevitable that man has natural ability to know himself. "Examine yourselves whether ye be in the faith; prove your own selves. Know ye not your own selves, how that Jesus Christ is in you, except ye be reprobates?"

Finally, we must properly understand passages such as

---

[1] The "volume just published" was a collection of nine lectures which had appeared in issues of *The Oberlin Evangelist* in 1840, just previous to this letter. It was originally titled, *Views of Sanctification* and is now available as *Principles of Sanctification*, (Minneapolis: Bethany House Publishers, 1986).

Psalm 19:12, "Who can understand his errors?" and Jeremiah 17:9, "The heart is deceitful above all things, and desperately wicked: who can know it?" These passages do not teach that men are naturally unable to know their personal characters, but that the deceitfulness of the heart is so great as to render such knowledge extremely difficult.

His difficulties also seem to be founded upon the second assumption that if men *are* able to know their present character, they can acquire this knowledge from some other source than their own consciousness. I remark, there appears to be confused notions among most people in respect to what consciousness is. I must, therefore, define what I mean by consciousness.

Consciousness is sometimes spoken of as a power or capacity of the mind, and sometimes as an act or effect of that power. It is commonly used in this latter sense, and may be defined to be—the mind's cognizance of its own existence and states or actions. If this is a correct definition, and I believe it cannot be doubted, we get our whole knowledge on all subjects from consciousness. We know absolutely nothing upon any subject unless it is revealed to us by consciousness. Every sensation, every thought, every volition, every impression upon the sensibility, every perception, every conception, every act of the imagination or fancy, every act of memory, every act of judgment, every affirmation of the reason, and every other possible or conceivable mental state, or act, is given to us by consciousness, and by consciousness alone. Whatever, then, a man knows upon any subject, he knows by his own consciousness, and in no other possible way. But it should be understood that consciousness never reasons, never forms a judgment, never feels. It consists simply in the mind's recognition of its own existence, actions, and whatever impressions are made upon it.

In the above extract, it appears to me that the brother confounds consciousness with those powers of mind, the action of which is revealed to us by consciousness. Other brethren have supposed that we are indebted, not to consciousness for a knowledge of our present characters, but that the appeal must be made to the word and Spirit of God. But to this I answer that to be sure, our opinions in respect to the law of God, and in respect to our own character, are to be formed under the light, and in accordance with the word and Spirit of God. But the question is, how are we to know what we think of the law of God, or what our opinions are in respect to its requirements? How do we gain the knowledge that we have any perception at all of the law of God, or any understanding of what it means? How do we know that we exist—that we think—that we read the Bible—that we have certain thoughts and emotions, certain judgments and affirmations of our reason respecting the law of God and our own course of feeling and conduct in view of it? To all this I answer, we know these things only by our consciousness. In no other possible way can we know them.

Again, I remark that I have felt not a little surprised that New School Divines, men who profess to believe the doctrine of the natural ability of men to do all their duty, should reason upon this subject as if they denied man's natural ability to know his own *present* character.

I should like to inquire of my brethren who take this ground, whether they mean to deny man's ability to know his own *present* character, or whether they maintain his obligation and still deny his natural ability? If they deny his obligation to know his own character, then of course they must admit that his ignorance of his own present character is not sinful, and that it is, therefore, in no sense inconsistent with his being in a state of entire sanctification. And if they admit his obligation, but deny his ability to know his present character, then they must give up the doctrine of man's natural ability to do whatever is required of him.

Should they admit man's natural ability to know his own present character, or any thing else whatever, I should esteem it a favor to be informed by them, in what other way they are to get this information, but by the testimony of consciousness?

I would inquire if a man is to have no opinion in respect to his present character; and if he is, on what this opinion is to be based? Is he to form the judgment that he is a converted or an unconverted man? On what ground does he form this opinion? If it is answered that he is to receive the testimony of Scripture, I ask, if the Scripture affirms anywhere that A. B., by name, is a converted man? And even if it did, how are we to become acquainted with this fact, but by being *conscious* of the perception of this truth taught in the Bible?

I suppose it will be universally admitted that so far as we are capable of knowing our own characters, we come at this knowledge by a comparison of ourselves with the law of God. But how does this comparison of all those acts of the mind that make up our character, with the law of God, and induces a final judgment in the case, come to be known by us? I answer simply and only by our own *consciousness*. I cannot therefore but express surprise that my brethren should stumble as they do at the assertion that Christians may know when they are in a state of sanctification by the testimony of their own consciousness.

But some fear that this assertion will lead individuals to deceive themselves, appealing to their own consciousness, instead of the Word of God. To this I answer, the same objection might hold true in respect to the question whether a man has been converted or not; whether he loves God at all or not; whether he believes, or whether he reads his Bible at all, or not. To this it has been said that he is not to judge from his own consciousness whether he is converted or not, but by his life and fruits. But to this I answer—it is indeed by his life and fruits that he is to be known, and know himself; but how does he know what his life is, and what his fruits are, but by his own consciousness? How does he know that he has such affection, puts forth such an action, goes to such a place, does or omits any thing whatever? I answer—he knows it only by his consciousness.

In my treatise just through the press, I have made the following remarks in relation to those states of mind of which we have but slight consciousness:

"While I say that consciousness is the only evidence we have or can have of our spiritual state, and of the exercises of our own minds, it should be distinctly remembered that many thoughts, emotions and affections go through our minds which we do not so distinctly recognize at the time as to remember them for an hour or perhaps for a moment. We must be indeed slightly conscious of their existence at the time; but our minds being occupied so much with other things prevents us from giving attention to them as to lodge them in our memories. Now of these thoughts, emotions and affections, which thus often pass through our minds in a great measure unnoticed, the following things should be said, deeply pondered, well understood, and always remembered: first, many of these thoughts, to say the least, must be sinful or holy. Second, if they are not distinctly noticed by consciousness, their moral character, whether sinful or holy, may be at the time overlooked by us. And third, as we have no distinct recollection of them, we may affirm that we are not *conscious* of sin, when as a matter of fact we may have been guilty of it in the exercise of these unnoticed thoughts and affections.

"So, all that a man in this state of existence may ever be able to affirm in respect to his moral character is that he is not *conscious* of sin, without being able to say absolutely that he does not, and has not within a given time, had any exercise of mind that is sinful. When his mind is strongly exercised, and his consciousness therefore very clear and distinct, he may be able to affirm with a good degree of confidence, if not with certainty, that he has had no sinful exercises perhaps for a given time. But of the general tenor of his life, I do not see how he can affirm any thing more with certainty than that he does not remember to have been conscious of any sin.

"This view of the subject will account for the fact to which I have already alluded: the way in which the Spirit of God always convinces of sin is by awakening in our memories the recollection of past consciousness, and often in this way revealing to us distinctly former states of mind of which we were but very slightly conscious at the time. The Holy Spirit makes us see that we have been guilty of committing sin of which we were not at all aware of before." [2]

"When, therefore, I say that by consciousness a man may know whether he is in a state of entire sanctification, I mean that consciousness is the real and only evidence that we can have of being in this state. When our minds are exercised strongly, and our consciousness therefore distinct, the testimony of consciousness is clear, explicit, and so satisfactory that we cannot doubt it. But under other circumstances and in other states of mind, when the exercises of the mind are such as to render consciousness less distinct and vivid, affections may be exercised by us, whether sinful or holy, that are not so distinctly noticed by consciousness, and so fully remembered by us that we can affirm absolutely of them that they were not sinful." [3]

This, then, is the sum of the whole matter. A man is able to understand the law of God aright, or he is not. If he is not, he is under no obligation to do so. If he has formed as correct a judgment in respect to what the claims of the law of God are, as in the present circumstances of his being, availing himself as he is able of such aids as God has extended to him, he has thus far done his duty, and knows the meaning of the law of God so far as he is at present bound to know it.

He is able to know whether he is at present in a state of obedience or disobedience to that law, or he is not able to know it. If he is not able to know, he is not under any obligation to know. If he has formed the most correct judgment of which he

---

[2] This quotation may be read in its context in *Principles of Sanctification,* "Knowing Your Relationship with God" pp. 125–126
[3] Between these two quotations, Finney discussed how the Apostle Paul must have recognized this principle. *Ibid.,* p. 127.

is naturally capable in the present circumstances of his being, with respect to his conformity or nonconformity to the law of God, he knows all upon that subject that he is at present bound to know. And if under these circumstances he cannot know whether he is or is not in a state of entire sanctification, then he cannot tell whether he is at present in rebellion against God, or whether he is rendering Him an acceptable service. He cannot tell whether he ought to repent of his present state of mind, or whether he ought to regard it as acceptable to God. Now I inquire, if, under these supposed circumstances of absolute inability to know whether we are or are not obeying God, we can possibly be required to know, or condemned for not knowing; and might we not just as well be condemned for not flying through the air, or for not having been present at the foundation of the world?

With respect to the liability of this statement to abuse, and to foster spiritual pride and self-delusion, I have at present only to say, it is the truth of God, and to be sure, like every other truth, is liable to perversion and abuse; but have ministers of the gospel yet to learn that this is no good reason why it should not be proclaimed upon the housetops?

The remaining objection is reserved for the next letter.

Your brother in the bonds of the gospel,
Charles G. Finney

CHAPTER 31

To the Editor of The Oberlin Evangelist

January 20, 1841

Dear Brother:

To present the second objection, I will now quote the remaining paragraph from the esteemed brother's letter, mentioned in my last letter, and make a few remarks upon it.

"One point is what you say of the claims of the law, in *The Oberlin Evangelist*, Vol. 2, p. 50: 'The question is, what does the law of God require of Christians of the present generation, in all respects in our circumstances, with all the ignorance and debility of body and mind which have resulted from the intemperance and abuse of the human constitution through so many generations?' [1] But if this be so, then the more ignorant and debilitated a person is in body and mind, in consequence of his own or ancestors' sins and follies, the less the law would require of him, and the less would it be for him to become perfectly holy—and, the nearer this ignorance and debility came to being perfect, the nearer would he be to being perfectly holy, for the less would be required of him to make him so. But is this so? Can a person be perfectly sanctified while particularly that 'ignorance of mind,' which is the effect of the intemperance and abuse of the human constitution, remains? Indeed, can he be sanctified at all, except as *this* ignorance is removed by the truth and Spirit of God; it being a moral and not a physical effect of sinning? I say it kindly; here appears to me at least, a very serious entering wedge of error. Were the effect of human depravity upon man simply physically to disable him, like tak-

---

[1] *Principles of Sanctification*, p. 117.

ing from the body a limb, or destroying in part or in whole, a faculty of the mind, I would not object; but to say, this effect is ignorance, a moral effect wholly, and then say, having this ignorance, the law levels its claims according to it, and that with it, a man can be entirely sanctified, looks not to me like the teachings of the Bible."

I have seen the passage from my lecture here alluded to, quoted and commented upon in different periodicals and uniformly with entire disapproval.

It has always been separated entirely from the exposition which I have given of the law of God, in the same lectures; with which exposition, no one, so far as I know, has seen fit to grapple. [2]

I believe, in every instance, the objections that have been made to this paragraph, were by those who profess to believe in the present natural ability of sinners to do all their duty.

I would most earnestly and respectfully inquire, what consistency there is in denominating this paragraph a dangerous heresy, and still maintaining that men are at present naturally able to do all that God requires of them?

I put the inquiry back to those brethren, by what authority do you affirm that God requires any more of any moral agent in the universe, and of man in his present condition, than he is at present able to perform?

I inquire, does not the very language of the law of God prove to be a demonstration that God requires no more of man than, in his present state, he is able to perform? Let us hear its language: "Thou shalt love the Lord thy God with all thy heart, and with all thy soul, and with all thy mind. Thou shalt love thy neighbor as thyself." Now here, God so completely levels His claims, by the very wording of these commandments, to the present capacity of every human being, however young or old, however maimed, debilitated, or idiotic, that "if it were possible to conceive of a *moral pigmy*, the law requires of him nothing more than to use whatever strength he has in the service and for the glory of God." [3]

I most respectfully but earnestly inquire of my brethren, if they believe that God requires as much of men as of angels, of a child as a man, of a half-idiot as of a Newton? I mean not to ask whether God requires an equally perfect consecration of all

[2]See especially, "What Is Sanctification" and "What Entire Sanctification Is Not", *ibid.*, pp. 15–43.
[3]Here Finney quotes from his own hearing the language or at least the sentiment of Prof. Hickock of Western Reserve College.

the powers actually possessed by each of these classes; but whether in degree, He really requires the same, irrespective of their present natural ability?

I wish to inquire whether my brethren do not admit that the brain is the organ of the mind, and that every abuse of the physical system has abridged the capacity of the mind, while it remains connected with this tenement of clay? And I would also ask whether my brethren mean to maintain with the same breath the doctrine of present natural ability to comply with all the requirements of God, and also the fact that God now requires of man just the same degree of service that He might have rendered if he had never sinned, or in any way violated the laws of his being? And if they maintain these two positions at the same time, I further inquire whether they believe that man has natural ability at the present moment to bring all his faculties and powers, together with his knowledge, on to as high ground and into the same state in which they might have been, had he never sinned? My brethren, is there not some inconsistency here?

In the paragraph from the letter above quoted, the brother admits that if a man by his own act had deprived himself of any of his corporeal faculties, he would not thenceforth be under an obligation to use those faculties. But he thinks this principle does not hold true in respect to the ignorance of man; because he esteems his ignorance a moral and not a natural defect. Here I beg leave to make a few inquiries:

1. Should a man wickedly deprive himself of the use of a hand, would not this act be a moral act? No doubt it would.

2. Suppose a man by his own act should make himself an idiot, would not this act be a moral act?

3. Would he not in both these cases render himself naturally unable, in the one case, to use his hand, and in the other, his reason? Undoubtedly he would. But how can it be affirmed, with any show of reason, that in the one case his natural inability discharges him from the obligation to use his hand, and that in the other case, his natural inability does not affect his obligation—that he is still bound to use his reason, of which he has voluntarily deprived himself, but not his hand? Now the fact is, that in both these cases the inability is a natural one, and the act that occasioned this inability in both cases, involves the guilt of all the moral default it causes.

4. I ask, if a man has willingly remained in ignorance of God, whether his ignorance is a moral or natural inability? If it is a moral inability, he can instantly overcome it by the right

exercise of his own will. And nothing can be a moral inability that cannot be instantaneously removed by our own volition. Do my brethren believe that the present ignorance of mankind can be instantaneously removed, and their knowledge become as perfect as it might have been had they never sinned, by an act of volition on the part of men? If they do not, why do they call this a moral inability, or ignorance, a moral defect? The fact is that ignorance is the natural effect of moral delinquency. Neglect of duty occasions ignorance; and this ignorance constitutes a natural inability to do that of which man is utterly ignorant—just as the loss of a hand, in the case supposed, is the natural effect of a moral act, but in itself constitutes a natural inability to perform those duties that might have been performed, were it not for the loss of this hand. The fact is that this ignorance does constitute, while it remains, a natural inability to perform those duties of which the mind is ignorant; and all that can be required is that from the present moment the mind should be diligently and perfectly engaged in acquiring what knowledge it can, and in perfectly obeying as fast as it can obtain the light. If this is not true, it is utter nonsense to talk about natural ability as being a *sine qua non* of moral obligation. And I would kindly, but most earnestly ask my brethren, by what rule of consistency they maintain with the same breath the doctrine of a natural ability to do whatever God requires, and also insist that He requires men to know as much and in all respects to render Him the same kind and *degree* of service as if they never had sinned or rendered themselves in any respect naturally incapable of doing and being, at the present moment, all that they might have done and been, had they never in any instance neglected their duty?

The brother, in the above paragraph, seems to feel troubled with the consideration, that if it is true that a man's ignorance can be any excuse for his not at present doing what he might have done, but because of this ignorance, it will follow that the less he knows the less is required of him, and should he become a perfect idiot, he would be entirely discharged from moral obligation. To this I answer: Yes, or the doctrine of natural ability, and the entire government of God, is a mere farce. If a man should annihilate himself, would he not thereby set aside his moral obligation to obey God? Yes, truly. Should he make himself an idiot, has he not thereby *annihilated* his *moral agency*; and of course his natural ability to obey God? And will my New School brethren adopt the position of Dr. Wilson of Cincinnati, as maintained on the trial of Dr. Beecher, that "moral obligation does not imply ability of any kind?" The truth is that for the time being a man may destroy his moral agency by rendering himself a lunatic or an idiot; and while this lunacy or idiocy continues, obedience to God is naturally impossible, and therefore not required. The guilt of this act is equivalent to all the default it causes.

But it is also true that no human being and no moral agent can deprive himself of reason and moral agency except for a limited time. There is no reason to believe that the soul can be deranged or idiotic when separated from the body. And therefore moral agency will in all cases be renewed in a future, if not in the present state of existence, when God will hold men fully responsible for having deprived themselves of power to render Him all that service which they might otherwise have rendered. But do let me inquire again, can my dear brethren maintain that an idiot or lunatic can be a moral agent? Can they maintain that any but a moral agent is the subject of moral obligation? Can they maintain that a man can be the subject of moral obligation any farther than he is in a state of sanity? Can they maintain that an infant is the subject of moral obligation previous to all knowledge? And can they maintain that moral obligation can in any case exceed knowledge? If they can and do, then to be consistent they must flatly deny that natural ability is a *sine qua non* of moral obligation, and adopt the absurd dogma of Dr. Wilson that "moral obligation does not imply any ability whatever." When my brethren will take this ground, I shall then understand and know where to meet them. But I beseech you, brethren, not to complain of inconsistency in me, nor accuse me of teaching dangerous heresy, while I teach nothing more than you must admit to be true, or unequivocally admit, *in extenso*, the very dogma of Dr. Wilson, as above.

I wish to be distinctly understood. I maintain, that *present* ignorance is *present* natural inability to use it. And I also maintain, that the law of God requires nothing more of any human being than that which he is at present naturally able to perform under the present circumstances of his being. Do my brethren deny this? If they do, then they have gone back to Dr. Wilson's ground. If they do not, why am I accounted a heretic by them for teaching what they themselves maintain?

In my treatise upon the subject of entire sanctification, I have shown from the Bible that actual knowledge is indispensable to moral obligation, and that the legal maxim, "ignorance of the law excuses no one," is not good in morals.

Professor Stuart, in a recent number of the *Biblical Repository*, takes precisely the same ground I have taken, and fully maintains that sin is the voluntary transgression of a *known* law. And he further abundantly shows that this is no new or heterodox opinion. Now Prof. Stuart, in the article alluded to, takes exactly the same position in regard to what constitutes sin that I have done in the paragraph upon which so much has been said. And may I be permitted to inquire why the same sentiment is orthodox at Andover, and sound theology in the *Biblical Repository*, but highly heterodox and dangerous at Oberlin?

Will my brethren of the New School, to avoid the conclusiveness of my reasonings in respect to the requirements of the law of God, go back to Old School-ism, physical depravity, and accountability, based upon natural inability, and all the host of absurdities belonging to their particular views of orthodoxy? I recollect that Dr. Beecher expressed his surprise at the position taken by Dr. Wilson, to which I have alluded, and said he did not believe that "many men could be found who could march up without winking to the maintenance of such a proposition as that." But to be consistent, I do not see but that my brethren, with or "without winking," are driven to the necessity, either of "marching up" to maintaining the same proposition, or they must admit that this objectionable paragraph in my lecture is the truth of God.

I have made these remarks in compliance with an intimation when I published those lectures that I might notice any thing that appeared to my brethren to be of serious importance in relation to their orthodoxy. But I did not then, nor do I now intend, either to fill the pages of the *Evangelist*, or occupy my own time, with any thing like a controversial discussion of this subject. I hate controversy. I have something else to do, besides engaging in it. But this much I must say, that after all I have heard and read upon the subject, I am more and more surprised at the amount of misapprehension and error that have been and still are prevalent in the Church of God on this subject.

I have made extracts from, and remarks upon the letter alluded to, not from any lack of fraternal regard for the brother from whom I received it, but because it brought these two objectionable points so fully up, and laid so legitimate a foundation for these remarks.

Your brother in the bonds of the gospel,
Charles G. Finney

CHAPTER 32

To the Editor of The Oberlin Evangelist

February 17, 1841

(Professor Finney returned from Cleveland in time to write the following letter for the last side of the paper.)

Dear Brother:

I have seen several remarks in the papers lately, and have heard several suggestions from various quarters, which have only increased the fear which I have for some time entertained, that multitudes of Christians and indeed many ministers have radically defective views of salvation by faith in Jesus Christ. To the doctrine of entire sanctification in this life, as believed and taught by some of us, it has been frequently objected lately, that prayers offered in accordance with this belief, and by a sanctified soul, would savor strongly of spiritual pride and self-righteousness. I have seen this objection stated in its full force recently, in a religious periodical, in the form of a supposed prayer of a sanctified soul—the objective of which was obviously to expose the shocking absurdity, self-righteousness, and spiritual pride, of a prayer, or rather thanksgiving, made in accordance with a belief that one is entirely sanctified. Now I must confess, that that prayer, together with objections and remarks which suggest the same idea, have created in my mind no small degree of alarm. I have no small fear that many of our divines, in contending for the doctrines of grace, have entirely lost sight of the meaning of the language they use, and have in reality but very little practical understanding of what is intended by salvation by grace, in opposition to salvation by works. If this is not the case, I know not how to account for their feeling and stating such an objection as this to the doctrine of entire sanctification.

Now, if I understand the doctrine of salvation by grace, both sanctification and justification are wrought by the grace of God, and not by any works or merits of our own, irrespective of the grace of Christ through faith. Now if this is the real doctrine of the Bible, what earthly objection can there be to our confessing, professing, and thanking God for our sanctification, any more than for our justification? It is true, indeed, that in our justification our own agency is not concerned, while in our sanctification it is. Yet I understand the doctrine of the Bible to be, that both are brought about by grace through faith, and that we should no sooner be sanctified without the grace of Christ than we should be justified without it. Now who pretends to deny this? And yet, if it is true, of what weight is that class of objections to which I have alluded? These objections obviously turn upon the idea, no doubt latent and deep seated in the mind, that the real holiness of Christians, in whatever degree it exists, is in some way to be ascribed to some goodness originating in themselves, and not in the grace of Christ. But do let me ask how is it possible that men who entertain, actually and practically, right views upon this subject, can by any possibility feel as if it must be proof conclusive of self-righteousness and Pharisaism, to profess and thank God for sanctification? Is it not understood on all hands, that sanctification is by grace; and that the gospel has made abundant provision for the sanctification of all men? This certainly is admitted by those who have stated this objection. Now if this is so, which is the most honorable to God, to confess and complain of our sins, triumphing and having dominion over us, or to be able truly and honestly to thank Him for having given us the victory over our sins? God has said, "Sin shall not have dominion over you, for ye are not under the law but under grace."

Now, in view of this and multitudes of kindred promises, suppose we come to God and say, "O Lord, thou hast made these great and precious promises, but as a matter of fact they do not accord with our own experience. For sin does continually have dominion over us. Thy grace is not sufficient for us. The blood of Christ does not cleanse us from all sin. We are continually overcome by temptation, notwithstanding thy promise, that in every temptation thou wilt make a way for us to escape. Thou has said the truth shall make us free, but we are not *free*. We are still the slaves of our appetites and lusts."

Now which, I inquire, is the most honorable to God, to go

on with a string of confessions and self-accusations, that are in flat contradiction to the promises of God, and almost, to say the least, a burlesque upon the grace of the gospel, or to be able, through grace, to confess that we have found it true in our own experience, "that if we confess our sins, He is faithful and just to forgive our sins and to cleanse us from all unrighteousness"—that His grace is sufficient for us—that as our day is so our strength is, as a matter of fact, and that sin does not have dominion over us, because we are not under the law but under grace?

To this I know it will be answered that in thus confessing our sins we do not impeach the grace or faithfulness of God inasmuch as all these promises are conditioned upon faith, and consequently that the reason of our remaining in sin is to be ascribed to our unbelief, and is therefore no disparagement to the grace of Christ. But I beg that it may be duly considered that faith itself is of the operation of God—is itself produced by grace; and therefore the fact of our being obliged to confess our unbelief is a dishonor to the grace of Christ. Is it honorable or dishonorable to God that we should be able to confess that even our unbelief is overcome, and that we are able to testify from our own experience that the grace of the gospel, as a matter of fact, is sufficient for our present salvation and sanctification? There is no doubt a vast amount of self-righteousness in the Church, which while it talks of grace really means nothing by it. For a man to go any farther than to *hope* that he is converted, seems to many minds to savor of self-righteousness. Now why is this, unless they themselves entertain self-righteous notions in regard to conversion? Many persons would feel shocked to hear a man in prayer unqualifiedly thank God that he had been converted and justified. And they might just as well feel shocked at this, and upon precisely the same principle, as to feel shocked if he should unqualifiedly thank God that he had been sanctified.

But again I say, that the very fact that a man feels shocked to hear a converted or a sanctified soul unqualifiedly thank God for the grace received, shows that down deep in his heart lies concealed a self-righteous view of the way of salvation, and that in his mind all holiness in Christians is a ground of boasting; and that if persons have become truly and fully sanctified that they really have a ground of boasting before God. I know not how else to account for this amazing prejudice. For my own part I do not conceive it to be the least evidence of self-righteousness when I hear a man sincerely and heartily thank God for converting and justifying him by His grace. Nor should I feel either shocked, horrified, or disgusted, to hear a man thank God that He had sanctified him wholly by His grace, if in either case or both cases I had the corroborative evidence of an apparently holy life, I should bless God, take courage, and feel like calling on all around to glorify God for such an instance of His glorious and excellent grace.

The feeling seems to be very general that such a prayer or thanksgiving is similar in fact, and in the principle upon which it rests, with that of the Pharisee noticed by our Savior. But what reason is there for this assumption? We are explicitly informed that that was the prayer of a Pharisee. But the Pharisees were self-righteous and explicitly and openly rejected the grace of Christ.

The Pharisee there boasted of his own goodness and not in the grace of Christ. Hence he did not thank God that the grace of Christ had made him unlike other men. Now this prayer was designed to teach us the abomination of any man's putting in a claim to righteousness and true holiness irrespective of the grace of God by Jesus Christ. But certainly this is an infinitely different thing from the thanksgiving of a soul who fully recognizes the grace of Christ, and attributes his sanctification entirely to that grace. And I cannot see how a man can suppose these two prayers to be analogous in their principle and spirit who has entirely divested himself of Pharisaical notions in respect to the doctrine of sanctification.

Your brother in the bonds of the gospel,
Charles G. Finney.

CHAPTER 33

To the Editor of The Oberlin Evangelist

March 31, 1841

Dear Brother:

Permit me, through your columns, to address the Church upon a subject of great delicacy, and yet of immeasurable importance. From repeated remarks in different religious periodicals, I have observed, that a very important distinction is overlooked, which appears to me calculated to work immeasurable mischief in the Church. The writers to whom I allude appear to confound *censoriousness* [1] with *Christian faithfulness*, above which a more ruinous error could scarcely be entertained or taught; and especially does this confusion seem to exist in their minds, and in their writings, in respect to whatever is said of the delinquencies of ministers of the gospel. They seem to assume, either that ministers of the gospel are universally in a state of entire and permanent sanctification, or if they are not, they are not, like other men, to be reproved for sin, and exhorted to repentance. It would seem, that nothing can be said of the sins of ministers, and that they cannot be reproved or warned, even in the utmost kindness and love, without its being regarded and treated by those writers, as of course censorious and denunciatory.

---

[1] In most of the previous letters, I substituted the word "hyper-critical" for "censorious." The mere word "critical" as a substitute seems too weak, and Finney would never say that we should not use "critical judgment" or be "critical listeners" in the sense of carefully evaluating, in the light of Scripture, the spirit of Christ and sound reason, all that we hear or read. Since Finney defines the word "censorious" in this letter, and since it seems to be the most appropriate word, I have left it throughout. The word "denunciatory" could also be defined as "judgmental" in our modern use of the word.

By the class of writers to whom I allude, it seems also to be supposed, that to speak plainly and pointedly of the sins of the Church, "to reprove, warn, exhort, and rebuke" them, in a pointed, though in an affectionate and earnest manner, is also censorious and denunciatory.

In short, it seems to be the practice of many writers of the present day, utterly to confound, as I said, Christian faithfulness with censoriousness. Now, if this confusion is allowed to pass without notice, till reproof, instead of being considered a virtue, shall be regarded as a vice, the Church is inevitably ruined. If, to reprove the sins of ministers, or of any class of Christians or men whatever, is to be regarded as of course censoriousness and denunciatory, then the power of the glorious gospel must be destroyed. Permit me to point out: what I suppose to be the true distinction between censoriousness and Christian faithfulness; to show that Christian faithfulness is universally obligatory; that ministers are as much bound to reprove their fellow-ministers, as any class of persons; that a disposition to complain of this, is conclusive evidence of a proud and turbulent spirit.

First, the difference between censoriousness and Christian faithfulness.

I consider censoriousness to consist in a disposition to censure, blame, or condemn others, and to manifest itself in speaking of the faults of others with a selfish and wicked intention. It manifests itself in passing severe and uncharitable judgments in regard to others' motives when their conduct appears to be right. It consists in giving publicity to their faults, in a manner that is not demanded by the great principle of benevolence.

I regard Christian faithfulness, in respect to the delinquencies of others, as consisting in reproving others for their sins, from love to God and the souls of men. In reproving, warning, and exhorting men to forsake their sins, for the honor of God and the good of His Church. Christian faithfulness, so far as reproof is concerned, consists in that plain, faithful, pointed, yet compassionate dealing with all classes of men, which was manifested by the prophets, by Christ and the apostles. The sins for which the inspired writers reproved and rebuked men, were not sins which they knew merely by inspiration, but sins which lay open to the public view, and sins of which they knew them to be guilty, by their own observation. In the reproofs, therefore, which they administered, we learn the great fundamental principles upon which reproofs and rebukes are to be administered. And we are to regard those principles as the laws of Christ's kingdom, and to administer reproof in accordance with them. Let me, therefore, be understood to say, that Christian faithfulness in regard to reproving sin, consists in a thorough, yet compassionate and benevolent withstanding, reproving, and, if need be, rebuking every form of sin, in high and low places. It consists in speaking freely, when the circumstances of the Church and the glory of God demand it, of the public sins of all classes of persons, in high as well as in low places. But again, I say, to speak unnecessarily, or from malicious motives, of the sins of any class of men, however public and outrageous their sins may be, is censoriousness.

Secondly, Christian faithfulness is universally obligatory.

This is an explicit command of the Bible: "Thou shalt in any wise rebuke thy neighbor, and not suffer sin upon him." There are a great many passages of scripture that explicitly enjoin this duty. The nature of the case shows, that it must be a universal duty. It is a plain dictate of benevolence. A benevolent man will just as naturally reprove others for their sins, and warn them to flee from the wrath to come, as he would give warning if his neighbor's house was on fire.

Next, as I said, ministers are as bound to reprove their fellow-ministers as to reprove any class of persons whatever.

When Peter was to be blamed, Paul withstood him to his face. Here, we have the example of an apostle reproving an apostle. Ministers are nowhere made an exception to the general law of Christ's kingdom—that all men are to be reproved for their sins. There is nothing in the nature of the case demanding that they should be made an exception. The sins of ministers are eminently injurious to the Church and to the world. There is, therefore, a special reason why they should be dealt with faithfully for their sins. Since they are regarded as public examples to the people, their sins should be especially pointed out, as sins, and publically reproved; lest their sinfulness should be overlooked by the people, and come to be imitated by them as virtues.

Their professions of piety are such, as to render them eminently deserving of reproof, if they do not walk uprightly. Just in proportion to the importance of their calling, is it important that they should be faithfully dealt with by all classes of men, and especially by their brother ministers. Respect should always be had to their official character, and reproof should be administered to them especially, and indeed to all men, in great candor, kindness, compassion, and yet with great and searching faithfulness.

Finally, to complain of this is evidence of a proud and turbulent spirit.

A disposition to resist or resent reproof, administered in a spirit of Christian faithfulness, is, on its face, wholly an antichristian spirit. If persons cannot be reproved, or even buffeted, for their faults, and yet take it patiently, they are certainly far enough from being in a Christian temper. Peter says, "What glory is it, if, when ye be buffeted for your faults, ye shall take it patiently? But if, when ye do well, and suffer for it, ye take it patiently, this is acceptable with God. For even hereunto were ye called; because Christ also suffered for us, leaving us an example, that ye should follow his steps: who did no sin, neither was guile found in his mouth: who, when he was reviled, reviled not again; when he suffered, he threatened not; but committed himself to him that judgeth righteously." Now the apostle plainly teaches, in this passage, that even to suffer rebuke or buffeting patiently, when we are really at fault, is no evidence of a Christian spirit, but a refusal to do so, must of course be an evidence of a proud and turbulent spirit.

When any class of men think themselves so far above reproof, either from their exalted station in life or great influence, that others have no right to reprove them for their sins, they must be in any thing but a Christian temper of mind; and especially, when they refuse reproof from their brethren, who are not only naturally but ecclesiastically their equals.

In short, when any men, or set of men, are in such a state of mind as to be unwilling to be reproved for sin by the merest child or novice, they are in a proud and impenitent state of mind. And in that state of mind, God cannot and will not bless them.

Permit me to conclude this letter with a few remarks.

It is greatly to be wished, that there were much more Christian faithfulness, in respect to administering reproof for every form and degree of sin, than there is, in the Church. There must be a great deal more of this, or the Church cannot prosper.

It is greatly desirable, that ministers should be much more faithful than they are in reproving each other, both in public and in private.

It is greatly to be desired, that this should be done in a much better spirit, than that in which it is generally done. That it should be done very thoroughly, and in a manner that will reach the very seat of the difficulty.

It is of infinite importance, that such plain dealing should be received in a right spirit, and that ministers especially should consider well the example of David, who, although a king, when he was personally and pointedly rebuked by Nathan, instead of resenting it, and complaining of censoriousness and denunciation, exclaimed with all humility, like a man of God, "I have sinned against the Lord."

As long as ministers are disposed to complain, and to treat all reproof, however kindly administered, as naturally being censorious and denunciatory, they need not expect the blessing of the Lord. When this complaint is made, we should examine carefully and prayerfully our spirit, motive, and manner of administering reproof; but should by no means be deterred from following up reproof, in a thorough, searching, benevolent, compassionate manner; either until there is reformation, or the case becomes so hopeless as to come within the principle laid down by Christ, when He commanded His disciples to let the religious teachers of His day alone, because "they were blind leaders of the blind."

Now, brethren, I have written this letter in the kindness and affection of my heart, and I am not without my apprehension, that even in this I shall be charged with censoriousness—and that what I know to be spoken in love, will be confounded with a spirit of censoriousness. But, my brethren, I cannot help it; I wish to call the attention of the Church and of the ministry, to this plain distinction, and beg of them duly and prayerfully to consider it, whenever they find themselves reproved. "Let the righteous smite me, it shall do me good. It shall be an excellent oil."

Your brother in the love and fellowship of the blessed gospel,
Charles G. Finney

CHAPTER 34

To the Editor of The Oberlin Evangelist

May 26, 1841

Dear Brother:

As I have continued to read what has been said in various publications, on the subject of entire sanctification, I have been more and more struck with the fact, that the difficulties in the way of a right understanding of the subject in most minds, and especially in the minds of ministers, are more fundamental than might have been expected on so plain a subject. In preparing my course of lectures for the press, I aimed mostly at placing the subject before the public simply as a Bible question, and avoiding, so far as I consistently could, the discussion of the metaphysical matters pertaining thereto. This, to the minds of common readers, I then supposed, and now suppose, to be the most acceptable and profitable method of presenting this great truth. But there is still a large class of minds who need to have their attention called to the consideration of certain metaphysical questions, which belong rather to the philosophy of the subject, than to the plain Bible announcement of it.

As the subject is continually up for investigation, and the interest of the Church in it perpetually increasing, I purpose, through your columns, to present still another view of this subject to the churches, not inconsistent with what I have before said, but in some respects a more fundamental and philosophical view of the subject. I have been considering the best method of presenting it, and have sometimes thought I would write a review of the leading articles that have been published in opposition to this doctrine. But I have ever been afraid even of the form of controversy, and greatly prefer to take up an original investigation of it, in my own way, without either the form or the spirit of controversy. In doing this I of course intend so to present the subject as to meet the principal objections and difficulties I have seen stated; but in a way that shall avoid any such collision with my brethren as might produce controversy. I shall endeavor to condense my articles as much as I can, and still have them intelligible. I design to write for thinkers, and for those who are willing to take the trouble to give the subject a somewhat fundamental examination.

That your readers may be informed of something like the outline of what I intend to present, I will in this article state the main positions I design to discuss, reserving to myself, however, the privilege of making any addition to, or alteration of the prescribed train of thought which may seem to be called for, from any new light that may dawn from any quarter upon the subject. The outline I shall give will contain a summary of the principal positions that seem at present to require investigation:

I. What is implied in moral obligation.

II. Wherein moral character consists.

III. What constitutes right character, or holiness.

IV. What constitutes wrong character, or sinfulness.

V. That moral character is always wholly right or wholly wrong, and never partly right and partly wrong at the same time.

VI. What entire sanctification is.

VII. That regeneration is entire sanctification.

VIII. The difference between entire sanctification, considered as an act, and entire sanctification, considered as a state; or, the difference between entire present sanctification and continued sanctification.

IX. That faith is entire sanctification, considered as an act, but as a state faith is a condition of entire sanctification.

X. Entire sanctification, as a state, is attainable in this life.

XI. It has been attained.

XII. In the Millenium this state will be the common attainment of Christians.

XIII. It is the duty and privilege of all persons to enter at once into this state.

XIV. Why they do not.

XV. Make some inferences and remarks.

Before I begin the discussion, perhaps it may be well to remark, that some of your readers may inquire why we dwell so much upon the subject of entire sanctification? To this I answer:

The subject needs to be and must be discussed, till it is understood by the Church.

There is now sufficient excitement in the Church upon the subject, to induce them to read what is written.

I have myself said comparatively little, directly upon the subject, except in the course of lectures which appeared in the last volume of your paper.

As a general thing, it is at present the most interesting and important subject of consideration and discussion, that is before the Church.

Although the minds of some may be so well settled as not to need further investigation, yet I am persuaded, that, as a general thing, no subject could be more acceptable and important to the general class of readers than this.

I will proceed with the investigation, and show:

I. *What things are implied in moral obligation.*

Moral obligation implies the possession of the powers of moral agency; namely, Understanding, Reason, Conscience, Free will, and Sensibility. Some of these powers may be possessed by mere animals. Reason, Free will, and Conscience, are the characteristics that distinguish moral agents from mere animals. It is, however, believed, at least by me, that a being would not be a moral agent, who did not possess ALL the above named powers and susceptibilities.

But here, for the benefit of many of my readers, it will be important to go a little into explanation, as it respects the meaning of these words.

By *Understanding*, I mean that power or faculty of the mind that receives the perception of the senses with respect to the existence and qualities of sensible objects, forms notions of them, combines, and classifies them, etc. This faculty is employed solely about sensible objects.

By *Reason*, I intend that power of the mind that is employed solely about absolute, eternal, infinite, and necessary truths. The reason takes knowledge of absolute and necessary truths, by a direct perception of them, just as the perceiving faculty takes knowledge of sensible objects by direct perception.

By *Conscience*, I mean that function of the reason that perceives and enforces moral obligation—that pronounces the sentence of condemnation or approbation, upon disobedience or obedience.

By *Free will*, I intend the power which a moral agent possesses of choosing in any direction in view of motives.

By *Sensibility*, I mean the susceptibility to pleasure and pain, or the faculty of feeling.

Moral obligation implies moral liberty, or natural ability. By this it is intended, that a moral agent must not only possess the faculties of a moral agent, but the power and ability to use them, according to his sovereign election, in acts of obedience or disobedience; being always responsible for the manner in which he uses his natural ability or moral liberty.

Moral obligation implies, so much light or knowledge, as to enable the agent to affirm *oughtness* of any action or occupation; that is, law, in order to be obligatory, must be prescribed, or published; and the agent, before he can be under a moral obligation to obey, must have sufficient light to perceive, that he ought or ought not, to do or omit the thing in question. If the powers of moral agency exist, it is of no use, unless the agent possess sufficient light to perceive obligation. And when obligation is perceived, the very perception of a thing as obligatory, implies that there is natural ability to obey or disobey. It should always, then, be understood, that moral obligation implies the possession of the powers of moral agency, natural power or ability to use them in the prescribed or required manner, together with so much light or knowledge as to produce the conviction of obligation; or, in other words, so much knowledge as to enable the conscience to affirm moral obligation.

And here it should be distinctly understood, that moral obligation can only be commensurate with natural ability, including in the idea of natural ability that degree of knowledge I have just mentioned. I know it has been denied by a certain class of philosophers, that moral obligation implies natural ability in the sense I have explained it. With this class of philosophers I have, at present, nothing to do, as I write to those and for those who have long professed to embrace the doctrine of natural ability, as indispensable to moral obligation.

Please do observe now, and bear it always in mind, that those who are called New School divines have all along, for many years, admitted the doctrine of natural ability as here explained, and have based their exhortations to sinners upon the fact, that men really possess natural faculties and powers to obey God; or, in other words, to do all their duty, and that, in every case, human responsibility and moral obligation are commensurate, and only commensurate with natural ability, including a knowledge of duty. And here let me say, that from this ground they can never be driven, so long as the law of God remains the rule of human action; for the very letter and spirit of the law of God require of men, just the use of all, and no more than all the strength that each moral agent possesses.

I have been surprised that some of the principal New School writers and reviewers, in their controversy with the doctrine of entire sanctification, should not only depart from and overlook the doctrine of natural ability, but make assumptions as the very foundation of their opposition, that are as far as possible from the New School admissions and views upon the subject of natural ability, and from their own well-known former views upon this subject. For example, in opposition to the doctrine of entire sanctification, it has been urged that men must be sure that they understand the law of God in all applications to human action, or they cannot be entirely sanctified, or know that they were, even if they were. Now who does not see that this objection assumes that men can be under moral obligation where they have no knowledge or light? In other words that something can be their duty of which they have no knowledge. But this is the same thing as to deny that moral obligation implies the possession of the powers of moral agency, together with sufficient light or knowledge to produce the affirmation of *oughtness* before obligation can in any case attach.

Again, it has been assumed in opposition to this doctrine, that a man must know the exact measure of his own ability, before he can know whether he fully obeys God. But this again assumes that he may be under obligation beyond what he is able to know to be his duty. As if an individual could be under a moral obligation to exert a greater measure of ability in the service of God than he knows himself to possess. In other words, that moral obligation can exceed that degree of light which produces the affirmation of *oughtness*. But this is a flat denial of the doctrine of natural ability as universally held by New School divines.

Again, it has been assumed that a man must be sure that his judgment is in every case infallible, before he can perfectly obey God, or know that he obeys Him, if he does. Now this again is not only a denial of the doctrine of natural ability as indispensable to moral obligation, but is an assumption of the direct opposite as truth; that is, it assumes that a man may be under obligation to do that, which according to the best light he has, he judges not to be his duty; in other words still, that his obligation may far exceed his light, which is a direct denial of natural ability.

Again, it has been assumed, that men are under obligation

to render to God just as high and perfect a service as if they had all the knowledge which they might have had, had they never sinned, and all the perfection of powers which they might have had, had they been fully developed, by the exercise of universal and perfect holiness. This, too, assumes the direct opposite of the doctrine of natural ability as true; for no one in his senses will pretend, that men have natural ability to render any such degree of service.

Now these, and several other objections of precisely a kindred character, are, strange as it may seem, brought forward by New School divines, as an unanswerable refutation of the doctrine of entire sanctification in this life: asserting and avowing as they do, that it is absurd to suppose that any human being can do these things. Now observe, these brethren maintain, that these things are really obligatory, notwithstanding it is absurd to suppose that any man has power to comply with these obligations. They insist on these things being essential to entire sanctification—that men are bound to be entirely sanctified—and yet, maintain the absurdity of their being able to yield this measure of obedience. Will the dear brethren look at the inconsistency of this. All such objections as these take it for granted, that a man is bound to know what he cannot know—that he may be under moral obligation, without any knowledge of such obligation—that he may sin, when he cannot know that he sins—which is the same thing as to affirm, that a law can be binding when it cannot be known; which is again to deny the doctrine, that natural ability, including a knowledge of duty, is indispensable to moral obligation.

Your brother in the love and fellowship of the blessed gospel, Charles G. Finney

CHAPTER 35

To the Editor of The Oberlin Evangelist

June 23, 1841

Dear Brother:

Before I pass to the second point to be discussed, I wish to call the attention of the brethren to the subject of my last letter; especially as circumstances, over which I had no control, prevented the present letter from having a place in the last issue of your paper. I might enlarge very much on the subject of natural ability; but perhaps have said enough for the class of readers to whom I principally address these letters. I am well aware, that with certain minds it may be eventually necessary, to enter into a still more fundamental discussion of the question of natural ability, in order to remove the false impressions made on many minds by the imaginary distinction between *natural* and *moral* ability. I say imaginary distinction; for I do not hesitate to say, that the distinction has no foundation in sound philosophy.

The moral ability and inability, of which so much has been said, by some divines, is, after all, when closely examined, nothing more nor less than *natural* ability and inability, properly so called. For this distinction, when stated in simple language, is just this—natural ability, according to them, consists in the power to do as you will; and a man is said to be naturally able to do that which he can do if he will. Moral inability, according to them, consists in a real inability to will, on account of the absence of sufficient light or motive to induce choice. The whole theory is based upon the assumption, that the will (or choice, of course and of necessity) is as the greatest apparent good is. Men are said, then, to be morally unable to will, in the absence of those considerations that really cause the given object to appear to be the greatest good. This moral inability, then, is simply this—an individual is unable to will, because he has not sufficient light to produce the conviction, that it is, upon the whole, best to will in the proposed manner. Now good is the very object of benevolence. The thing required by the law of God is good-willing, or willing good. And the law requires, that every good shall be willed, according to its relative value, as perceived by the mind. This is the very essence, substance, and spirit of the law of God—to regard, will, intend to promote every interest, according to its relative value, is the very thing, and the only thing required by the spirit of the law of God.

Now Pres. Edwards' theory is, that "the will always is as the greatest apparent good is." If this is so, I affirm that every moral being is perfect, and only perfect, and that continually. Indeed, if his theory is true, that the will is of course and of necessity as the greatest apparent good is, there never was, never will be, and never can be such a thing as sin in the universe; for, as a matter of fact, that state of the will that chooses or wills every interest, according to its perceived relative value, for its own sake, is holiness, and nothing else is holiness. And President Edwards himself, when considering the nature of virtue, maintains this sentiment, in all its length and breadth.

The great position which Pres. Edwards labors to establish, and which others have fondly cherished, and strenuously defended, is, that "the will is as the greatest apparent good is." Now he does not mean, that the will is as the greatest apparent good to self is; for he is laboring to establish the philosophy of choice, whether in good or evil beings—whether in good-willing or evil-willing. He is laboring to show what it is that always determines the will, or produces choice—whether the choice be holy or sinful. He regards the will as determined in all instances by the highest motive, and considers that the highest motive, which appears to the mind, to be the greatest good. He brings forth his giant strength, to show the absurdity of supposing, that the will is not, in all cases, as the greatest apparent good is. By apparent good is intended, that which appears, is apprehended, or perceived by the mind to be the *greatest*. By *apparent good*, then, is and must be intended, that which is perceived and considered by the intelligence as the greatest good.

Now with respect to this position of Pres. Edwards, that "the will is as the greatest apparent good is," I beg permission to say; first, it is exactly what the law of God enjoins on every moral being; and all that the law of God can justly enjoin. The law legislates only over the voluntary power. It requires only right willing. Hence, love, or good-willing, is the fulfilling of the law. Good-willing is the willing of every interest according to its perceived relative value. In other words, every good is to be willed, for its own sake—to be regarded and treated according to its relative value, as perceived by the mind. I say, as *perceived*, for knowledge or light is plainly a condition of moral obligation, and indispensable to natural ability. If this is not so, an unborn infant may as well be required to obey the law of God, as one who has arrived at years of understanding. It is, then, the duty and the whole duty of every moral agent, to will that which is the greatest good, and if it be the true doctrine, that the will universally is as the greatest apparent good is, there is not, never was, and never can be a sinner in the universe.

Secondly, no sinner's will is, or while he is a sinner, ever will be or can be as the greatest apparent good is. But his will, or choice, universally, is the direct opposite of the greatest apparent good. The reason of every sinner in the universe affirms, that the good of God, and of all beings in the universe, is a greater good than his own. And sin universally consists in preferring a lesser to a greater apparent or perceived good. *This is the true definition of sin. Sin is the willing of the lesser of two apparent goods.* A sinner's own happiness is a good. But he knows, and cannot but know, that it is the less and not the greater good. Now the giving of his own happiness the preference, over other and higher goods, *is the very essence of sin.* God's law requires him to will every interest according to its perceived or apparent value, but between two apparent goods he chooses the least. So that the position of Pres. Edwards, in respect to sin, is universally false; and with respect to holiness, it is universally true. That is—it is true, that holiness consists in the will's being as the greatest apparent good is. I do not mean to admit, that the *will* chooses the greatest apparent good, of *necessity*; but only that holiness itself must necessarily consist in willing as the greatest apparent good is.

Now what is *moral inability*, according to this philosophy? It lies in the lack of sufficient light to produce the conviction, that the thing required to be chosen is the greatest good. This is called a moral inability. But why a *moral* inability? This inability can have no moral character. It is to all intents and purposes, as really a *natural* inability, while it exists, as the lack of a perceiving faculty would be. I come back, then, because

I am forced back by sound philosophy and common sense, to that view of natural ability, that makes it consist of the following elements: the powers of moral agency; the ability to use or refuse to use them in the required manner; sufficient light to produce the conviction or affirmation of *oughtness*, in relation to any point of duty.

Were this the place, and could it be done in a mere newspaper, I should like to enter somewhat into detail, in refutation of the absurd distinction between moral and natural ability and inability, as sometimes contended for. But most of your readers will, I am persuaded, consent to the definition of natural ability which I have given, and do actually consider a *moral* inability that consists in the absence of sufficient light to produce the conviction of *oughtness* to be, after all, a real *natural* inability. My reason affirms, that I ought to treat every interest according to its relative value. If, therefore, I have not sufficient light to affirm that a certain interest ought to be chosen, or willed, as a greater good than some other interest, I am not only not bound to choose that interest, which, with my present light, I am unable to regard as the greater good, but with the light I now have, I have no right, and it would be sin in me to will it. And now what I wish to say to the brethren, is this—I speak now to those who admit the doctrine of natural ability as generally maintained by New School divines—*whenever you make out a definition of entire sanctification, will you see to it, that your definition does not include or imply a denial of the doctrine of natural ability, in any of its essential elements, as these elements have just above been pointed out?*

Again, will you, my ministerial brethren, when you preach upon the subject, *be careful not so to define entire sanctification, or use any such arguments in opposition to the doctrine as to deny, explicitly or impliedly, the doctrine of natural ability? Will you not test your definition and your arguments by bringing them into the light of the definition of natural ability in all its essential elements?*

Again, *when you read any definition of entire sanctification, or any arguments that are arrayed against it, will you not bring them into the light of the true doctrine of natural ability, and know assuredly, that if they explicitly or impliedly contradict this, they are fundamentally false and erroneous? The Law of God has for ever settled the moral obligation of men upon the foundation of natural ability. And whatever is inconsistent with this doctrine is false.*

And to my Christian brethren in general, I wish to say, if

you hear ministers preach upon the doctrine of entire sanctification, or if you read in periodicals, or elsewhere, essays upon
the subject, *will you remember to compare their definitions of
entire sanctification, and the arguments they use in opposition
to it, with the doctrine of natural ability, as stated in this and
my former letter?*

I am the more particular, to call the attention of my readers
to this point, and request the editor to emphasize these paragraphs, from the fact, that nearly all that I have seen, either
in the way of definition or argument, in opposition to the doctrine of entire sanctification in this life, has assumed or implied
a denial of the doctrine of natural ability. If ministers and
Christians would be guarded and consistent upon this point, in
their writings and reasonings upon this subject, they would not
so perplex themselves and others "by multiplying words without knowledge." It is very easy to show, that some of the principal writers upon this subject, and whose writings have had
the most extensive influence against the doctrine of entire sanctification in this life, have been guilty of gross blunders and
entire inconsistency, both in their definitions of entire sanctification and in the arguments with which they have endeavored
to overthrow the doctrine. Both in their definitions and arguments, nothing has been more common, than for them to blun-
der into flat denial of the doctrine of natural ability, while they
themselves are known to be strenuous maintainers of this doctrine. I do not mean that they have denied the doctrine in words,
for this would have shocked them. But I do mean, that their
definitions, in many cases, and their arguments have assumed
the opposite of the doctrine of natural ability as true. I need
not name these writers. All who have read, or will take the
trouble to read what has been said within the last two or three
years, will readily recollect or perceive the truth of this statement.

I come now to the second point to be discussed:

II. *Wherein moral character consists.*

By *moral character*, I mean praise or blameworthiness.
Moral character does not consist in the nature or substance of
soul or body; for no man can be praised or blamed, for the substance of his nature, either of soul or body.

Nor does moral character consist in those acts or states of
mind that are properly involuntary. Praise or blame cannot be
affirmed of that over which a moral agent has no control—
which he cannot do or prevent. This follows of course, from the
doctrine of natural ability, as maintained in this and in my last
letter.

Moral character does not consist or belong to unintelligent acts. An idiot, or maniac, or a man in his sleep, or acting under perfect ignorance of moral obligation, can neither be praised or blamed in such circumstances. This also is affirmed by our natural sense of justice, and is a part of the doctrine of natural ability.

Of course moral character does not consist in emotions, or mere feelings; because these are involuntary states of mind, and cannot be controlled by the will. No man can directly force himself into a given state of emotion or feeling. Nor can he, under circumstances calculated to excite emotions, prevent them by willing their prevention. Mere emotions, or feelings, then, lie beyond the boundary of natural ability, and of course moral character cannot consist in them.

That moral character cannot consist in emotions or feelings is evident from the fact, that they are not required by the law of God. The law of God legislates over the voluntary power of the mind, or rather, over the mind in the exercise of its voluntary power, the will. It requires good-willing, or benevolence. And this benevolence, or good-willing is the fulfillment of the law. This is evident for several reasons.

1. From the nature of the case, moral character must lie solely in acts of will. All virtue is summed up in one word, benevolence, good-willing. God is said to be love, or benevolence, and all His virtue is only some modification of good-willing.

2. Moral freedom lies solely in the power of willing. Moral character, therefore, must attach solely to acts of will. Actions of the body, and many actions of the mind, are connected with the will by a natural necessity. The moral character does not attach to the outward act, or motion of the arm or limb, but to the act of willing, which produces, by a natural necessity, this motion. Just so it is with those thoughts, or emotions and feelings, that are connected with the actions of the will by a natural necessity.

3. The Bible recognizes acts of will, as constituting obedience or disobedience. "If there be first a willing mind, it is accepted according to what a man hath, and not according to what he hath not." I might quote many passages in confirmation of this truth; but as they will readily come to your mind, I will move on with my subject.

Moral character does not attach to every act of will. For, as I have said, there may be acts of will without light or knowledge. And again, volition may be in a sense necessitated by choice or intention. If I choose or intend to go to the city of New York, as soon as I possibly can this intention will in a sense necessitate the volitions that move the muscles, and carry me forward. I do not suppose, that these volitions are strictly necessitated, because the agent can at any time change his intention, and refuse the volition. But while the intention *exists*, the consequent volitions, emotions, and actions must exist.

I conclude that *moral character lies solely in the ultimate choice, or intention of the mind.* A man's character is as his supreme and ultimate intention is. An ultimate choice or intention is, the choice of a thing, or an intention to do it, for its own sake, and not as a means to some other more remote and higher end. For example—a man labors to get money, to purchase tools, to pursue a calling, to glorify God. Now the great reason for his laboring, that is, his ultimate intention is to glorify God. His proximate intention is to obtain money. His next intention is to purchase tools. A third object is to pursue a calling. But all these are only means to promote one ultimate end, the glory of God. Now his conduct is, in every instance, holy or sinful, according as his ultimate end or intention is selfish or supremely and disinterestedly benevolent. Let it be borne in mind, then, that in all instances, the moral character of any act, or state of mind, is as the ultimate intention of that act or state of mind is. If the intention is wholly right, there may be mistake, and a violation of the *letter* of the law; but there cannot be *sin*, or a violation of the *spirit* of the law; for, right intention is nothing else than the very thing which the law of God requires—namely, supreme, disinterested benevolence: or, in other words, choosing, willing, or intending the highest glory of God, and the greatest good of universal being. When the ultimate intention is wrong, there cannot be holiness. There may be obedience to the *letter*, but there cannot be obedience to the *spirit* of the law; for this ultimate, or selfish intention, willing, or choosing, is the very thing which the law of God forbids.

Now, beloved, I beg of you, let what I have said upon this subject, be thoroughly pondered, and prayed over, until my next letter.

Brethren, will you think?

Your brother in the love and fellowship of the blessed gospel,
Charles G. Finney

CHAPTER 36

To the Editor of The Oberlin Evangelist

June 23, 1841

Dear Brother:

I have recently been both surprised and grieved, to find in the "Supplement" of the Comprehensive Commentary (a book that possesses many excellencies) a commentary designed particularly for the use of Sunday Schools, an article on the divine inspiration of the Bible, which appears to me to be of a most dangerous tendency. It seems to me, that ministers, and all classes of Christians, should have their attention called particularly to the infidel character and tendency of that article. The ground taken by the writer is that the historical parts, especially of the New Testament, are not inspired, not even with the inspiration of such a degree of divine superintendence as to exclude error and contradiction from them. He takes the ground that there are palpable inconsistencies and flat contradictions between the writers of the gospels, and points out several instances, it appears to me, very much with the art and spirit of infidelity, which he affirms to be irreconcilable contradictions. The ground taken by him is that the *doctrinal* parts of the New Testament are inspired, but that the *historical* parts, or the mere narrative, are uninspired.

Now upon this piece I feel constrained to say the following things:

The piece is eminently calculated to diffuse among the young, and indeed among all classes of persons who have not thoroughly examined the subject, a spirit of infidelity and contempt for the Bible. For who will not see at first blush, that if the writers were mistaken in recording the acts of Christ, there

187

is equal reason to believe they were mistaken in recording the doctrines of Christ? Who does not know that the record of the doctrines preached by Christ is mere narrative and history, just as much as the journeyings, conversations, and acts of Christ? To say that the narrative of the gospel is uninspired, with the inspiration of superintendence, is the same thing as to say that the whole gospel is uninspired. For, what are the Gospels, but narratives or histories of Christ's birth, life, preaching, conversations, miracles, death, resurrection, ascension, etc.? Now what an inadmissible distinction is attempted, when it is affirmed that the *didactic* or *doctrinal* portions of the gospel are inspired, while the *narrative* is uninspired? Only convince the world and the Church that the narrative of the gospel is uninspired—that there are irreconcilable contradictions between the writers, and who will, or who can consistently believe, that they may not have committed errors in stating the *doctrines* of the gospel?

That this is a dangerous article, I am convinced from the fact that my attention was first called to it by a young man who had read it, and seemed ready to adopt the views of the writer. The article, to be sure, when examined by one used to such investigations, is easily seen to be a weak production. But to those who are not acquainted with the principles upon which such questions are to be settled, the article in question would be, as I have said, of most dangerous tendency.

The cases brought forward by this writer, supposed by him to be irreconcilable contradictions, are specimens of just that class of *apparent* discrepancies which forbid the idea of collusion among the witnesses. When such apparent discrepancies as these exist among witnesses in courts of justice, and it is found, on a thorough examination, that they can be reconciled with each other, such apparent discrepancies are considered as greatly corroborative of the truth, and add much to the credibility of the witnesses, upon the ground that they forbid the supposition of collusion among them. Now nothing is to be regarded as a contradiction, except that which cannot by any possibility be reconciled. And there is no serious difficulty in any of the cases adduced by the writer, in showing that the account of each of the Gospel writers may be strictly true, one omitting some circumstances mentioned by others.

It is, I suppose, unnecessary for me to take up those cases and show how their statements can be easily reconciled with each other, as this has so often been done in answer to the objections of infidels. It seems strange to me, that such an article as that should have found a place in such a work, under the superintendence of such an editor. And I must say, that my surprise and grief that such a thing should have occurred has been very great. I would not have mentioned the article, but from the deep conviction pressed upon my mind, that unless the attention of the Church and of ministers was called to this point, the book, in the hands of Sunday School teachers, would, unobserved, diffuse a spirit of infidelity among the rising generation. It is amazing that the writer of that article should not have ingenuity enough, if he had never seen the subject examined, to discover some way in which those writers could be easily enough reconciled with each other, and their apparent discrepancies satisfactorily explained. In all such cases we are bound to show, only, that they *may* be consistent with each other.

In conversation with a brother minister a few days ago in reference to the article in question, he remarked that he knew the writer and understood the dangerous tendency of the article, and that on this account he had never owned and would not have the book in his library.

I do not mention this to injure the credit of the book; for as I have said, it is, in many respects, a valuable work, and on this very account, this striking defect in it should be pointed out. I plead with ministers of the gospel to call the attention of their congregations where this commentary, with this Supplement is in their hands, to the false and dangerous character of the article in question. It may be found in Part III., pp. 113–16, of that work.[1]

Charles G. Finney

---

[1] Certainly, Bible believing Christians today need to take Finney's warning to heart with regard to the inerrancy of Scripture and the certain results of denying the truth or validity of the historical portions of the Bible. The Bible is true in all that it affirms.

CHAPTER 37

To the Editor of The Oberlin Evangelist

July 7, 1841

Dear Brother:

On reexamining Pres. Edwards on the WILL, since my last letter, I perceive that I misapprehended the meaning of his proposition, that the will or choice universally is as the greatest apparent good is. He so explains the sense in which he uses the term *good*, as to mean by the proposition, only, that the will is as the most *agreeable* is. This sets aside the inconsistency mentioned in my last letter between his treatise on the will and that on the nature of virtue. I hasten to make the correction as my misrepresentation of his meaning was wholly unintentional.

However, neither this correction, nor anything else that I can discover, at all sets aside the absurdity of the distinction which he labors to establish between natural and moral ability and inability. This natural ability consists in the established connection between volition and its sequences, so that, according to him, a man is naturally able to do that which he will, without at all touching his ability to will otherwise than he does. But this is no natural ability to obey God. Choice, or good-willing, is the very thing required by God. Therefore, a natural ability to be holy must consist in an ability to originate and put forth the required acts of will, or choice. He makes *willing* and *the most agreeable* identical. A man, therefore, is unable to will except in accordance with that which under the circumstances appears most agreeable to him. Moral ability, according to Pres. Edwards, consists in the presence of such motives as to make the required course of conduct appear the most agreeable.

The absence of these motives is what he means by a moral inability. But who does not see that this is a natural inability, or that there is no such thing as a natural inability? If I am not entirely mistaken, modern New School divines mean by moral inability a very different thing from this. They intend by it only an unwillingness.

Before I introduce the next topic of discussion, I wish to add the following remarks.

The brethren to whom I alluded in my last letter admit that all men possess natural ability to do their whole duty. They also admit that entire sanctification in this life is the duty of all men, and that this obligation is conditioned upon the natural ability to be so sanctified. They admit and maintain that a state of entire sanctification in this life is attainable on the ground of natural ability.

Now that which has seemed strange to me is, that, with these admissions on their lips, they should approach the doctrine of entire sanctification in this life, and begin with a definition of what constitutes entire sanctification, that includes various things which men are naturally unable to do—that at the same breath they should admit that men are naturally able to be entirely sanctified in this life, and that this natural ability is the condition of their obligation, and still include that in their definition of entire sanctification which renders the supposition of its being attainable in this life an absurdity. For example, one maintains that men must actually know all the relations they sustain to God and all beings, before they can either be entirely sanctified or know it if they are so. This brother assumes, of course, that a man can be under obligation to fulfill relations which he does not and cannot know himself to sustain. And thus it is, in his opinion, an absurdity to maintain the attainability of this state in the present life.

To this brother it might be said, that if this degree of knowledge be essential to a state of entire sanctification, it never is, and never will be attainable by any being but God; for a knowledge of all our relations must imply absolute omniscience.

Another brother includes in the idea of entire sanctification, the rendering to God all that degree and perfection of service, that might have been rendered by us, if our powers had been fully developed by universal holiness. Hence, he very justly infers, that no such state is attainable in this life. And I add, he might also have said that it will be equally unattainable in the life to come, by those who have neglected their duty here. These must serve as specimens of the manner in which this subject has been treated, and the doctrine of natural ability either explicitly denied or its denial strongly implied in their definitions of entire sanctification. What does all such arguing as this prove?

I come now to show:

III. *What constitutes right character or holiness.*

You will remember, that in my last letter I laid down the position that moral character belongs to and consists in the ultimate choice or intention of the mind. Furthermore, the whole of *right* character resolves itself into supreme, disinterested benevolence. This means that the ultimate, supreme, disinterested intention to promote, to the utmost extent, the glory of God and the good of the universe, properly constitutes the whole of right character. While this intention, or supreme, disinterested good-willing remains, there may be mistakes, but there cannot be sin. There may be a violation of the *letter*, but cannot be a violation of the *spirit* of the law of God. This is self-evident, inasmuch as this state of the will is the very thing and the whole that the law of God requires. This state of will is connected, by a natural necessity, with those outward actions, and inward states of feeling, or of the sensibility, that make up the evidences and constitute the happiness of Christian character. Supreme benevolent intention, or good-willing, is holiness. It is obedience to the law of God. And while this state of the will exists, holy living must exist. While this intention exists no selfishness can possibly co-exist in the same mind. But more of this in a future issue.

Supreme, disinterested benevolence, good-willing, or good-intending, is all that the law of God demands, or can justly demand of any being. Right character, then, is summed up in one word, LOVE or in supremely benevolent intention. And now let me say, by *supreme love*, or supremely benevolent intention, I mean, that it is a sincere and honest intention, or willing, to do the utmost that can be done, to promote the universal good of being—the individual always being left to the exercise of his own judgment under the best light he can obtain, in respect to the particular amount of time, energy, and feeling to be expended at any one moment, or in the discharge of any one particular form of duty—the individual always acting right, whenever he comes up to the best light which, under the circumstances of the case, he can obtain. In other words, when he does, says, omits, just what, under the circumstances he judges to be right.

Here let me anticipate an objection. Some may say that Paul

"verily thought he ought to do many things contrary to the name of Jesus of Nazareth." In answer to this let me reply:

Paul was wholly wrong, because his ultimate intention was wrong. His judgment was wrong because his ultimate intention was wrong. He neither intended nor judged according to the best light he had. But suppose his intention had been right, if then he had acted according to the best light he had, which he must have done, if his intention had been right, his conduct would not have been sinful.

Again, it is objected, that the doctrine, that moral character consists in intention, would seem to justify the maxim, that the end sanctifies the means. To this I reply that right character is, by the law of God, made to consist in good-willing or intending. And whatever objection lies against this sentiment, lies against the law of God. A man cannot intend the glory of God and the universal good of being, and knowingly disobey God, as a means for the promotion of this end. It is therefore absurd to say, that good intention can sanctify the use, or make it right to use unlawful or prohibited means.

In concluding this third topic, let me request you to notice again, in what right character consists: it belongs to and consists in supreme disinterested love, benevolence, or in the supreme intention to promote, to the utmost of your ability, the glory of God and the good of the universe; and that, while this intention exists, sin cannot co-exist with it; because the intention is just what, and all that the law of God requires. Outward actions being connected with this intention by a natural necessity. I speak now of the *spirit* of the law. The *letter* of the law often requires outward actions, and certain states of the emotions; but the performance of these actions, or the exercise of these emotions are not recognized by the law as obedience; that is, they are not compliance with the *spirit* and *meaning* of the law, only as they are the result of perfect and universal benevolence, or a right intention. So that right character always resolves itself into a compliance with the spirit, and not merely the *letter* of the law of God.

IV. *What constitutes wrong character.*

It has been shown, that character lies in and belongs to the ultimate intention of the mind, and that right character consists in supremely disinterested benevolent intention. *Wrong character*, then, consists in any intention or choice *known* to be inconsistent with the law of God. In some of the late issues of the *Biblical Repository*, Prof. Stuart has shown that sin, all sin, consists in the voluntary transgression of a *known law*. In those able articles he shows that this is not only the doctrine of the Bible, but has long been held as truth by those whose orthodoxy will not probably be called in question. This sentiment is in precise consistency with the doctrine of natural ability as maintained by the New School divines.

Selfishness is wrong character. Selfishness is the preference of self-interest or other considerations over higher interests. It consists in the intending or willing to gratify self, or to promote self-interest, in opposition to the command of the law, to exercise universal benevolence. Selfishness, or self-gratification is always an act of the will, and is always an ultimate intention of the mind, *self-interest always being chosen for its own sake*, which constitutes it an ultimate intention.

Wrong character, or wrong ultimate intention, or selfishness, does not necessarily imply the choice of, or the intention to do what is wrong, *because* it is wrong; but nevertheless it is known to *be* wrong. *Selfishness is always a supreme affection or choice of the mind.* For, in every selfish choice, the mind chooses what it does in defiance of the authority of God, and in a reckless disregard of the highest interests of the universe.

While selfishness exists in the mind, there may be compliance with the *letter* but never with the *spirit* of the law of God. Selfishness is the carnal mind, or minding the flesh, "which is enmity against God; which is not subject to the law of God, neither indeed can be."[1]

Your Brother in the love and fellowship of the blessed gospel,
Charles G. Finney

---

[1] For Finney's thorough discussion of love and selfishness in their relation to one another, along with three important sermons on love, see, *Principles of Love*, (Minneapolis: Bethany House Publishers, 1986).

CHAPTER 38

To the editor of The Oberlin Evangelist

September 1, 1841

Dear Brother:

My next topic of discussion is:

V. *Moral character is always wholly right or wholly wrong, and never partly right and partly wrong at the same time.*

In the commencement of this letter, I must again remind your readers of that in which moral character consists, and occupy a few moments in stating, what I have already said, that moral character belongs solely to the *ultimate intention* of the mind, or to choice, as distinguished from *volition*. The law of God requires supreme disinterested benevolence, and all holiness, in the last analysis, resolves itself into some modification of supreme disinterested benevolence, or good-willing. Benevolence, or good-willing, is synonymous with good-intending, or intending good. Now the true spirit of the requirement of the moral law is this—that every moral being shall choose, will, or intend to promote every interest according to its relative value as perceived by the mind. This is holiness. It is exercising supreme love or good will to God, and equal love or good will to our neighbor.

This is a *choice* or intention, as distinguished from a *volition*. It is also an *ultimate* intention, as distinguished from *proximate* intention.

Choice is the selection of an end. Volition is produced by choice, and is the effort of the will to accomplish the end chosen. An ultimate intention, or choice, is that which is intended or chosen for its own sake, or as an ultimate end, and not something chosen or intended as a means to accomplish some other and higher end. A proximate end is that which is chosen or intended, not as an ultimate end, but as a means to an ultimate end. If I choose an end, I, of course, put forth those volitions which are requisite to the accomplishment of that end. Holiness, or virtue, consists in the *supreme ultimate intention, choice, or willing the glory of God and the highest good of His kingdom.* Nothing else than this is virtue.

As holiness consists in ultimate intention, so does sin. And as holiness consists in choosing the glory of God and the good of the universe, for its own sake, or as the supreme ultimate end of pursuit; so sin consists in willing, with a supreme choice or intention, self-gratification or self-interest. Preferring a less to a greater good, because it is our own, is selfishness. All selfishness consists in a supreme ultimate intention. By an ultimate intention, as I have said, is intended that which is chosen for its own sake as an end, and not as a means to some other end. Whenever a moral being prefers or chooses his own gratification, or his own interest, in preference to a higher good, he chooses it as an end, for its own sake, and as an ultimate end; not designing it as a means of promoting any other and higher end. Every sin, then, consists in an act of will. It consists in preferring self-gratification, or self-interest, to the authority of God, the glory of God, and the good of the universe. It is, therefore, and must be, a supreme ultimate choice, or intention.

Sin and holiness, then, both consist in supreme, ultimate, and opposite choices, or intentions, and cannot by any possibility, co-exist.

But for the sake of entering more at large into the discussion of this question, I will examine a little in detail the philosophy of the question, and bring the philosophy into the light of the Bible.

In discussing the philosophy of the question, I would observe, that five suppositions may be made, and, so far as I can see, only five, in respect to this subject.

First, it *may* be supposed that selfishness and benevolence can co-exist in the same mind.

Second, it *may* be supposed that the same act or choice may have a complex character on account of complexity in the motives which induce it.

Third, it *may* be supposed that an act or choice may be right or holy in kind, but deficient in intensity or degree.

Fourth, it *may* be supposed that the will, or heart, may be right, while the affections, or emotions, are wrong.

Fifth, it *may* be supposed that there may be a ruling, latent, actually existing, holy preference, or intention, co-existing with opposing volitions.

Now unless one of these suppositions is true, it must follow, that moral character is either wholly right or wholly wrong, and never partly right and partly wrong at the same time. Therefore, now to the examination:

First, it has been shown, that selfishness and benevolence are supreme, ultimate, and opposite choices, or intentions. They cannot, therefore, by any possibility, co-exist in the same mind.

Second, the same act or choice cannot have a complex character, on account of complexity in the motives. Motives are objective or subjective. An objective motive is that thing external to the mind that induces choice or intention. Subjective motive is the intention itself. Character, therefore, does not belong to the objective motive, or to that thing which the mind chooses; but moral character is confided to the subjective motive, which is synonymous with choice or intention. Thus we say, a man is to be judged by his motives, meaning that his character is as his intention is. There may be complexity in the objective motive, but can by no possibility be such complexity in the subjective motive, to which character belongs, as to include both sin and holiness. Multitudes of considerations, external to the mind itself, may have concurred, directly or indirectly in their influence, to induce choice or intention; but the intention or subjective motive is always necessarily simple, and indivisible. In other words, moral character consists in the choice of an ultimate end, and this end is to be chosen for its own sake, else it is not an ultimate end. If this choice be the glory of God and the good of the universe—if it be the willing or intending to promote and treat every interest in the universe according to its perceived relative value, it is a right, a holy motive, or intention. If it be anything else it is sinful. Now whatever complexity there may have been in the considerations that led the way to this choice or intention, it is self-evident that the *intention must be one, simple, and indivisible.*

Whatever complexity there might have been in those considerations that prepared the way to the settling down upon this intention, the mind in a *virtuous* choice has and can have but one reason for its choice, and that is the intrinsic value of the thing chosen. The glory of God, the good of the universe, and every good according to its perceived relative value, must be chosen for one, and only one reason, and that is, the intrinsic value of the good that is chosen for its own sake. If chosen for any other reason, the choice is not virtuous. It is absurd to say, that a thing is good and valuable in itself, but may be chosen, not for that but for some other reason—that God's glory and happiness, and the happiness of the universe, are an infinite good in themselves, but are not to be chosen for that reason, and on their own account, but for some other reason. Holiness, then, must always consist in singleness of eye or intention. It must consist in the supreme disinterested choice, willing, or intending the glory of God and the good of the universe, for its own sake. In this intention there cannot be any complexity. If there were, it would not be holy, but sinful. It is, therefore, stark nonsense to say that one and the same choice may have a complex character, on account of complexity of motive. For that motive in which moral character consists, is the supreme, ultimate intention, or choice. This choice, or intention, must consist in the choice of a thing as an end and for its own sake. The supposition, then, that the same choice or intention may have a complex character, on account of complexity in the motives, is wholly inadmissible.

If it be still urged, that the intention or subjective motive may be complex—that several things may be included in the intention and aimed at by the mind—and that it may, therefore, be partly holy and partly sinful; I reply that if by this it is meant that several things may be aimed at or intended by the mind at the same time, I inquire what things? It is true that the supreme, disinterested intention to glorify God may include the intention to use all the necessary means. It may also include the intention to promote every interest in the universe, according to its perceived relative value. These are all properly included in one intention; but this implies no such complexity in the subjective motive as to include both sin and holiness.

If by complexity of intention is meant that it may be partly disinterestedly benevolent and partly selfish, which it must be to be partly holy and partly sinful, I reply that this supposition is absurd. It has been shown that selfishness and benevolence consist in supreme ultimate and opposite choices and intentions. To suppose, then, that an intention can be both holy and sinful, is to suppose that it may include two supreme opposite and ultimate choices or intentions at the same time. In other words, that I may supremely and disinterestedly intend to regard and promote every interest in the universe according to its perceived relative value, for its own sake; and at the same time, may supremely regard my own self-interest and self-gratification, and in some things supremely intend to promote my selfish interests, in opposition to the interests of the universe and the commands of God. But this is naturally impossible. An ultimate intention, then, may be complex in the sense that it may include the design to promote every perceived interest according to its relative value; but it cannot, by any possibility, be complex in the sense that it includes selfishness and benevolence, or holiness and sin.

The third supposition is that holiness may be right, or pure in kind, but deficient in degree. On this I remark that we have seen that moral character consists in the ultimate intention. The supposition, therefore, must be, that the intention may be right, or pure in kind, but deficient in the degree of its strength. Our intention is to be tried by the law of God, both in respect to its kind and degree. The law of God requires us to will, or intend the promotion of every interest in the universe according to its perceived relative value, for its own sake. In other words, that all our powers shall be supremely and disinterestedly devoted to the glory of God and the good of the universe. This cannot mean that any faculty shall at every moment be kept upon the strain, or in a state of intense tension, for this would be inconsistent with natural ability. It would be to require a natural impossibility, and therefore unjust. It cannot mean that at all times and on all subjects the same degree of exertion shall be made, for the best possible discharge of duty does not always require the same intense degree of intense mental or corporeal exertion.

The law cannot, justly or possibly, require more than that the whole being shall be consecrated to God—that we shall fully will or intend the promotion of every interest according to its perceived relative value, according to the extent of our ability.

Now the strength, or intensity of the intention must, and ought, of necessity, to depend upon the degree of our knowledge or light in regard to any object of choice. If an obligation is not to be proportioned by the light we possess, then it would follow that we may be under obligation to exceed our natural ability, which cannot be.

The importance which we attach to objects of choice, and consequently the degree of ardor or intenseness of the intention, must depend upon the clearness or obscurity of our views, of the real or relative value of the objects of choice.

Our obligation cannot be measured by the views which God has of the importance of those objects of choice. It is a well-settled and generally admitted truth, that increased light increases responsibility, or moral obligation. No creature is bound to will anything with the intenseness or degree of strength with which God wills it; for the plain reason that no creature sees its importance, or real value, as He does. If our obligation were to be proportioned by God's knowledge of the real or relative value of objects, we could never be entirely sanctified, either in this world or the world to come, nor could any being but God be in a state of entire sanctification.

Our obligation cannot be measured by the views or knowledge which angels may have of the intrinsic or relative value of the glory of God, the worth of souls, and the good of the universe. Nor can the obligation of a heathen be measured by the knowledge and light of a Christian. Nor the obligation of a child, by the knowledge of a man. The fact is, that the obligation of every moral being must be proportioned by his knowledge.

If, therefore, his intention be equal in its intensity to his views, or knowledge of the real or relative value of different objects, it is right. It is up to the full measure of his obligation; and if his honest judgment is not to be made the measure of his obligation, then his obligation can exceed what he is able to know; which contradicts the doctrine of natural ability, and is, therefore, false.

If conscious honesty of intention, both as it respects the kind and degree of light possessed, is not entire sanctification, then there is no being, in heaven or earth, who can know himself to be entirely sanctified; for all that any being can possibly know upon this subject is, that he honestly wills or intends, in accordance with the dictates of his reason, or the judgment which he has of the real or relative value of the object chosen.

If something more than this can be required, then a law can be binding further than it is prescribed, or so published that it may be known, which is contradictory to natural justice, and absurd. No moral being can possibly blame, or charge himself with any default, when he is conscious of honestly intending, willing, or choosing, and acting, according to the best light he has.

Nothing less than this uprightness of intention, both in kind and degree, is virtue or obedience at all. Good-willing or intending is, in respect to God, to be at all times supreme, and in respect to other beings it is to be in proportion to the relative value of their happiness as perceived by the mind. This is always to be the intention. The volitions, or efforts of the will to promote these objects, may and ought to vary indefinitely in their intensity, in proportion to the particular duty to which, for the time being, we are called.

But further, we have seen that virtue consists in willing every good according to its perceived relative value, and that nothing short of this is virtue. But this is perfect virtue for the time being. In other words, virtue and moral perfection, in respect to a given act, or state of the will, are synonymous terms. Virtue is holiness. Holiness is uprightness. Uprightness is that which is just right, just that which, under the circumstances, it should be; and nothing else is virtue, holiness, or uprightness. Virtue, holiness, uprightness, justice, moral perfection—when we apply these terms to any given state of the will, are synonymous. To talk, therefore, of a virtue, holiness, uprightness, justice—right in kind, but deficient in degree—is to talk sheer nonsense. It is the same absurdity as to talk of sinful holiness, an unjust justice, a wrong rightness, an impure purity, an imperfect perfection, a disobedient obedience.

The fact is, virtue, holiness, uprightness, etc., signify a definite thing, and never anything else than conformity to the law of God. That which is not entirely conformed to the law of God is not holiness. This must be true in philosophy, and the Bible affirms the same thing. "Whosoever shall keep the whole law, and yet offend in one point, he is guilty of all."

God has no right to call that holy which is defective in degree. Unless every perceived interest is, for the time being, willed or intended according to its relative value, there is no virtue. Where this intention exists there can be no sin.

The fourth supposition is that the will, or heart, may be right while the affections or emotions are wrong. Upon this I remark that this supposition overlooks that in which moral character consists. It has been shown that moral character consists in the supreme ultimate intention of the mind, and that this supreme, disinterested benevolence, good-willing, or intention, is the whole of virtue. Now this intention begets volitions. It directs the attention of the mind, and, therefore, produces thoughts, emotions, or affections. It also, through volition, begets bodily action. But moral character does not lie in outward actions, the movement of the arm, nor in the volition that moves the muscles; for that volition terminated upon the action itself. I will to move my arm. Moral character belongs solely to the intention that produced the volition, that moved the muscles, to the performance of the outward act. So intention produces the volition that directs the attention of the mind to a given object. Attention, by a natural necessity, produces thought, affection, or emotion. Now thought, affection, or emotion, are all connected with volition by a natural necessity; that is—if the attention is directed to an object, corresponding thoughts and emotions must exist of course. Moral character no more lies in emotion, than in outward action. It does not lie in thought, or attention. It does not lie in the specific volition that directed the attention; but in that intention, or design of the mind, that produced the volition, which directed the intention, which again produced the thought, which again produced the emotion. Now the supposition, that the intention may be right, while the emotions or feelings of the mind may be wrong, is the same as to say, that outward action may be wrong, while the intention is right. The fact is, that moral character is and must be as the ultimate intention is. If any feeling or outward action is inconsistent with the existing ultimate intention, it must be so in spite of the agent. But if any outward action or state of feeling exists, in opposition to the intention or choice of the mind, it cannot, by any possibility, have moral character. Whatever is beyond the control of a moral agent, he cannot be responsible for. Whatever he cannot control by intention, he cannot control at all. Every thing for which he can possibly be responsible, resolves itself into his intention. His whole character, therefore, is and must be as his intention is. If, therefore, temptations, from whatever quarter they may come, produce emotions within him inconsistent with his intention, and which he cannot control, he cannot be responsible for them.

As a matter of fact, although emotions, contrary to his intentions, may, by circumstances beyond his control, be brought to exist in his mind; yet, by willing to direct the attention of the mind from the objects that produce them, they can be banished from the mind. If this is done as soon as in the nature of the case it can be, there is no sin. If it is not done as soon as in the nature of the case it can be, then it is absolutely certain, that the intention is not what it ought to be. The intention is to devote the whole being to the service of God and the good of the universe, and of course to avoid every thought, affection and emotion, inconsistent with this. While this intention exists, it is certain that if any object be thrust upon the attention which excites thoughts and emotions inconsistent with our supreme ultimate intention, the attention of the mind will be instantly diverted from those objects, and the hated emotion hushed. For, while the intention exists, corresponding volitions must exist. There cannot, therefore, be a right state of heart or intention, while the emotions or affections of the mind are sinful. And, as I said, the supposition overlooks that in which moral character consists, and supposes it to consist in that over which the law does not properly legislate; for love, or benevolence is the fulfilling of the law.

But here it may be said, that the law not only requires benevolence, or good-willing, but requires certain kind of emotions, just as it requires the performance of certain outward actions, and that therefore there may be right intention where there is a deficiency, either in kind or degree, of right emotions. To this I answer that outward actions are required of men, only because they are connected with intention, by a natural necessity. And no outward act is ever required of us, unless it can be produced by intending and aiming to do it. If the effect does not follow our honest endeavors, because of any antagonist influence, opposed to our exertions, which we cannot overcome, we have by our intention complied with the spirit of the law, and are not to blame that the outward effect does not take place. Just so with emotions. All we have power to do, is, to direct the attention of the mind to those objects calculated to secure a given state of emotion. If, from any exhaustion of the sensibility, or for any other cause beyond our control, the emotions do not arise which the consideration of that subject is calculated to produce, we are no more responsible for the absence or weakness of the emotion, than we should be for the want or weakness of motion in our muscles, when we willed to move them, in consequence of exhaustion or any other preventing cause, over which we had no control. The fact is, we cannot be blameworthy for not feeling or doing that which we cannot do or feel by intending it. If the intention then is what it ought to be for the time being, nothing can be morally wrong.

The last supposition is, that a latent preference, or right intention, may co-exist with opposing or sinful volitions. Upon this I remark that I have formerly supposed, that this could be true, but am now convinced, that it cannot be true; for the following reasons.

Observe, that the supposition is, that the intention, or ruling preference may be right—may really exist as an active and virtuous state of mind, while, at the same time, volitions may exist inconsistent with it.

Now what is a right intention? I answer: Nothing short of this—willing, choosing, or intending the glory of God and the good of the universe, and to promote this at every moment, to the extent of our ability. In other words—right intention is supreme, disinterested benevolence. Now what are the elements which enter into this right intention? One, the choice or willing of every interest, according to its perceived relative value. And two, to devote our entire being, now and forever, to this end. This is right intention. Now the question is, can this intention co-exist with a volition inconsistent with it? Volition implies the choice of something, for some reason. If it is the choice of whatever can promote this supremely benevolent end, and for that reason, the volition is consistent with the intention; but if it is the choice of something perceived to be inconsistent with this end, and for a selfish reason, then the volition is inconsistent with the supposed intention. But the question is, do the volition and the intention co-exist? According to the supposition, the will chooses, or wills something, for a selfish reason, or something perceived to be inconsistent with supreme, disinterested benevolence. Now it is plainly impossible, that this choice can take place while the opposite intention exists. For this selfish volition is, according to the supposition, sinful or selfish; that is, something is chosen for its own sake, which is inconsistent with disinterested benevolence. But here the intention is ultimate. It terminates upon the object chosen for its own sake. To suppose, then, that benevolence still remains in exercise, and that a volition co-exists with it that is sinful, involves the absurdity of supposing, that selfishness and benevolence can co-exist in the same mind, or that the will can choose, or will, with a supreme preference, or choice, two opposites, at the same time. This is plainly impossible. Suppose I intend to go to the city of New York as soon as I possibly can. Now if, on my way, I will to loiter unnecessarily a moment, I necessarily relinquish one indispensable element of my intention. In willing to loiter, or turn aside to some other object, for a day, or an hour, I must, of necessity, relinquish the intention of going as soon as I possibly can. I may not design to finally relinquish my journey, but I must of necessity relinquish the intention of going as soon as I can. Now virtue consists in intending to do all the good I possibly can, or in willing the glory of God and the good of the universe, and intending to promote them to the extent of my ability. Nothing short of this is virtue. Now if, at any time, I will something perceived to be inconsistent with this intention, I must, for the time being, relinquish the intention, as it must indispensably exist in my mind in order to be virtue. I may not come to the resolution, that I will never serve God any more, but I must of necessity relinquish, for the time being, the intention of doing my utmost to glorify God, if at any time I put forth a selfish volition. Therefore, a holy intention cannot co-exist with a selfish volition.

It must be, therefore, that in every sinful choice, the will of a holy being must necessarily drop the exercise of supreme, benevolent intention, and pass into an opposite state of choice; that is—the agent must cease, for the time being, to exercise benevolence, and make a selfish choice.

Having briefly examined the several suppositions that can be made in regard to the mixed character of actions, I will now answer a few objections; after which, I will bring this philosophy as briefly as possible, into the light of the Bible.

Objection, Does a Christian cease to be a Christian, whenever he commits a sin? I answer:

Whenever he sins, he must, for the time being, cease to be holy. This is self-evident. Whenever he sins, he must be condemned. He must incur the penalty of the law of God. If he does not, it must be because the law of God is abrogated. But if the law of God is abrogated, he has no rule of duty; consequently, he can be neither holy nor sinful. If it is said that the precept is still binding upon him, but that with respect to the Christian the penalty is forever set aside, or abrogated, I reply that to abrogate the penalty is to repeal the precept; for a precept without penalty is no law. It is only counsel or advice. The Christian, therefore, is justified no further than he obeys, and must be condemned when he disobeys, or Antinomianism is true.

Therefore, when the Christian sins, he must repent, and 'do his first works,' or he will perish. Until he repents he cannot be forgiven. In these respects, then, the sinning Christian and the unconverted sinner are upon precisely the same ground.

In two important repects the sinning Christian differs widely from the unconverted sinner:

First, in his relations to God. A Christian is a child of God. A sinning Christian is a disobedient child of God. An unconverted sinner is a child of the devil. A Christian sustains a covenant relation to God. Such a covenant relation as to secure to him that discipline which will reclaim and bring him back, if he wanders away from God. "If his children forsake my law, and walk not in my judgments; if they break my statutes, and keep not my commandments; then will I visit their transgression with the rod, and their iniquity with stripes. Nevertheless my loving-kindness will I not utterly take from him, nor suffer my faithfulness to fail. My covenant will I not break, nor alter the thing that is gone out of my lips" (Psalm 89:30–34).

The sinning Christian also differs from the unconverted man, in the state of his sensibility. In whatever way it takes place, every Christian knows that the state of his sensibility in respect to the things of God, has undergone a great change.

Now it is true, that moral character does not lie in the sensibility. Nevertheless our consciousness teaches us, that our feelings have great power in inducing acts of choice. In every Christian's heart there is, therefore, a foundation laid for appeals to the sensibilities of the soul, that gives truth a decided advantage over the will. And multitudes of things in the experience of every Christian, give truth a more decided advantage over his will than is the case with unconverted sinners.

Objection. Can a man be born again, and then be unborn? I answer: If there were anything impossible in this, then perseverance would be no virtue. No one will maintain, that there is anything naturally impossible in this, unless it is those who hold to the doctrine of physical regeneration.

If regeneration consists in a change in the ruling preference of the mind, it is plain, that an individual can be born again and afterward cease to be virtuous. That a Christian is able to apostatize, is evident, from the many warnings addressed to Christians in the Bible.

Regeneration designates the first holy act, whether it is love, repentance, or faith. Now it is plain, that there can be but one first holy act, and therefore can be but one regeneration. But a Christian may be converted sundry times. Christ said to Peter, doubtless after he had been converted— "When thou art converted strengthen thy brethren." A Christian may certainly fall into sin and unbelief, and afterward be renewed, both to repentance and faith.

Objection. But how is this theory consistent with the statement: "Whosoever is born of God doth not commit sin; for his seed remaineth in him; and he cannot sin, because he is born of God" (1 John 3:9)? I answer: What does this passage mean? Should we understand it strictly, we should be obliged to admit that no Christian can, by any possibility, commit a sin. But this would contradict multitudes of other passages of the Bible. What is the "seed" here spoken of, that "remaineth in him"? Does it imply a physical change—some root or seed implanted in the very constitution? Then, to be sure, sin would be naturally impossible. This, then, is not the meaning. Is this "seed" the love of God? But in what sense does this always remain in a man? Not constantly, as an exercise or voluntary state of mind. For this, as we have seen, would render all sin impossible.

It may mean, that while this "seed" remaineth he cannot sin. If this seed really does mean supremely benevolent intention, it is true, as we have seen, that while this intention exists no sin can exist with it. Or it may mean, consistently with other scriptures, and with the nature of the case, that such a change has taken place in his sensibility, and in his volitions, as to secure him against living in habitual sin, and prevent his apostasy.

In this epistle, John seems to be speaking in very general terms, and in scarcely any part of it can we understand him in any other way, without making him contradict himself and every other writer of the Bible. He says, in another passage, "Whosoever sinneth hath not seen Him, neither known Him"; which, understood strictly, would make him affirm, that if a man committed one sin, he had never been a Christian. Every attentive, intelligent, and candid reader of this epistle, must know, that John is speaking of the habitual character, as distinguished from individual acts, either of sin or holiness. In this ninth verse, then, he undoubtedly means to affirm, that the new birth does secure a man, or render it certain, that he will not live in sin. As he says in another place, "Whatsoever is born of God overcometh the world." By this, certainly, he does not mean to say, that in no instance is one who is born of God overcome by the world, and led into sin, but that he who is born of God habitually overcomes the world; that this is his real, bona fide experience.

Objection. Can there be no such thing as weak faith, weak love, and weak repentance? I answer: If you mean comparatively weak, I say, yes. But if you mean weak, in such a sense as to be sinful, I say no. Faith, repentance, love, and every Christian grace, properly so called, does and must consist in an act of will, and resolve itself into some modification of supreme, disinterested benevolence. I shall, in a future issue, have occasion to show the philosophical nature of faith. Let it suffice here to say, that faith necessarily depends upon the clearness or obscurity of the intellectual apprehensions of truth. Faith, to be real or virtuous, must embrace whatever of truth is apprehended by the intelligence for the time being.

Various causes may operate to direct the intelligence from the objects of faith, or to cause the mind to perceive but few of them, and those in comparative obscurity.

Faith may be weak, and will certainly necessarily be weak, in such cases, in proportion to the obscurity of the views. And yet, if the will or heart confides so far as it apprehends the truth, which it must do to be virtuous at all, faith cannot be weak in such a sense as to be sinful; for if a man confides so far as he apprehends or perceives the truth, so far as faith is concerned, he is doing his whole duty.

Faith may be weak in the sense, that it often intermits and gives place to unbelief. But this does not show, that faith and unbelief can co-exist. Unbelief, as might easily be shown, were this the place, when it is spoken of in the Bible as a sin, is disbelief. It is the rejection of truth perceived. Faith is the reception of truth perceived. Faith and unbelief, then, are opposite states of choice, and can by no possibility co-exist.

Faith may be weak, in respect to its objects. The disciples of our Lord Jesus Christ knew so little of Him, were so filled with ignorance and the prejudices of education, as to have very weak faith in respect to the Messiahship, power, and divinity of their Master. He complains of them as having but little confidence, and yet it does not appear that they did not implicitly trust Him, so far as they understood Him. And although, through ignorance, their faith was weak, yet there is no evidence, that when they had any faith at all they did not confide in whatever of truth they apprehended.

Objection. But did not the disciples pray, "Increase our faith?" I answer: Yes. And by this they must have intended to pray for instruction; for what else could they mean? Unless a man means this, when he prays for faith, he does not know what he prays for. Christ produces faith by enlightening the mind. When we pray for faith we pray for light. And faith, to be real faith at all, must be equal to the light we have. If apprehended truth is not implicitly received, and confided in, there is no faith; but unbelief. If it is that, faith is what it ought to be, wholly unmixed with sin.

Objection. But did not one say to our Lord, "Lord, I believe, help thou my unbelief," thus implying, that he was in the exercise both of faith and unbelief at the same time? I answer: Yes. But this was not inspiration. It is not certain, that he had any faith at all. If he had, and prayed understandingly, he meant nothing more than to ask for an increase of faith, or for such degree of light as to remove his doubts in respect to the divine power of Christ.

These are the principal objections to the philosophical view I have taken of the simplicity of moral action, that occur to my mind. I will now briefly advert to the consistency of this philosophy with the scriptures. [1]

The Bible everywhere seems to assume, the simplicity of

---

[1]See "Unity of Moral Action" and "Obedience Entire" in *Finney's Systematic Theology*, (Minneapolis: Bethany House Publishers, 1976), pp. 32–59. For Finney's sermons on faith see *P inciples of Faith*, (Minneapolis: Bethany House Publishers 1988).

moral action. Christ explicitly informed His disciples, that they could not serve God and Mammon. Now by this He did not mean, that a man could not serve God at one time and Mammon at another; but that he could not serve both at the same time. The philosophy that makes it possible for persons to be partly holy and partly sinful at the same time, does make it possible to serve God and Mammon at the same time, and thus flatly contradict the assertion of our Savior.

James has explicitly settled this philosophy, by saying, that "Whosoever shall keep the whole law, and yet offend in one point, he is guilty of all." Here he must mean to assert that one sin involves a breach of the whole spirit of the law, and is therefore inconsistent with any degree of holiness existing with it.

Christ has explicitly taught, that nothing is regeneration, or virtue, but entire obedience, or the renunciation of all selfishness. "Except a man forsake all that he hath, he cannot be my disciple."

The manner in which the precepts and threatenings of the Bible are usually given, show that nothing is regarded as obedience, or virtue, but doing exactly that which God commands.

The common philosophy, that maintains the co-existence of both sin and holiness in the mind at the same time, is virtually Antinomianism. It is a rejection of the law of God as the standard of duty. It maintains that something is holiness which is less than supreme disinterested benevolence, or the devotion for the present time of the whole being to God. Now any philosophy that makes regeneration, or holiness, consist in anything less than just that measure of obedience which the law of God requires, is Antinomianism. It is a letting down, a rejection of the law of God.

The very idea of sin and holiness co-existing in the same mind, is an absurd philosophy, contrary to scripture and common sense. It is an overlooking of that in which holiness consists. Holiness is obedience to the law of God, and nothing else is. By obedience, I mean entire obedience, or just that which the law requires. Anything else than that which the law requires is not obedience and is not holiness. To maintain that it is, is to abrogate the law.

I might go to great lengths in the examination of scripture testimony, but it cannot be necessary, or in these letters expedient. I must close this letter, with a few inferences and remarks.

It has been supposed by some, that the simplicity of moral action, has been resorted to as a theory by the advocates of entire sanctification in this life, as the only consistent method of carrying out their principle. To this I reply: That this theory is held in common, both by those who hold and those who deny the doctrine of entire sanctification in this life. The truth of the doctrine does not depend at all upon this philosophical theory for its support; but may be established by Bible testimony, whatever the philosophy of holiness may be.

Growth in grace consists in two things: In the stability or permanency of holy exercises. In their intensity or strength. As knowledge increases Christians will naturally grow in grace, in both these respects.

The theory of the mixed character of moral actions, is an eminently dangerous theory, as it leads its advocates to suppose that in their acts of rebellion there is something holy. It is dangerous because it leads its advocates to place the standard of conversion, or regeneration, exceedingly low; to make regeneration, repentance, true love to God, faith, etc., consistent with the known or conscious commission of present sin. This must be a highly dangerous philosophy. The fact is, that regeneration, or holiness, under any form, is quite another thing than it is supposed to be by those who maintain the philosophy of the mixed character of moral action.

Your brother in the love and fellowship of the blessed gospel,
Charles G. Finney

CHAPTER 39

To the Editor of The Oberlin Evangelist

September 15, 1841

Dear Brother:

I come now, according to my plan, to show:
VI. *What entire sanctification is.*

It is agreed on all hands, that entire sanctification consists in entire obedience to the law of God. The great point of inquiry, therefore, is, what is the spirit, or real meaning of the requirement "Thou shalt love the Lord thy God with all thy heart, and with all thy soul, with all thy mind, and with all thy strength, and thy neighbor as thyself"? Now the love required by the law of God cannot be complacency [1] in the form of an emotion, for the following reasons:

Emotions are involuntary states of mind, and therefore, strictly speaking, without the tint, both of morality and legislation.

We are required to love our neighbor as ourselves. But whether we are under an obligation to feel complacency at all in our neighbor must depend upon his character. He may be deserving of more or less complacency than ourselves; and certainly the law of God would not require us to exercise complacency toward our neighbor, unless his character were holy. The love which the law of God enjoins must be benevolence, or good-willing: because this is voluntary, and because it must be the same kind of love that God exercises toward all men, and the kind of love that must constitute the holiness of God. Certainly

---

[1] Complacency means self-satisfaction or an approving contentedness. See especially, "Love is Complacent," *Principles of Love*, (Minneapolis: Bethany House Publishers, 1986), pp. 51–56.

it was not *complacency* in men, that led Him to "give his only begotten Son to die for his enemies."

Entire sanctification, then, must consist in supreme, disinterested benevolence to being. In other words—it consists in willing the highest good of being for its own sake, and supremely intending to live wholly for the promotion of that end. In other words still, it is entire consecration to the glory of God and the good of the universe. But here I must repeat what I have in some of my letters previously said—that there is a grand distinction between the choice of an end or intention and those volitions that are the natural result of this choice, and which are put forth by the will as efforts to secure the end chosen. The thing which the law requires is, the exercise of supreme perfect benevolence, or willing the good of being as an end. The choice of an end naturally, and while the choice continues, necessarily produces volition, or those causative acts of will which are necessary to secure the proposed end. While the benevolence required by the law is in exercise, corresponding volitions and actions must be. As I said in my last letter, the agent has power to change his intention, or the benevolent state of his will. But while that benevolent state of will exists, there can be no sin; because that benevolent state of will is the very thing which the law of God requires, and produces corresponding acts and states of mind by a natural necessity. Let it be understood, then, that right ultimate intention—entire consecration to the glory of God and the good of the universe—obedience to the law of God—supreme, disinterested benevolence, all mean the same thing, and either of them expresses the true idea of entire sanctification. To make anything else than this entire sanctification, is to depart from the Bible, and make holiness consist in something else than obedience to the law of God, or to include in entire sanctification that which the law of God does not require.

Your brother in the love and fellowship of the blessed gospel,
Charles G. Finney

CHAPTER 40

To the Editor of The Oberlin Evangelist

September 29, 1841

Dear Brother:

I come now, according to my plan, to show:

VII. *That regeneration is entire sanctification, considered as an act in opposition to a state.*

Regeneration, or a change of heart, is a change in the ultimate intention, or in the choice of the great end or object of life; or, it is a turning from disobedience to obedience; or, from selfishness to supreme, disinterested benevolence.

It is described in the Bible as a radical change of moral character. It must, therefore, consist in a change of ultimate intention, or the end or object of life.

The Bible speaks of regenerate ones as sanctified; because, whatever they may now be, they must have been sanctified at their regeneration. In other words, they must have obeyed God at least once, if they are regenerate.

Regeneration is the condition of justification, pardon, and acceptance with God. This could not be, unless it consisted in obedience to God. It has been generally insisted on, by divines of all schools, that the new birth consists in giving the *whole heart* to God, or in an act of *entire consecration to God*. Nothing can be a condition of pardon and acceptance with God short of a state, for the time being, of entire obedience to God. God has no right to pardon until rebellion is given up, and sin, at least for the time being, wholly rejected. And besides, it must be the intention of the mind, to give up sin wholly and forever. Nothing short of this can be regeneration. Nothing short of this can be the condition of justification. If anything short of this is the condition upon which God pardons, accepts, and justifies the sinner, He has departed from the principles of His own government, abrogated the law, and introduced another rule of action. But this cannot be.

The uniform representation of the Bible is, that regeneration is an act or state of entire consecration to God. "Except a man forsake all that he hath he cannot be my disciple." "If any man will come after me, let him deny himself daily, and take up his cross and follow me." "Ye cannot serve God and Mammon." It cannot be necessary to dwell any longer upon this subject; for if regeneration consists in a change of the ultimate intention of the mind, it must constitute entire sanctification, considered as an act.

VIII. *The difference between sanctification considered as an act, and entire sanctification considered as a state.*

Sanctification as an exercise or act, may consist in any exercise or act of obedience.

Sanctification as a state consists in an abiding right ultimate intention. Or, in abiding, supreme, disinterested benevolence; including all its modifications as circumstances vary.

IX. *Faith is entire sanctification, considered as an act; but as a state, faith is a condition of entire sanctification.*

Faith is not conviction, or mere assent to truth. Faith is not an emotion, or felt assurance of mind. Faith is an act of will, or it could not be a holy act. It is that act of will by which the truth is received. It is the yielding, or giving up of all the powers, by the will, to the influence of truth perceived, and an attitude of waiting for further light. A truth may be fully believed, so far as conviction is concerned, where there is no evangelical faith. Sinners and devils often believe the truth; but they have not faith that yields the mind up to its influence. This yielding, or committing of the mind to the influence of truth, constitutes the peculiarity or characteristic of evangelical faith.

Faith may exist and be viewed, either as a generic, or as a specific exercise of mind. As a generic exercise it has not necessarily any moral character. At least it is not necessarily holy. The mind may be yielded up to the influence of mathematical, philosophical, or historical truth, which, in the generic sense of the term, is an exercise of faith. But, evangelical faith is not a conviction that the Bible is the word of God—nor that it is true—nor is it a perception of its meaning, with the assurance that it is true. Evangelical faith is a *species*, in distinction from a *genus*. It is a willing to receive, or rather the actual reception by the will of the testimony of God. It is the mind's choice, intention, or willing to be governed by His truth, because it is the truth of God. It is the yielding up of the whole being to be influenced by His testimony concerning His Son and by His Son.

Faith must be a holy act, because it is a compliance with obligation. It is, therefore, in the sense of an act, entire sanctification, or consecration to God.

But it is only a compliance with an initial obligation. It is a consent to be duly influenced by the will and truth of God, and waits for the truth and will of God more and more to be made known. The state of Paul's mind at the time of his conversion will illustrate my meaning. When Paul was struck to the ground, and informed that it was Jesus who had spoken to him, he cried out, "Lord, what wilt thou have me to do?" This faith is that attitude of the mind or will that says, "Speak, Lord, thy servant heareth. My purpose is to obey. Only let me know thy will, and I will do it." Faith is not repentance, nor love; but from its very nature must be the condition of all other acts of obedience except itself. It is a consent to receive His Word, or truth, and be influenced by it. It is the will taking the attitude of obedience, or submission, and needs only to know duty to be ready to do it. Faith, then, must be the condition of entire sanctification as a state. Faith as an act, viewed by itself, is not universal obedience, nor does it constitute the whole of religion; but is only a modification or one form of true religion.

Certainly there is no difficulty in supposing one holy act to be conditioned upon another, or holiness as a state to be conditioned upon one holy act. And, indeed, holiness as a state must be conditioned upon some first or initial act. Faith in the testimony or truth of God, must be a condition of all heart obedience to the law of God, as such; that is, because He requires it. Let it be remembered, then, that faith is the receiving of the truth and testimony of God for its own sake, and on its own account, as worthy of implicit confidence, and as excellent in itself.

It is easy to see that in its last analysis faith is a modification of benevolence, as justice, truth, mercy, repentance, etc., are. But it is not the whole of Christian character. I say again, in the last analysis, faith, and every other holy exercise, resolve themselves into a modification of benevolence. And, therefore, strictly speaking, holiness is a unit; love or benevolence comprehending the whole moral character of every holy being. The different Christian graces may be, however, and often must be viewed separately, and as presenting so many different phases of benevolence.

When faith is viewed by itself, it is easy to see, that it sustains to the other Christian graces which make up a *state* of sanctification, the relation of a condition, as it consists in the consent of the will, to receive and be influenced by the testimony of God.

Your brother in the love and fellowship of the blessed gospel, Charles G. Finney.

CHAPTER 41

To the Editor of The Oberlin Evangelist

October 13, 1841

Dear Brother:

Let us now notice:

X. *That a state of entire sanctification is attainable in this life.*

By this proposition I mean, that this state is attainable in a *practical sense*, and in such a sense as to render *the expectation of making this attainment* rational to those who set their hearts upon it. To me it has appeared remarkable, that in so many articles which have been written by the opposers of this sentiment, there should be so much of the *appearance* of admitting the attainability of this state in the sense I have explained, while, in fact, they *do not* fully admit it.

In the celebrated article of Dr. Woods upon this subject, while he fully admits that it *may* be attained, he denies that it is attainable in such a sense as that we may rationally expect to make this attainment in this life. I do not recollect his words, but the sentiment is this: that if such men as Paul, and other eminent saints, have failed to make this attainment, the expectation on our part of making it is irrational. Now admitting that Paul did not make this attainment, and that as yet it has never been made by any being merely human; yet it no more follows that it never will be made, or that it is irrational in the saints, in all future time to expect to make this attainment, than it would be irrational in them to expect the world's conversion, because it never had been converted.

It has been common with the opposers of this doctrine to admit, in general language, the attainability of this state, while

217

their general course of argument makes it plain, that they do not consider it attainable in any such sense as that we may rationally expect to make this attainment in this life. They have refused to take issue with us upon the question of attainability, obviously because they have felt, that before God and the church it would not do to deny the *attainability* of this state; and that neither the Bible nor the church would bear them out in making such denial.

Furthermore, they have admitted the necessity of aiming at a state of entire sanctification as indispensable to any degree of religion in the soul; and yet, I do not recollect that any one of them has marched right up to the admission, that this *state* is attainable in such a sense that we may expect, and are bound to expect to make this attainment. They have strangely maintained, that we were bound to intend and really mean to be perfectly holy in this life—while it has been considered irrational to expect to be so; and even dangerous to entertain any such expectation.

As I have so repeatedly argued the attainability of this state, in your paper, recently, I will not repeat the arguments in this place, but refer your readers to what they may find on this subject in my reply to the Troy Presbytery, and also in my "Views of Sanctification in this Life."[1]

I have only introduced this head here for the sake of calling attention to the fact, that while there has been so much of the appearance of admitting the attainability of this state in this life; yet, as a matter of fact, it does not seem to have been admitted to be attainable in any practicable sense; that is, in

---

[1]The next letter in this book, number 42, contains the action of the Troy Presbytery to Finney's teachings on sanctification, along with Finney's analysis of their misrepresentation of his ideas. In every subsequent unfavorable theological analysis of Finney's views with which I am familiar, his opponents have not considered Finney's reply included here. In many cases, his critics have simply parroted the Troy Presbytery's analysis of Finney's views instead of ever reading Finney in the primary sources to see what he actually taught or considered his replies to his critics. Since I believe Finney's reply is outstanding, shedding much light on the topic, and because I believe his views need to be fairly represented by those who appreciate his thought as well as by those who disagree with him, I have included both the action of the Troy Presbytery and Finney's reply in this book. As I said earlier in this book, Finney's "Views of Sanctification in this Life," is now printed as *Principles of Sanctification*. For his most mature views, see *Finney's Systematic Theology*, pp. 309–416; and *Principles of Union with Christ*.

such a sense that anybody ever has made, or will make it, or can rationally expect or hope to make such an attainment.[2]

Your brother in the love and fellowship of the blessed gospel, Charles G. Finney

---

[2]Finney does not complete points XI-X in any succeeding letters. In 1843, he does preach a series of sermons on "Holiness in the Present Life," and these can be found in *Principles of Godliness* (Minneapolis: Bethany House Publishers, 1984).

CHAPTER 42

CHRISTIAN PERFECTION

September 15, 1841

(Editor's Note: The following is a news item, an official document, and a letter of reply from Charles G. Finney. Because of the serious nature of these official statements, and because scholars may want to study *exactly* what the Presbytery declared and compare *exactly* Finney's reply, no words have been edited or changed, and the numbering and lettering of paragraphs remains the same for easy reference to the disputed points in these formal documents or Finney's letter.)

TROY (N.Y.) PRESBYTERY

The following editorial note is taken from the *New York Evangelist* of July 10; the same issue which contains the "Action of the Troy Presbytery," published below. It is a little remarkable, that the same paper from which the editor extracts our "wish" that he would copy Mr. Finney's letters, states, so conspicuously that it could not well be overlooked, that in the next issue we should commence the publication of Dr. Wood's review. How then could he say, "It is hardly fair that we should be expected to publish both sides, while that paper confines itself entirely to one?"

The *Oberlin Evangelist*, referring to our notice of Mr. Finney's letters on Perfection, expresses a wish that we would copy them. We shall with pleasure publish anything which comes from the pen of Mr. Finney, indicating a wish to return to correct views on this subject. We have a strong confidence that the logical mind of that distinguished preacher will not long retain its present position, and that his known frankness and humble disposition will lead him to declare his conviction of the error, as soon as he shall feel it. In the mean time, will not the *Oberlin Evangelist* insert the action of the Troy Presbytery? It is hardly fair that we should be expected to publish both sides while that paper confines itself entirely to one.

In the same connection is the following editorial note:

"**TROY PRESBYTERY ON PERFECTION**. We cannot omit to call special attention to the able and convincing document which we publish on the first page, from this ecclesiastical body. The style is chaste, clear, and forcible. The real point at issue is stated with great precision. It gives us great pleasure to see the truths on which we have so strenuously insisted, vindicated by so much abler hands. We hope all our readers will give this important article a candid perusal. We consider that it *finishes* the question, and is unanswerable. Nobody can object to its manner and spirit."—*New York Evangelist*.

Immediately on the receipt of the paper, Prof. Finney wrote to Bro. Johnson, the editor, asking him if he would publish a review of the Troy Presbytery article. In the same letter we wrote to him, stating that we should comply with his request, and publish the article itself, as soon as our columns were relieved from Dr. Woods' articles and Pres. Mahan's reply. We stated to him, that an article which "*finishes the question, and is unanswerable*," ought certainly, and should be given to our readers. Accordingly we give the article entire below. We copy from the *New York Observer* as the *New York Evangelist's* version contained many mistakes. Our readers can see whether it "*finishes the question*."

It should also be stated, that no letter has been received from Bro. Johnson, nor has he in his paper given any answer to the request to publish Mr. Finney's review. For this reason we publish that in connection with the article. It was prepared some six weeks ago, for the *New York Evangelist*, and is published as prepared for that paper. Is it too much to ask Bro. Johnson to insert the review, or to recall his statement, that the *Oberlin Evangelist* "concerns itself entirely to one side?"

ACTION OF THE TROY PRESBYTERY

Copied from the *New York Observer*

Messrs. editors: The Troy Presbytery, at its recent session in Hoosic Falls, adopted the following statement and resolutions, in relation to the subject of "Christian Perfection."

STATEMENT OF DOCTRINE

In the progress of human investigation it not unfrequently hap-

pens, that truth and error are *so* connected, that the work of distinction becomes as indispensable, as that of refutation. In this
form error is always the most dangerous, not only because it is
least likely to be perceived, but because, from its relation it is liable
to share in that confidence, which the mind is accustomed to assign
to admitted truth. In this form, also, it is often, relatively to our
perceptions, the same as the truth; but the moment this unnatural
union of repellent elements is sundered, both assume their distinctive and peculiar marks.

These prefatory thoughts find an ample illustration in the
present state of opinion, in some sections of the church, relative to
the doctrine of "Christian Perfection." That all the sentiments of
this system are false, it would be difficult to prove; and as difficult
to show their entire truth. The system is a subtle combination of
truth and error. Any partial prevalence that it may have had, is
easily explained on this principle. Where the truth is made most
prominent, the whole assumes an imposing aspect; but an inver-
sion of this error will as signally mark its defects. The work, therefore, of exposing the one without injury to the other, becomes a
duty with every devout and honest inquirer. This is what your
committee propose to undertake; and for this purpose it will be
sufficient to answer the two following questions: 1. *What is the
controverted point in this system?* 2. *What is truth in relation to
that point?* Let us take up these questions in the above order.

1. In the first place, What is the controverted point—what is
the real issue?

That there is some issue, admits of no doubt. What is it? It is
not, whether by the requirement of the moral law, or the injunction
of the gospel, men are commanded to be perfectly holy; not whether
men are under obligations to be thus holy; not whether, as moral
agents, such a state is to them a possible state; not whether the
gospel system is competent to secure actual perfection in holiness,
if its entire resources be applied; not whether it is the duty and
privilege of the church to rise much higher in holy living, than it
has ever yet done in our world. To join the issue on any, or all of
these points, is to make a false issue; it is to have the appearance
of a question without its reality. Some, or all of these points, form
a part of the scheme of "Christian Perfection"; but certainly they
do not invest it with any peculiar character, for they involve no
new sentiment differing from the ground taken by the great body
of orthodox Christians in every age. It cannot be supposed that
their advocacy has led to the various and fearful solicitudes of
learned and pious men in regard to the truth and tendency of this
system. It must therefore be fraught with some other element.

What is that element? The assertion that Christian men do attain in some cases during the present life, to a state of perfect holiness, excluding sin in every form, and that for an indefinite period they remain in this state. This position requires a moment's analysis, that it may neither suffer, nor gain, by an ambiguous use of terms.

1. A state of *perfect holiness* is the general thing affirmed under several relations—such holiness, as leaves not a solitary point of the divine requirements, either in kind or degree, that is not absolutely and completely met by the subject of this predicate—such holiness as involves entire conformity to God's law, and excludes all sin. Any thing short of this is not perfect holiness, even at the time when its possession is alleged; such a state would be one of imperfect or incomplete sanctification. In establishing the reality of this assumed attainment it is not allowable to abate, or decrease the purity and rigor of the Divine law—this would at once change the nature of both categories involved in this question, that is, sin and holiness. We must take the law as it is, and use it as the infallible standard of measurement.

2. This affirmation of a fact is made under several relations. The first is one of speciality, that is, that some Christians have reached this state. It is not contended that it is a state of all Christians, and by consequence, that none are Christians, but those who are perfectly sanctified. The second involves two relations of time, that is, that this attainment has been made in the present life, and that it has remained the permanent state for a period more or less indefinite, as a day, a week, a month, a year, or years. It is not denied that it is a state in which defection is possible; hence a Christian in this state may relapse into one of imperfect sanctification. Such a phenomenon would be apostasy from perfect to imperfect holiness, and might be succeeded by a return to the former state. These relapses and restorations may be of an indefinite number, for they admit of no necessary limitation, but the life of the individuals. They are not, however, to be confounded with that theory of moral action, which regards each as totally good, or totally bad, for they contemplate a longer period of time, than is assigned to the production of any given moral act.

Such is the real question at issue—such is the import of "Christian Perfection," so far as it has any peculiarity. This is the question to be decided; to argue any other, is to lose sight of the real one—it is to meet an opponent where there is no debate, but entire agreement.

II. In the second place it is proposed to inquire, What is truth in relation to this point?

It is obvious that the burden of proof lies with him who affirms the truth of the sentiment. He must moreover direct his proof to the very thing affirmed, and not to something else. It is easy to carry a question by stating one proposition and proving another. If the proposition in debate be established, the discussion is at an end—the doctrine of "Christian Perfection" must then be acknowledged.

1. It may be well therefore in the first place, to insist on our logical rights, and inquire—"has the proposition yet been proved?" This question involves a variety of subordinate ones, a brief allusion to which is all that can be made.

(a) It has sometimes been urged, that because perfection in holiness is attainable in this life, therefore it is actually attained. How much validity this argument possesses, we shall be able to judge, if we state it in a syllogistic form. It would be thus: whatever is attainable in this life is actually attained in this life; a state of perfect holiness is attainable in this life; therefore, it is actually attained in this life. It must be confessed, that this syllogism has the attribute of logical conclusiveness; but ere we grant the truth of the inference, it may be well to decide the truth of the premises. Is the first or major premise true? If so, then every sinner, who hears the gospel, must attain to actual salvation; then not some, but all believers must be perfectly sanctified in the present life; then every man actually reaches in the present life, the highest possible, intellectual and moral good of his being. It must be palpable to every discriminating mind, that this reason takes for granted a false premise; and although conformable to the rules of logic, it is liable to prove an untruth; it confounds the broad distinction between what is merely possible and what is actual.

(b) Again, it is urged in defense of this system, that the gospel contains *adequate provisions* for the perfect sanctification of believers in this life, and therefore, *some* believers are thus sanctified. The logical formula will place this reasoning in its true light. It would stand thus: whatever is possible by the provisions of the gospel in this life, will take place in this life; the perfect sanctification of some believers in this life is possible by these provisions; therefore it will actually take place in this life. This is a most extraordinary method of reasoning. With some slight changes, it will prove, what the advocate of "Perfection" himself will be slow to admit. In the second or minor proposition substitute the word "all" for "some"; and then it proves, that all believers are perfectly sanctified in the present life. Again, in the same proposition, in place of *some* or *all believers*, insert the words, *all men*, then it proves, that *all* are perfectly sanctified in this life. There must, therefore, be some radical difficulty in the first or major proposition. What is the difficulty? It lies in a limitation, which is not expressed, but which the moment it is seen, overturns the whole argument. The provisions of the gospel are sufficient for perfect sanctification at any time and place, if they be fully applied, but not otherwise. Their partial or full application contemplates the action of a rational and voluntary agent. Hence, while competent, they may fail of this effect, owing to the non-application, and not any fault in the provisions themselves. Before, therefore, this argument is entitled to the least weight, it must be proved that some believers, or all, fully appropriate these provisions in the present life. This being done, then all is clear. This has never yet been done; but it has been lately assumed, as if it were an undisputed truth. The main argument of President Mahan on "Perfection" is embarrassed with this very fallacy.

(c) Again, in support of this scheme, much use has been made of the *commands, promises*, and *prayers* recorded in the Bible.

In relation to the commands, it will be sufficient to say, that, although the Bible does command a state of perfect holiness in the present life, it does not follow, that the command is in any instance fully obeyed on earth. Before we can arrive at this conclusion, we must adopt the following principle, that is, that whatever is commanded in the Bible is actually performed by the subjects of that command. This would exclude the existence of all sin from the world; it would prove all men to be holy, without a single exception; it would establish the perfect sanctification, not of some, but all believers. It is certainly a most favorable engine of demonstration, too potent for an ordinary hand to wield.

So also the argument based on the promises of God, involves fallacies of reasoning not less apparent. It is a glorious truth, that God has promised to all believers, a final victory over sin, which undoubtedly will be accomplished in some period of their history. But does it follow that because believers are to be perfectly sanctified at some time and somewhere, the present life will be the time and place of this perfect sanctification? Let a promise be adduced, if it can be, that fixes the period of this event to the present life. The divine promises, like the provisions of the gospel, are conditioned as to the degree of their results, by appropriative acts on the part of the believer. Hence the fallacy of the argument is apparent, in that it takes for granted that some believers in the present life do fully comply with all the conditions contemplated in the promises themselves. Without this assumption, it proves nothing. Besides, it is not to be forgotten, that the promises are general, addressed alike to all believers; and hence the rules of reasoning by which they are made to prove the perfect sanctification of some Christians in the present life, equally proves the same of all, in every period of time, past, present, and future. The argument from promises has no relation to, or limitation by, any specific time. But two alternatives seem to be possible: either the reasoning must be abandoned as not valid, or we must admit that every regenerated man is sinless, and that too, from the moment of his conversion.

Similar defects characterize the arguments drawn from the prayers which the Bible records, as well as those which it authorizes Christians to make. It is true, that Christ prayed for his disciples in language the most elevated— "Sanctify them by thy truth." The same may be said of the great Apostle, when he prayed: "And the very God of peace sanctify you wholly." We are directed to pray that God's will may be done on earth as in heaven; and in general authorized to pray for a perfect victory over all sin at every time. These are the facts. Now, what is the inference? The advocate of "Perfection" responds—*that some believers are perfectly sanctified in the present life.* These and kindred facts we offer, to prove this conclusion. Is there then between the two a certain connection? If we admit the one, must we logically admit the other? Facts speak a very different language. Were those included in the prayer of Christ, thus sanctified, and that from the moment of its utterance? Was the same true of all the Christians of Thessalonica? Has the will of God yet been done on earth as perfectly as in heaven? Has every believer, who has hungered and thirsted after righteousness, attained to sinless perfection in this life? Did not Paul most fervently pray for the salvation of Israel; and have not thousands of Jews died since in their sins? Did he not pray that the thorn in his flesh might be removed, and was it removed? The grand mistake in this reasoning is, that it fixes what the *nature and terms* of prayer do not fix; that is, the *time when* and the *place where* the sought blessing shall be obtained. Applied as evidence to any believer who claims to be wholly sanctified, it would prove his sanctification an hour, a week, month, or year before he was thus sanctified, as really as at the moment in which he professed to have made this high attainment. Contemplated in its most general form, it would prove, that every thing which is a proper object of prayer, and which will be obtained in some state of being, will actually be obtained in the present life. There is a vast abyss between the facts and the conclusion, which the utmost ingenuity is unable to remove.

(d) Finally, on this branch of the argument, we remark, that a variety of *proof-texts* has been summoned to the service of this system. A critical examination of all these is inconsistent with the limits of the present statement. It will be sufficient to advert to the false principles of interpretation to which they have been subject. These are three in number.

(1) The first consists in a misapplication of passages; as when Paul says, "I take you to record this day, that I am free from the blood of all men," or when Zacharias and Elizabeth are spoken of as "walking in all the commandments and ordinances of the Lord blameless."

(2) The second consists in regarding certain terms as proofs of perfection in holiness, which are merely distinctive of Christian character, as contrasted with the state of the unregenerate. These are such words as "holy, saints, sanctified, blameless, just, righteous, perfect, entire, etc." That these and kindred terms are designed to be *characteristic*, and not descriptive of the degrees of holiness, is proved by the fact that they are indiscriminately appropriated to all Christians, and that in many cases they are applied, when the context absolutely charges sin upon their subjects.

(3) The third false principle consists in interpreting certain passages in an absolute and unrestricted sense, where evidently they are designed to have only a qualified sense. This error may perhaps be best illustrated by a single passage. Take that remarkable saying of the Apostle John: "Whosoever is born of God doth not commit sin; for his seed remaineth in him; and he cannot sin, because he is born of God." Stronger language, or better proof-text cannot well be conceived. In an unrestricted sense, it affirms not only that every regenerated man is sinless, but an impossibility that he should be otherwise; it dislodges all sin and moral agency from a converted mind, at a single blow. What will the advocate of "Perfection" do with this passage? Will he acknowledge either or both of these consequences? This can hardly be supposed. How then will he escape them? There is but one way for him—this lies in placing a restricted and qualified sense upon the passage, and in a moment all is plain and harmonious. But why subject so plain a passage to the law of interpretation, and deny it to others much less obvious and decisive? No reason can be perceived but the one which grows out of the necessities of a favorite theory. Indeed, there is logically no stopping place to this system, short of the bold affirmation, that all believers are perfectly sinless from the moment of conversion. Every argument in its last analysis must terminate in this extraordinary result. To arrest the inference at any point, is to betray a logical inconsistency. Are the advocates of "Perfection" prepared for this bold and unbiblical doctrine? If not, it is time they had reviewed their arguments and abandoned principles fraught with such a conclusion. Their weapons of defense are not

less *destructive* than *constructional* in their character.

2. Having tried the merits of the positive testimony on this subject, we remark in the second place, that in the present state of the question, the position is absolutely incapable of proof. When a man affirms his own sinless perfection for any given period, as a day, a week, or a year, he affirms his own infallible knowledge on two points; that is, that at the present moment he can recall every moral exercise during that period, every thought, feeling, desire, purpose, and that he does infallibly judge of the moral character of each exercise. Will any pretend to this knowledge? To do so, manifests the last degree of presumption, as well as ignorance, both of facts, and the truths of mental science. Every effort to recall the whole of our mental exercises for a single day, must always be a failure; it can only be partially successful. This shows how little weight is due to the testimony of a man who asserts his own perfection; he may be honest but this is no proof of the truth of his statement. If a case of "perfection" were permitted to be real, still it is impossible in the present state of our faculties, to find it and predicate certain knowledge of it. The evidences of "Christian Perfection," are then not only inconclusive, but its main proposition is absolutely unknowable to us.

3. In the third place we remark, that this proposition is disproven by an amount of evidence that ought to be considered conclusive. To secure the greatest brevity of statement, this evidence may be condensed into the following series of propositions: The Bible records defects in the characters of the most eminent saints, whose history it gives; it speaks in moderate terms of the attainments of the pious, when put in contrast with those of Christ, who hence is an exception to our race; it points the believer to the heavenly world, as the consummation of his hopes and exemption from all sin and sorrow; it describes the work of grace as going forward by successive and progressive stages, and fixes no limit to these stages antecedent to the period of death; it speaks of those as being self-deceived, who deny their own sinfulness—"If we say that we have no sin, we deceive ourselves, and the truth is not in us"; it represents Christians here as in an imperfect state—"For in many things we offend all" [the word "all" in the original, qualifies "we," and not "things"]; it exhorts Christians to lowly and humble views of their own attainments; it declares Christians in the present life to be under a process of providential discipline, the object of which is to make them more fully partakers of God's holiness; the most eminent saints that have lived, since the days of the Apostles, have uniformly expressed a painful consciousness of remaining sin, and spoken of their attainments, in language far different from that of

self-confidence; the higher Christians have risen in holiness, the more deeply have they been humbled with their own sinful imperfections, owing to a clearer discernment, both of God and themselves. These propositions might, each of them be amplified into as many arguments. Taken together, they seem conclusively to set aside the pretensions of any class of men, who claim for themselves sinless perfection in the present life. We cannot but think, that, however sincere such persons may be, they labor under a most dangerous delusion. With them we have no controversy; our controversy is with their system. It appears to us in no other light than that of a system, totally disconnected with its proposed evidence, demonstrably unknowable, by the present state of our faculties, and in direct contravention to an amount of proof, biblical and experimental, that must forever discredit its claims.

RESOLUTIONS

1. Resolved, That in the judgment of this Presbytery, the doctrine of "Christian Perfection" in this life, is not only false, but calculated in its tendencies, to engender self-righteousness, disorder, deception, censoriousness, and fanaticism.

2. Resolved, That it is contrary to the Faith, adopted by the Presbyterian Church in the United States. See chap. 12, sec. 2.

3. Resolved, That it is the duty of all orthodox ministers to acquaint themselves with this error, and at such times and in such measures, as may seem to them most expedient, to instruct their people on this point.

4. Resolved, That we view with regret and sorrow, the ground taken on this subject by the Theological Professors at Oberlin.

5. Resolved, That we hail with joy every improvement in human opinion that conforms to the Bible, and promises in its practical tendency, to decrease the sins, or increase the moral purity of the church.

6. Resolved, That the above statement and resolutions be signed by the Moderator and Stated Clerk, and published in the *New York Evangelist*, *New York Observer*, the *Christian Observer*, and the *Presbyterian*.

Fayette Shipherd requested that his dissent from the above report of the Committee be appended to it, entered on the records of the Presbytery, and published with it. The request was granted. All the other members present voted in the affirmative.

Thos. J Haswell, Moderator.

N. S. S. Beman, Stated Clerk.

Troy, June 20, 1841.

TO THE TROY (NEW YORK) PRESBYTERY

Dear Brethren:

Permit me to make a few remarks upon your report on the subject of Christian Perfection. I have read with attention most that has come to hand upon the subject of your report, and have thought it of little or no use to reply, until some opponent of our views should throw his objections into a more tangible form than any one had hitherto done. Your report embraces, in a condensed form, almost all that has been said in opposition to our views. For this reason, as well as for the reason that I have a high respect and fervent love for those of your number with whom I am acquainted, I beg leave to be heard in reply.

What I have said was prepared for and should have been published in the *New York Evangelist*. I wrote to the editor, making the request to be heard through his columns; to which he has made no reply. I still hope he will not fail to do me, yourselves, and the church the justice, to give this article a place in his columns. The truth demands it. For no other reason, I am sure, than to subserve the interests of truth, would I say one word. Without further preface, I quote your statement of the real point at issue. You say: "That there is some issue, admits of no doubt. What is it? It is not, whether by the requirements of the moral law, or the injunctions of the gospel, men are commanded to be perfectly holy; not whether men are under obligations to be thus holy; not whether as moral agents, such a state is to them a possible state; not whether the gospel system is competent to secure actual perfection in holiness, if its entire resources be applied; not whether it is the duty and privilege of the church to rise much higher in holy living, than it has ever yet done in this world. To join the issue on any, or all of these points, is to make a false issue; it is to have the appearance of a question without its reality. Some, or all of these points, form a part of the scheme of 'Christian Perfection'; but certainly they do not invest it with any peculiar character, for they involve no new sentiment differing from the ground taken by the great body of orthodox Christians in every age. It cannot be supposed that their advocacy has led to the various and fearful solicitudes of learned and pious men in regard to the truth and tendency of this system. It must therefore be fraught with some other element. What is that element? The assertion that Christian men do obtain in some cases, during the present life, to a state of perfect holiness, excluding sin in every form, and that for an indefinite period they remain in this state."

Upon this I remark:

I. *You have made a false issue.* Proof:

1. What *our proposition is.* It is, and always has been, *that entire sanctification is attainable in this life, in such a sense as to render its attainment a rational object of pursuit, with the expectation of attaining it.*

This proposition, it would seem, you admit; but on account of "the *various and fearful solicitudes of learned and pious men,*" you take it for granted, there must be heresy somewhere, and accordingly proceed to take issue with us, upon *one of the arguments* we have used in support of our proposition; and reply to our other arguments, as if they had been adduced by us in support of the proposition, upon which you have erroneously made up the issue.

2. Some of the arguments by which we have attempted to establish this proposition are—

(1) That men are naturally able to obey all the commandments of God.

(2) That this obedience is unqualifiedly demanded of men in this life.

(3) That the gospel *proffers sufficient grace* to secure their entire sanctification in this life; and that nothing is wanting but "appropriative acts," on the part of Christians, to realize this result.

(4) That the entire sanctification of Christians in this life was made the subject of prayer by inspired men, and also that Christ taught his disciples to pray for it.

(5) That this state has actually been attained.

These are among our arguments: and as they are the only ones to which you have professed to reply, I will mention no others.

3. I will put our arguments into the form of syllogisms in their order.

First Argument. Whatever is attainable in this life, on the ground of natural ability, *may* be aimed at with a rational hope of success. A state of entire sanctification in this life is attainable on the ground of natural ability. Therefore, it may be aimed at with a rational hope of success.

Again, Whatever men are naturally able to do in this life, they may aim at doing with a rational hope of success. Men are naturally able to do all their duty, which is to be entirely sanctified. Therefore, they may aim at entire sanctification with a rational hope of being entirely sanctified.

You admit both the major and the minor premises, in these syllogisms. Can the conclusion be avoided?

Second Argument. Whatever God commands to be done by men in this life, *may* be done by them. God commands men to be entirely holy in this life. Therefore, a state of entire holiness in this life is possible. You admit both the major and minor premises. Can the conclusion be avoided?

Third Argument. Whatever attainment the gospel *proffers sufficient grace* to secure in this life, *may* be made. The gospel proffers sufficient grace, should any one "apply its entire resources," to secure a state of entire sanctification in this life. Therefore, this state may be secured, or this attainment may be made. Here again, you admit both premises. Can the conclusion be denied?

Fourth Argument. Whatever was made the subject of prayer by the Spirit of inspiration may be granted. The entire sanctification of the saints in this life was prayed for by the Spirit of inspiration. Therefore, Christians may aim at and pray for this state, with the rational expectation of being entirely sanctified in this life.

Again. What Christ has made it the universal duty of the church to pray for, may be granted. He has made it the duty of all Christians to pray for the entire sanctification of the saints in this life. Therefore, these petitions may be granted, and Christians may expect to be entirely sanctified in this life. Both premises in these syllogisms are admitted. Are not the conclusions inevitable?

Fifth Argument. Whatever men have done, men can do. Men have been entirely sanctified in this life. Therefore, they may be so sanctified. The *minor* premise, in this syllogism, you deny; and, strange to tell, you affirm, over and over again, that *this one argument of ours is the main proposition to be established!* And you reply to all our other arguments in support of the main proposition as if they had been adduced to prove this! Now it would have been equally fair, and just as much in point, so far as our argument in support of the main proposition is concerned, if you had made an issue with us on any other argument adduced by us in support of that proposition—insisted that this was the main question—and replied to our arguments as if they had been adduced in support of that.

4. *You misrepresent our logic.* Assuming that the *fact of actual attainment* is the main proposition which we are laboring to establish, and in support of which we adduce the fact of actual attainment *only as an argument,* you misrepresent our reasoning. To put this matter in the clearest light, I will place, side by side, the syllogisms which you put into our mouths, and *our own* syllogisms.

Your syllogisms imputed to us	*Our own syllogisms*
1. Whatever is attainable in this life is actually attained in this life. A state of perfect holiness is attainable in this life. Therefore it is actually attained.	1. Whatever is attainable in this life *may* be aimed at, with the rational hope of attaining it. Entire sanctification is attainable in this life. Therefore, the attainment of this state *may* be aimed at with the rational hope of success.
2. Whatever is possible, by the provisions of the gospel in this life, will take place in this life. The perfect sanctification of some believers is possible by those perfect provisions. Therefore it will take place in this life.	2. Whatever attainment is possible, by the provisions of the gospel in this life, *may* be aimed at by those under the gospel, with a rational hope of attaining it. The sanctification of believers is actually possible by these provisions. Therefore, believers *may* aim at making this attainment, with a rational hope of success.
3. In relation to the commands, it will be sufficient to say, that although the Bible does command a state of perfect holiness in the present life, it does not follow, that the command is in any instance fully obeyed on earth.	3. Whatever the Bible commands to be done in this life, *may* be done. The Bible commands Christians to be perfect in this life. Therefore, they *may* be perfect in this life.

Now, brethren, I ask if you will deny the major premise, in either of the above syllogisms? You cannot deny either. I beseech you, then, to consider what injustice you have done to yourselves, to us, your brethren, and to the cause of truth, by such an evasion and misrepresentation of our logic.

The syllogism would stand thus: Whatever is commanded by God is actually performed. Perfect holiness is commanded. Therefore, all men are perfectly holy.

Before we can arrive at this conclusion, we must adopt the minor premise, or the the following principle; that conclusion, is, that whatever is commanded in the Bible is actually performed by the subjects of that command.

5. *What your logic must be to meet our argument as we have stated it.* If you would state, in syllogistic form, an argument that shall meet and set aside our reasoning, it must stand thus: That a thing is attainable in this life, is no proof that it can be attained. This must be assumed as a major premise, by any who would answer our logic. But who does not see, that this amounts

to a denial of an identical proposition? The same as to say—that a thing being attainable in this life, is no proof that it is attainable in this life. But to waive this consideration, and state the argument as it must stand in syllogistic form, to meet and refute our logic, it must stand thus: 'That a thing is attainable in this life is no proof that it can be attained. Entire sanctification is attainable in this life. Therefore, its attainability is no proof that it can be attained.' Who does not see, that the major premise is false, and that therefore the conclusion is? Now observe, we admit, that its attainability is no proof that it *will* be attained. But we insist, that its attainability is proof that the attainment may be aimed at with a rational hope of success.

Again, would you meet our second argument with a syllogism, it must stand thus: 'That God commands a state of entire sanctification in this life, is no proof that such a state is attainable in this life. God does command a state of entire sanctification in this life. Therefore, the *command* is no proof that such a state is attainable.' Brethren, this argument would have the attribute of logical conclusiveness, if the major premise was not false.

The very same course must be pursued by you, would you meet and set aside our reasoning in respect to our other arguments. This is so manifest, that I need not state the syllogisms.

II. In respect to our inference in favor of the doctrine of entire sanctification in this life, drawn from the prayers of inspiration, and the fact that all Christians are commanded to pray for the entire sanctification of believers in this life, you say as follows: "Similar defects characterize the arguments drawn from the *prayers* which the Bible records, as well as those which it authorizes Christians to make. It is true, that Christ prayed for his disciples in language the most elevated: 'Sanctify them by thy truth.' The same may be said of the great Apostle, when he prayed: 'And the very God of grace sanctify you wholly.' We are directed to pray that God's will may be done on earth as in heaven; and in general authorized to pray for a perfect victory over all sin at every time. These are the facts. Now, what is the inference? The advocate of 'Perfection' responds—*that some believers are perfectly sanctified in the present life.* These and kindred facts we offer, to prove this conclusion. Is there then between the two a certain connection? If we admit the one must we logically admit the other? Facts speak a very different language. Were those included in the prayer of Christ, thus sanctified, and that from the moment of its utterance? Was the same true of all the Christians of Thessalonica? Has the will of God yet been done on earth as perfectly as in heaven? Has every believer, who has hungered and thirsted after righteousness, attained to sinless perfection in this life? Did not Paul most fervently pray for the salvation of Israel; and have not thousands of Jews since died in their sins? Did he not pray that the thorn in his flesh might be removed, and was it removed? The grand mistake in this reasoning is, that it fixes what *the nature and terms* of prayer do not fix; that is, the *time when* and the *place where*, the sought blessing shall be obtained."

On this I remark:

This appears to me a most remarkable paragraph. Here you quote a part of 1 Thess. 5:23: "And the very God of peace sanctify you wholly," and then stop, assuming that nothing can be affirmed in respect to the *time when* the Apostle prayed that this blessing might be granted. Now, beloved brethren, why did you not quote the whole passage? When it would have been most manifest, that the Apostle actually prayed for this blessing to be granted in this life. I will quote it and see if this is not so: "The very God of peace sanctify you wholly; and I pray God your whole spirit, and soul, and body, be preserved blameless unto the coming of our Lord Jesus Christ."

As the sanctification of the "body," as well as the "soul and spirit," is prayed for, and that the whole being may be "preserved blameless unto the coming of our Lord Jesus Christ," how can you say as you do, "The grand mistake in this reasoning is, that it fixes what the nature and the terms of prayer do not fix; that is, the *time when* and *place where*, the sought blessing shall be obtained." Does not this prayer contemplate the bestowment of this blessing in this life? Who can reasonably deny it? Again: You say, "We are directed to pray that God's will may be done on earth as in heaven, and in general authorized to pray for a victory over all sin at every time." Now how can you make this admission, and still add the assertion just quoted, that "prayer does not fix the *time when* this blessing is to be expected?" Certainly, the *time when* is, in this prayer, limited to this life. In order to meet our argument, based upon the prayer of the Apostles, and the injunction of Christ, to pray for the entire sanctification of believers in this life, you must argue as follows. Here again I put the syllogisms into separate columns, that you may see them in contrast.

Your reasoning put in syllogistic form	*Our syllogisms*
That the Spirit of inspiration prayed for the entire sanctification of believers in this life, is no evidence that an answer to this prayer may be expected by saints in this life. Paul, under the Spirit of inspiration, did pray for the entire sanctification of the saints in this life. Therefore, this prayer is no evidence, that saints may aim at being entirely sanctified in this life, with a rational hope of being so sanctified.	Whatever state was prayed for by the Spirit of inspiration, Christians may aim at with a rational hope of attaining it. The Spirit of inspiration prayed for the entire sanctification of saints in this life. Therefore, Christians may aim at this attainment with the expectation of success.
Again. That Christ has made it the universal duty of saints to pray for the entire sanctification of Christians in this life, is no evidence that they may offer this prayer, with a rational expectation of being answered. Christ made it the universal duty of Christians to pray for entire sanctification in this life. Therefore, this is no evidence that they may offer this prayer, with the rational hope of being heard and answered.	Again. Whatever state Christians are required to pray for in this life, they may pray for with the expectation of being heard and answered. Christians are required to pray for a state of entire sanctification in this life. Therefore, they may pray for this attainment with the expectation of being heard and answered in this life.

Now, brethren, whose logic is the most conclusive?

III. In one paragraph of your report you admit and deny, at the same breath, that entire sanctification is promised in this life. You say— "It is a glorious truth, that God has promised to all believers, a final victory over sin, which undoubtedly will be accomplished in some period of their history. But does it follow, that because believers are to be perfectly sanctified at sometime and somewhere, the present life will be the time and place of this perfect sanctification? Let a promise be adduced, if it can be, that fixes the period of this event to the present life. The divine promises, like the provisions of the gospel, are conditioned as to the degree of their results, by appropriative acts on the part of the believer. Hence, the fallacy of the argument is apparent, in that it takes for granted that some believers in the present life do fully comply with all the conditions contemplated in the promises themselves. Without this assumption it proves nothing."

In the first part of this paragraph, you deny that God, anywhere in the Bible, promises a state of entire sanctification in this life, and request that one promise be adduced, that fixes the period of this event to the present life. And then you seem immediately to admit, that the blessing is *promised*, on the condition of "appropriative acts on the part of the believer." This you must intend to admit, inasmuch as you have before admitted, that "should a believer avail himself of all the resources of the gospel," he might make this attainment. Certainly you will not pretend to have any authority for such an admission, unless the promises, when fairly interpreted, do proffer such a state to Christians, upon condition of "appropriative acts." How shall we understand such a denial and admission at the same breath as this paragraph contains?

But you request that one promise may be adduced that fixes the period of entire sanctification to the present life. I might quote many. But as you ask for only one, I will quote one, and the one, *a part of which* you have quoted— 1 Thess. 5:23, 24: "The very God of peace sanctify you wholly; and I pray God your whole spirit, and soul, and body, be preserved blameless, unto the coming of our Lord Jesus Christ. Faithful is He that calleth you, who also will do it."

IV. *You deny that Christians can know that they are in a state of sanctification.*

You say: "If a case of 'Perfection' were admitted to be real, still it is impossible, in the present state of our faculties, to find it and predicate certain knowledge of it."

Here, assuming as you do, that the main proposition respects the fact of actual attainment, you insist that this fact, did such cases exist, would be entirely insusceptible of proof. Indeed! Does God command man to do what he cannot know that he does, even if he does it? This would be passing strange. You admit that God requires men to be entirely sanctified—condemns them if they are not—but yet deny that they could know that they obeyed, even if they did. This would, indeed, be a singular requirement—to command a man, on pain of eternal death, to do that which he could not by any possibility know that he did, even if he did it. This denial of ability to know, whether we are in a state of entire sanctification, is a total denial of the doctrine of natural ability as I presume it is held by every member of your body. Do not every one of you, my brethren, hold that natural ability to obey a command is the *sine qua non* of moral obligation to obey it? Do you not hold that a man cannot be under a moral obligation to do what he does not know himself to possess—to employ his faculties in any kind or degree of service which he cannot know to be his duty? Now if a man does all that he is able to know himself capable of doing, is he under a moral obligation to do any thing more? And if he is unable to know that he falls short of his duty, does he fall short of it? Brethren, will you give us light upon this subject? *Do you—will you* seriously maintain, that a man is naturally unable to know whether he obeys the commands of God, and yet, that he is condemned, and liable to be damned, for coming short, when he could not know that he came short? Brethren, will you maintain this?

V. *Your answer to our proof-texts is a very summary one.* It consists simply in *affirming* that we have misapplied them—that we regard certain terms as proof of perfection, which are only distinctive of Christian character—and, that we interpret them in an absolute and unrestricted sense—without so much as naming one of them. You have, indeed, quoted one passage, and affirmed, that a "better proof-text cannot well be conceived." But we have never regarded or quoted it as a proof-text at all. Your disposal of our proof-texts is really a short-hand method of getting over them. But there was one difficulty in the way of your quoting and answering them, which was—that had you quoted them, it would have appeared to everybody, that they were used by us to prove another proposition than that which you were controverting.

VI. *Our arguments in support of the fact of attainment you have passed over, almost in silence.* At the same time, you have taken our arguments, adduced to prove the *practical attainability*, and replied to them as if adduced to prove the fact of *actual attainment.* Brethren, we think we have reason to feel grieved at this.

VII. *You find yourselves obliged to be exceedingly indefinite in regard to the measure of attainment which Christians may rationally hope to make in this life.* You say: "The question is not, whether it is the duty and privilege of the church to rise much higher in holy living than it has ever yet done in this world." Now, brethren, I ask you, *how much higher* attainments Christians may make in this world than they have ever yet made? This is, with us, and must be with the church, a question of all absorbing interest. Do you answer to this question, that Christians may make indefinitely higher attainments than they have yet made? I ask again, on what authority is this affirmation made? Do you argue it from the fact, that the gospel has promised sufficient grace to Christians, on condition of "appropriative acts," to secure in them a much higher state of holiness than has ever yet been attained? But if Christians may rationally hope to attain a higher state of holiness than has ever yet been attained, by appropriating to themselves promises which proffer entire sanctification in this life, why may they not rationally aim at attaining all that the gospel has promised to them? Brethren, will you answer this question?

Appended to your report is a resolution, expressing "regret and sorrow, at the ground taken on this subject, by the Theological Professors at Oberlin." Will you permit us to reciprocate your "regret and sorrow," and express our deep grief, that the Presbytery of Troy have taken such ground upon this subject—so misapprehended, and of course so misrepresented the arguments of their brethren?

I must close this communication with a few remarks.

1. We admit, you had a right to take issue with us on the question of actual attainment, if you were dissatisfied with our course of argument on that position. But you had no right to misrepresent our argument in support of another position as you have done. You had no right to represent our argument, in support of the practical attainability, as have been adduced in support of the fact of actual attainment. This you have done, and by so doing, you have done your brethren and the cause of truth great injustice.

2. To what I have said in this article, you may reply, that you never denied the practical attainability of a state of entire sanctification, and that, therefore, on that question, you had no controversy with us. Why, then, my brethren, did you not admit, that in our main position you agree with us, and that you only deny one of the arguments by which we attempted to support that position? This, as Christian men, you were bound to do. But instead of this, you have said nothing about admitting our main position; but made the transfer of our arguments from the support of one proposition to the support of the one upon which you take issue, and thus represent our logic as absurd and ridiculous.

We shall be happy to discuss the question of actual attainment with our brethren, when they ingenuously admit that the main position we have taken, (namely, the practical attainability of a state of entire sanctification in this life) is a truth of the Bible.

3. Permit me to ask my brethren, what opponent, or course of argument, might not be rendered ridiculous, by the course you have taken—that is, by stating another proposition than that intended to be supported, and then representing the whole course of argument as intended to support the substitute proposition?

4. Should you say, that your report was not intended as a reply to *our* course of argument, I ask, who has ever argued in support of this doctrine in the manner you represent? Who ever inferred, that, because men have natural power to obey God, that, therefore, they do obey Him? I have read, with attention, almost everything

that has come to hand upon this subject, and I never saw or heard of any such course of argumentation as that to which you profess to reply.

5. Will your Presbytery, in reply to what I have written, excuse themselves, by saying, that their treatment of our argument was an oversight—that they had supposed us to reason in the way they have represented us as reasoning? To this I must reply, that you were bound to understand our argument, before you replied to it, in your public, or in any other capacity. And especially were you under this obligation, inasmuch as I had twice written to a leading member of your body, beseeching him, in the bowels of Christian love, to examine this subject, and to be sure he did it in a spiritual frame of mind, before he committed himself at all upon the question.

6. Will you, dear brethren, permit me to ask, how long the opposers of the doctrine of entire sanctification in this life expect to retain the confidence of the church, and prevent their understanding and believing this doctrine, by such a course of procedure as this? You are, no doubt, aware, that your course is not a novel one; but that it has been substantially pursued by several other opposers of this doctrine.

And now, beloved brethren in the Lord, do not understand me as entering into a war of words with you, or as entertaining the least unkind feeling in my heart toward you. I most cheerfully leave to your deliberate and prayerful consideration, the remarks I have freely made upon your report. I cannot, however, refrain from saying, that when I saw the name of one whom I greatly loved, and with whom I had often taken sweet counsel, attached to that report, my heart felt a kind of spontaneous gushing, and I almost involuntarily exclaimed, "et tu brute."[1]

Yours in the bonds of Christian love,
Charles G. Finney

---

[1] Here Finney probably refers to Beman.